The Economic Crisis
in Latin America

The Economic Crisis in Latin America

WILLIAM WITHERS

Queens College of the City University of New York

THE FREE PRESS OF GLENCOE
Collier-Macmillan Limited, London

PREFACE

FROM 1950 TO 1957 LATIN AMERICA EXPERIENCED A VIGOROUS economic boom. Average total production rose over 5 percent a year, per capita production 2½ percent a year. But after 1957 the boom collapsed, and a serious economic and political crisis developed. Several of the leading countries suffered from extreme inflations which were followed by depressions and a decline in per capita real income. Communism became a genuine threat because of economic deterioration, and the Castro revolution in Cuba.

But optimism continued despite these adverse conditions because of the triumph of middle-class democratic governments under such men as Alessandri, Frondizi, Quadros, Prado, Betancourt, Lleras Camargo, and Echandi Jimenez. It was strengthened by the leadership of the late President John F. Kennedy in establishing the Alliance for Progress, and by its universal acceptance through the Charter of Punta del Este. In 1960 and 1961 a slow recovery began, and some of the countries, notably Argentina, Bolivia, Chile, and Colombia made progress in controlling inflation. But by 1962 the situation again became adverse. The great flight of capital was resumed. The Alliance for Progress had gotten under way very slowly and did not compensate for the capital outflow. Moreover, businessmen and politicians alike, both in the United States and Latin America, lost confidence in the ability of the Alliance for Progress to solve Latin America's economic and political problems. They even lost faith in the possibility of solution through democratic government. By 1963, as Tad Szulc put it, Latin America "had come close to midnight." Pessimism expressed itself in a number of alarmist books and in the growing cynicism and rejection of Latin America in general, and the Alliance for Progress in particular.

v

This is not, however, one of the pessimistic books. It is optimistic, and its optimism is based on faith in the great power of education. In some ways, the most urgent need of Latin America today is education. Through education, Latin American countries will be able to increase their standard of living and solve their almost insuperable problems. But more education *in* Latin America must be accompanied by more education *about* Latin America. We in the United States especially need to know more about Latin America. Its future critically affects us, and our failures in leadership in this area arise in no small measure because we do not know enough about it to understand it. But, as the world leader in the fight against communism, the United States needs to lead intelligently in Latin America more than in any other underdeveloped region in the world.

Thus, this book is essentially an educational venture. It undertakes to provide a survey of the economic conditions and problems in Latin America, both as a whole, and in specific countries. It attempts also to formulate an economic theory that will serve as the basis for Latin American economic and political policy. At present, Latin America is in a critical stage in the great social revolution which is occurring in underdeveloped countries throughout the world. A transition is taking place in which Latin American nations may turn communist or develop socialist systems. They may also remain primarily capitalist. The policy of the United States can be the deciding factor. But wise policy depends on knowledge. Not only the policy makers but the general public as well must be rapidly educated as to the economic, political and social problems of Latin America.

In recent years Latin American culture has had a direct impact on the United States through the influx of Puerto Ricans in the east and Mexicans in the southwest. Puerto Ricans comprise one tenth of the population of New York City, and Mexicans one third of Los Angeles—our two largest cities. A rapidly increasing cultural influence is being felt not only through these migrations but through increasing tourism in Mexico and the Caribbean islands. We have also been forced to think about Latin America because of the Cuban Revolution, which brings communism and its atomic missiles within 90 miles of our shores. It can be argued that Latin Americans are now exerting almost as much influence on us as we are on them. The emotional drive

that went into the writing of this book is partly a result of re-
acting to the political and cultural impact of Cuba, Mexico, and
Puerto Rico.

The author has been indebted to a great number of persons.
Some have provided stimulation and encouragement such as
Professor Adolph Berle, Jr. Others, such as Dr. Raoul Prebisch
and Professor Pedro Teichert, have provided two basic ideas,
the peripheral and economic policy revolution concepts. Still
others have given concrete advice such as Colonel C. F. Fiori
and Professor Henry S. Miller. The author is especially indebted
to his secretaries, Mrs. Eleanor Hodgdon, Mrs. Helen Picado,
and Mrs. Phyllis Breedlove, and to his language assistant, Miss
Delia Tolentino.

The author has spent many years in anticommunist activities.
He had personal contact while in Castro's Cuba in 1959 with the
anticommunist underground. To read about the threat of
communism is one thing. To be in contact with it personally
on the spot is another. It creates a strong emotional incentive
to learn more and to find nontotalitarian answers for the problems of the underprivileged *Latinos*.

WILLIAM WITHERS

Eatontown, New Jersey
March, 1964

CONTENTS

Part V: THE FUTURE OF LATIN AMERICA

I

The Crisis in Latin America

ONE

THE CRISIS IN PERSPECTIVE

IN THE VAST AREA BELOW THE RIO GRANDE, INCLUDING THE ISLANDS of the Caribbean Sea and Central and South America, live over 200,000,000 Latin Americans. These people are similar in that their languages and some elements of their culture are derived from Spain and Portugal. They are also similar because they are a part of the great social revolution now occurring throughout the world among underprivileged people. Like the inhabitants of many parts of Asia, Africa, and the Middle East, they suffer from low incomes, low productivity, unused or poorly used resources, population pressure, and what the economist, Ragnar Nurkse, has called "the vicious circle of poverty."

The world social revolution of the underprivileged critically affects us in the United States. Since World War II the world has become polarized between the East and West. But a vast middle ground exists between the two poles containing the majority of the world's population. Both Russia and the United States are vigorously competing for leadership and control in this "no man's land." Subject to pressure from both sides, the underprivileged people of the middle can turn either east or west. But they have a third choice. They can evolve new socio-economic systems which are neither wholly capitalist nor communist. The ensuing changes resulting from the great world social revolution will affect seriously the national independence and prosperity of the United States. We cannot afford to allow these areas to go communist, and if they do not go either capitalist or communist, the new socialized economic systems they develop may also have serious consequences for our economic and political life.

The social revolution in the world at large began during and immediately after World War II. Oddly enough, it is not the result of poverty alone. Years before, the people in the revolu-

3

tionary areas were even poorer. Two other factors are involved. One of these is adverse comparison. A man can be content with his poverty if he regards it as inevitable and finds that others are equally poor. But if he learns that his neighbors are living much better than he is and that his poverty is not inevitable, he becomes discontented and revolts against those who seem to be holding him down. World War II caused a great increase in communication. Millions of men from the more prosperous parts of the world entered less prosperous regions and brought news of a better economic life. The mass media of communication also increased and spread the news. The underprivileged began to feel that the time for self-improvement had come. But in addition, a second factor operated—the rise of nationalism among people who had formerly had a semicolonial status.

At various locations the world revolt has entered a stage of crisis. The pressure for change has become so great that immediate or rapid improvement is demanded, violence occurs, and the chances of extreme solutions such as fascism or communism become real. In this situation no time is to be lost either by the Russians and Chinese in their efforts to convert these areas to communism, or in our efforts to prevent it. Even a third world war could be touched off in this explosive political and social atmosphere.

In Latin America the areas of crisis are numerous. Social revolution has reached a critical stage in Argentina, Bolivia, Brazil, Chile, Colombia, the Dominican Republic, Ecuador, and Venezuela. Communism is not impossible in any or all of these countries. The communist revolution of Cuba points the way. Out of Cuba a group of trained and indoctrinated *penetracionistas* have been sent to all parts of Latin America. A similar group has trained in Mexico City. In addition, Latin American-China towns in various countries have become centers of communist intrigue, and communist "peace corps" have been organized.

Apart from the specific evidences of crisis in Latin America, those who know the common people at first hand report the growth of an acute crisis psychology. The poor city worker or *obrero,* the *campesinos* or peasantlike workers on the farms, and the lower ranks of white-collar workers reveal a mounting hysteria. Depression conditions and extreme inflation have contributed to these attitudes. The hysterical workers and poor farmers say that "something terrible is going to happen." Their mental outlook is that of persons predicting the end of the world in a few months. But fear is mingled with hope. As in the end of the world when the judgment day comes, some hope to be the few chosen for the better life. Communists in Latin America understand and enhance this fatalistic attitude. They exploit it as a device to propagandize for a judgment day in which Heaven will be the communist system.

It is conceivable, of course, that middle-of-the-road political tactics, the ameliorating effect of United States aid, and the return of greater prosperity may prevent extreme reactions in Latin American politics in the next five or ten years. The Latin American crisis may subside. But the threat of communism will continue because it is due to persistent economic problems.

American Interest in Latin America

For years Americans have had a casual and rather specialized interest in Latin America. Businessmen of various types, ranging from adventurers and promoters like Kieth to more conservative corporate executives like W. R. Grace, have attempted to make money in Central and South America. By 1960 American direct investments in Latin America exceeded $9 billion and almost every conceivable type of business was represented. Naturally these business groups, especially Standard Oil of New Jersey, the Chase-Manhattan Bank, W. R. Grace and Company and the United Fruit Company, have been keenly concerned with Latin American affairs.

But apart from this specialized business interest, American interest has been casual. Many millions of tourists have visited Cuba, Haiti, Mexico, and the Dominican Republic; other millions have become accustomed to Latin American music and some of the products of these nations, especially coffee. Until the threat of communism after World War II and the Cuban revolution, however, the average American was largely indifferent to his Latin neighbors. His interests were oriented in east-west directions. Latin American countries are not the homelands of North Americans. Their tourist attractions, except for Mexico and the Caribbean, do not interest us very much and on the whole are still too expensive.

6   THE CRISIS IN LATIN AMERICA

The Cuban revolution temporarily aroused great concern. Much more attention was given to Latin America by the Federal government, the press, and other media of communication. Latin American research increased, and extensive plans were made for the study of Latin America on the university level through Latin American institutes. One of the leading Latin American economists, Dr. Raoul Prebisch, was brought into President Kennedy's world economic brain trust, the "nine wise men." The aroused interest resulted in extremely important economic and political measures such as the establishment of the Inter-American Development Bank, the Charter of Punta del Este and the Alliance for Progress. Renewed efforts were made to establish effective hemispheric cooperation in the fight against communism.

Yet the upsurge of interest in 1960 and 1961 had considerably subsided by 1962 despite the missile crisis in that year. Business men selling or investing in Latin America continued to be keenly interested. But the vast majority of our people were only a little more concerned about their southern neighbors than they had been before the rise of Castro and the invasion fiasco. Registration in college courses in Spanish or in Latin American area study rose very little. Latin American institutes remained largely in the planning stage. Virtually no effort was made to revise high school and elementary school curricula to include more Latin American content. It is remarkable how casual and specialized our interest remained. One of the problems of Latin America is that of raising our concern to a level equivalent to the Latin American's concern about us.

Capacity to be interested in a subject depends on our knowing something about it. No one can deny that we should be intensely concerned about Latin America at the present time, but our indifference is partly due to ignorance. The reverse is true also. We know little because we are not interested. At some point, however, this vicious circle must be broken. Probably we should start by learning more. Obviously, learning more means that more time and space must be devoted to Latin America in our mass media, more Latin American courses and course content must be introduced into the curricula of our schools and colleges, more of us must try to learn Spanish, and more time and money must be devoted to Latin American research. The means of learning must be provided. Educational means, however, are only a part of the need. To learn more, we must have attitudes conducive to learning, and a general conception of the problems of Latin America to serve as a focus for study.

Attitudes Toward Latin America

Many years ago—1922, in fact—a college professor at the University of Nebraska named Jacob Warshaw wrote a book in which he sought to reveal the true nature of Latin America.[1] He contended that there were five fantasies which not only distorted our view of Latin America, but resulted in attitudes which prevented us from trying to learn much about it. Suppose, as Warshaw contended, that Americans regard Latin Americans as (1) inferior, (2) immoral, (3) aborigines, who are (4) politically unstable, and (5) can be completely "typed." Would the people of our "superior" nation bother to learn about these "inferior" people?

American attitudes toward Latin Americans have changed greatly since 1922, but serious vestiges of the five fantasies remain. For example, the attitude that they are inferior persists. No one will deny that Latin Americans on the average have a lower standard of living and lag far behind us economically. But the inferiority we attribute to them goes beyond economics, and is applied to intelligence, morals, and cultural achievement. Part of this attitude is due to ignorance. Few of us are aware of the substantial literary and artistic accomplishments of Latin Americans. Few know that many of their well-trained engineers are employed in the United States and other advanced countries.

In addition to ignorance, the Spanish-American war has caused some of these invidious attitudes. Victory over another nation generates a sense of superiority in the victors which lasts for years. Such superiority feelings are irrational, especially when, as in the case of the Spanish-American war, they are applied to other nations speaking the same language, and when victory itself was due to size and economic superiority rather than to the mental or moral inferiority of the vanquished. Rationally or not, however, the Spanish war affected us more than we realize, and the stigma of inferiority is still applied indiscriminately to Hispanic peoples. Why should we study the language and culture of an inferior people? Spanish is for "mere business courses," or else it is studied to bask in the glories of the bygone age of Philip II.

Enough is now known about anthropology and the ethnic composition of Latin America to dispel the notions that all Latin Americans are really aboriginal Indians and that the Indian part of the population is mentally inferior to the whites. However, belief in Latin American immorality—another of the Warshaw fantasies—still persists. This attitude is not so much concerned with sex as with business immorality and with the alleged indolence of the Latin American. It is true, of course, that all over over Latin America one finds versions of the "squeeze" and "under-the-table." Different countries have their names for it such as *coima* (tip) in Argentina, *mordida* (the bite) in Mexico and *chivo* (the goat) in Cuba. The history of Latin America is full of examples of presidents, dictators, and other politicians who became enormously wealthy by milking the public. Thousands of American businessmen have felt obliged to pay graft for government or private business privileges. But the violations of business morality have occurred in many other under-developed areas and even in the United States, especially in our early economic history. The situation in this respect, moreover, is vastly better than it was several decades ago, and there is reason to hope that some day Latin American business and public morality may approximate our own. In the meantime, however, it is irrational to shut our minds to the study of an area which has vital concern for us because business immorality exists. The "laziness" of the Latin American has also been exaggerated, but we will have more to say about that in a later chapter.

Similarly, political instability cannot be denied, and it is likely to disgust Americans who are accustomed to a more peaceful and orderly handling of political affairs. But even political instability until recent years has been more apparent than real. Although Latin Americans have changed their governments through revolution and bloodshed about as often as through peaceful and constitutional means, the underlying social structure has remained about the same. Foreign business interests have seldom been seriously affected except in Cuba, Bolivia, Mexico, Nicaragua, and Haiti. But the point here is that bad or unstable government is not a good reason for indifference or aversion on our part.

Nor is the "typing" of Latin Americans a good reason for lack of study. When typing goes beyond the assignment of a few traits such as laziness and emotionalism, it becomes so complicated that the "uniform" Latin is no longer uniform. No group of people numbering two hundred million can all be, as one writer suggests, emotional, defeatist, impulsive, volatile, brilliant, introverted, circumlocutory, gallery-playing, egocentric, courteous, epicurean, lackadaisical, cosmopolitan, friendship-conscious, poetic, passive, status-minded, vehement, procrastinating, and pagan.[2] And yet these are the traits one has to list to include all Latin Americans if "typing" is undertaken. Obviously, many people in Latin America have some of these qualities, but few of them have the whole list. Moreover, great cultural differences exist in the twenty-two nations. Mexicans differ from Cubans, Colombians, and Venezuelans. Argentinians differ from Brazilians and Chileans. Within one country, such as Brazil or Colombia, the differences internally may be so great that unity as a nation is seriously threatened. Instead of all Latin Americans being exactly alike, their cultural and ethnic differences are extreme.

It can be concluded that an understanding of Latin Americans is predicated upon avoidance of the inimical attitudes implicit in the five fantasies. As Warshaw said years ago, "probably the most important factor in our intercourse with Latin America will be the willingness to accept Latin American customs, manners, and morals as equivalent to our own."[3]

The Essence of the Crisis

The study of the Latin America Crisis requires a focal theory about which the institutional and statistical facts can be organized and interpreted. The theory put forth here is that the crisis results from the failure of recent economic policies in Latin America to solve the basic problems of economic underdevelopment.

Underdevelopment means poverty. In 1953 the average per capita income of the United States was $1,908. The per capita income of Venezuela was higher than that of any other Latin American country, yet it was only $530. However, the per capita income of Bolivia, the poorest country, was $55. In that year only three Latin American nations and Puerto Rico had per capita incomes above $350 a year. Fourteen of the nations had per capita incomes between $296 and $136.[4] To say merely that Latin American nations lag behind the United States in economic development is an understatement. Their lag is of truly tragic proportions, and the rate at which they would have to grow to catch up with us even in twenty years is inconceivably large. The uneducated and illiterate poor people of these countries are now aware of the great differences. They have been told that they can overtake us if proper political measures are adopted. Delay in the expected economic progress now leads to social revolution.

Underdevelopment in Latin America also means economic dependency. Most of the nations rely heavily on exports of a few raw materials and food products. The Central American countries, the Dominican Republic, Colombia, Ecuador and Brazil export bananas, sugar, and coffee. Venezuela is a great oil exporter. Argentina and Uruguay depend to a considerable extent on their exports of meat and wool. Chile, Bolivia, and Peru depend on mineral exports, notably tin and copper. The prosperity of these nations is seriously affected by a drop in the prices of their exports. For many years there has been a long-run downward trend in the value of their exports in terms of the cost of imports.[5] As industrial nations like the United States grew richer, the prices of machinery and manufactured goods rose and the prices of sugar, coffee, bananas, and wool fell. Dependence on the sale of exports at falling prices limited the long run rise in Latin American incomes. Great distress was caused by depressions in the United States or Great Britain which reduced these export prices still further. The growing nationalism in Latin America heightened economic resentment and gave rise to a strong desire for economic independence for political as well as economic reasons. The situation is now critical because a large segment of the literate population feels that the dependency can no longer be tolerated, that it must be ended once and for all. Economic nationalism of this nature is especially strong in Mexico, Brazil, Argentina, Chile, and Cuba.

The Nature of Economic Development

Dependent and poor underdeveloped areas become peripheries, hinterlands, or colonies for the advanced centers or heartlands of development. The peripheries are raw material or food producers. Manufacturing does not grow rapidly. As modern technology and capital are applied in the peripheries, they go into raw material production and one-product specialized agriculture rather than general manufacturing. These areas resemble athletes like fencers who overdevelop certain muscles because of the nature of the sport. Their economic bodies do not grow as a whole. Thus, the problems of poverty and dependency can only be solved if *over-all* development occurs.

Economic development is a new branch of economics. For many years economists, influenced by the pessimism of David Ricardo and Thomas Malthus, were not interested in such an optimistic notion as economic development. In fact, they could hardly conceive of development as a problem, of economics as a developmental science. Economic life followed static, universal, and immutable laws which doomed large portions of the world's population to wages barely above the level of subsistence. With this outlook, there could be no laws of development or attention to a "problem" of development. Even the upward-downward movement of economic conditions known as the business cycle was not seriously studied until the crises of the 1920s made it imperative. Long-run change or secular growth is even a more modern topic. Today, however, theories of growth, and data of growth in the United States and in other parts of the world, have come into their own as subjects of investigation. The key to the solution of most Hispanic problems lies in the study of growth.

Simple elements of growth may be delineated. Imagine a primitive society of some nature. It can be an island of the South Pacific, or an Indian village with pueblo huts in the Far West. In either case, there are several basic characteristics. Resources are inadequate and there is very little specialization in production. There is primitive technology and cultural institutions oppose change. Our Indian Village or Island Compound can remain for hundreds or even thousands of years in a state of economic suspension if no changes intrude upon the cultural arrangement to upset it by causing either a more elaborate division of labor or advanced technology. It can be asked, therefore, Why does any primitive culture ever change, or why, in any part of the world at any time, has man's lot improved? Why did the primitive Greeks of the sixth and seventh centuries A.D. ever become the Greeks of the Athenian Empire? Why did Roman civilization ever arise? Or why did the so-called Dark Ages ever become brighter? The answer lies in some stimulus to cultural change, some social or economic revolution. Resources, technology, institutions, and the division of labor are the elements in the economic development of a people and growth and well-being arise from changes in the combination of these elements induced by a cultural revolution. Such a revolution is occurring in Latin America, and we shall now trace its origins.

References

1. J. Warshaw, *The New Latin America*, Thomas Y. Crowell Company, New York, 1922.

2. Cf. Harry Stark, *Latin America*, W. C. Brown, Dubuque, Iowa, 1961, p. 28.

3. Warshaw, *op. cit.*, p. 7.

4. C. P. Kindleberger, *Economic Development*, McGraw-Hill, New York, 1958, p. 6.

5. Economists call this a decline in the "terms of trade."

THE ORIGINS OF THE CRISIS

CHANGE IN ALL ADVANCED NATIONS REVEALS COMMON ELEMENTS. As we have pointed out, every social system evolves through an increase in specialization, more efficient use of resources, creation and application of advanced technology, and formation of institutions which promote rather than resist advancement. But rapid change or revolution will not occur unless there is a severe shock of some kind which forces people to alter their social system. The shock occurs primarily in the cultural aspects of life, in the morals, attitudes, beliefs, values, and aims of a people. The old culture must be modified or rejected. Old ways must be "modernized" or discarded for new ways.

New values challenging the old may arise *within* a nation or be imported. The older civilizations of Greece and Rome developed largely from indigenous causes. The transformation of western Europe through the breakdown of feudalism, the rise of mercantilism, the growth of individual enterprise, and the appearance of industrialism also had internal causes. But the current social revolution affecting Latin America is largely external in origin, except for the creative originality of two countries, Mexico and Uruguay. Except for the great influence of these nations, new aims and values have come into Latin America from abroad, principally from the United States, Great Britain, Russia, and China. These new perspectives struggle with a resistant culture derived from Spanish and Portuguese colonialism.

To understand the origins of the Latin American crisis one must go back to this early colonial history. A revolution consists of two protagonists, *what was* versus *what is*. When then is the nature of the old Latin American cultural fabric which now struggles against modernism? Broadly viewed, it is a composite

13

of (1) racial intermixture with the blending of the cultures of these races, (2) the effects of early colonial exploitation, (3) the agrarian feudalism of the Spanish, Portuguese, Incas, and Aztecs, (4) the superficial imposition of democratic ideals and institutions derived from the United States and western Europe, (5) the mercantilism of the Spanish and (6) the economic liberalism and colonialism of Porfirio Diaz. We shall consider these various elements in turn.

Racial Backgrounds

Latin America, like the United States, is the product of a great mixture of racial and cultural elements. The main components are Indian, Negro, and Iberian. Many other European nationalities, however, have contributed their influence in addition to Spain and Portugal. In Argentina, Brazil, and Chile especially, Italians, Germans and Irish have settled and intermarried with other national and racial groups. They have greatly influenced business, agriculture, and politics.

The oldest racial and cultural influence is Indian. Before Columbus discovered the islands of the Caribbean Sea and the eastern coast of South America, great Indian civilizations existed in Mexico, Yucatan, Guatemala, Honduras, and Peru. The first of these was the Mayan culture centering in Yucatan which lasted from the fourth to the tenth centuries A.D. when it was broken into three dynasties and deteriorated because of civil wars, pestilence, and hurricanes. A later civilization, that of the Aztecs, had developed during the eleventh to the fourteenth centuries in the valley of Anahuac in Mexico, and it was this culture that Cortes subdued when he invaded the mainland. About A.D. 1200 an inconspicuous tribe began to dominate the valley of Cuzco in Peru and later founded the great empire of the Incas which was also in existence when the Spaniards arrived in America. Lesser Indian cultures existed in Colombia, Ecuador, and Chile.

The Indian empires of the Aztecs and Incas were subdued by the Spanish in the years 1519 to 1535. Following the subjugation of the Indians by the *conquistadores,* the colonial period began. It was to last from 1535 to 1824 when the independence of the

colonies was finally won at the decisive battle of Ayacucho in
Peru. Under Charles I, and later Philip II, the colonies established in various parts of Latin America had prospered. A great
stream of gold and silver flowed from Mexico, Colombia, and
Peru which enriched the mother country temporarily, but ultimately caused inflation there and in the rest of Europe. Although
the precious metals enriched some of the *conquistadores,* their
soldiers, and the royal governors, the greatest wealth was to
come from the agricultural produce of the colonies such as
sugar and tobacco.

Exploitation and Feudalism

The basis of the old culture of Latin America is to be found
in the colonial period. It was characterized by exploitation and
semifeudalism. The *conquistadores* came to steal the wealth and
exploit the labor of the natives and their interest in colonization
was secondary. Wealth was obtained not through productive
farming or business but through extraction based on the physical
force, protection, and encouragement of the state. A tendency
to rely on government protection and position as means of obtaining wealth thus became a tradition. The Latin American
world has never at any period fully accepted the doctrine of
laissez-faire. Even today, government, not free individual
economic effort, is often considered the chief means of becoming
wealthy because, through government, economic power is obtained which can be used for personal enrichment.

The colonial period was not only statist but feudalistic. To
some extent the feudalism was merely the continuation of
Indian feudalism with Spanish soldiers and noblemen replacing
the Indian overlords. This was the situation in Mexico and
Peru where feudalism had been well established before the
Spaniards arrived. In other parts of Latin America the Indians
had not developed elaborate feudal cultures, and feudalism
was imposed by the Spanish. The sovereigns of Spain granted
their subjects great *encomiendas* which originally were rights
to the labor of Indians within a given area. In actuality, however, they were grants of land on which the Indians lived and
farmed, and they included personal and political rights over

them. Thus Charles I rewarded Cortes by making him the
Marquis of the Valley of Oaxaca in Mexico, an area of 25,000
square miles with a population of a hundred thousand Indians.[1]
His great castles can still be visited in and near Cuernavaca.

It is important to realize that feudalism has continued in Latin
American despite increases in the personal and political rights
of the peasant or peon population. The widespread system of
large estates is essentially feudalistic, although the "serfs" have
become tenants or wage workers and are not bound to the land
legally. They have political and personal freedom on paper.
But in effect they are held on the land through debt, lack of
capital to buy their own land, lack of industrial skill to enable
them to move off the land and earn a living in the cities, and
through ignorance, lack of education, illiteracy, and violation
of their personal and political rights.

Latin American feudalism has important consequences for
the current Latin American crisis. Feudalism creates attitudes of
class status, conservatism, and the importance of the great man
or leader. It establishes the belief that men must be ruled rather
than rule. It is essentially undemocratic and casts serious doubt
on the capacity of the common man to govern himself. The
national political organization resulting from feudalism carried into modern times is dictatorship and benevolent paternalism through the leadership of a "great man." Much of the
governmental instability of Latin America can be attributed
to the fact that democratic political institutions were imposed
on a feudalistic culture. Although lack of education and illiteracy have had an important influence in making democracy
function badly, the underlying cultural factors are more important. Latin America was conditioned by its feudal history to
accept dictatorship of either the right or the left. As the common man senses the need for a better life, it is natural for him
to turn to a leftist dictatorship if rightist dictatorship has not
helped him. This has been true in other parts of the world.
Where feudalism continued into the twentieth century and
where there was not a large and thriving middle class of long
standing, imbued with solid traditions of freedom and individualism, the doctrine of proletarian dictatorship took root.
Communism threatens Latin America today because of its persistent feudalism.

"Democracy"

The superimposition of democracy and liberal doctrines in Latin America came early in the revolutions which by 1824 established the independence of the Latin American nations. Had these nations followed their revolutions with the development of business enterprise, the elimination of the feudalistic land system, and the encouragement of a middle class, democratic traditions and practices might now be as firmly entrenched in South as in North America. But there were negative influences at work that prevented this. The revolutions merely overthrew the yoke of old Spain. They did not dislodge the landed aristocracy, which continued to oppose political and economic changes and the development of realistic democracy. Absence of capital and the emphasis on agriculture retarded the growth of business and industry and a middle class based on them. Democratic doctrine was an ideology accepted only by Latin American intellectuals and used as a political device to rally mass support and at the same time hide the underlying control of a privileged few.

Thus the revolutionary heroism of Bolivar, San Martin, Miranda, Hidalgo, Morelos, Moreno, and Sucre became a liberal tradition and did not result in genuine democratic practices until a century or more later. Except in Mexico, Chile, Costa Rica, and Uruguay, democracy hardly functioned in any genuine sense prior to World War II. As a tradition rather than a practice, it must not be underestimated, however. Where democratic ideology is strong and has social prestige, it is difficult to substitute a fascist or communist ideology and the attendant totalitarian systems.

From the time of the revolutions for independence until the era of Porfirio Diaz in Mexico, Latin American countries passed through a series of dictatorships based upon a superficially democratic electoral and constitutional structure. Although democratic principles were voiced and the heroes of the revolution venerated, the landed aristocracy and the army controlled the governments. There was, in fact, no functioning ideology either political or economic. Democracy was merely a fetish. With Diaz, in 1876, Latin America entered a new period, however, in which governments and intellectuals combined to agree upon and implement a new economic ideology, economic liberalism, or internationalism. In this, the nations of Latin America followed Mexican leadership with the exception of Uruguay.

Economic Liberalism in Latin America

The regime of Porfirio Diaz was welcomed in Mexico which had been in a state of political turmoil since the days of Hidalgo sixty-six years earlier. Diaz, one of Juarez's ablest generals, revolted against him because he believed that due credit and privilege had not been given to the army for its revolt during the French invasion and the regime of Maximilian. After plotting in Texas against Lerdo, Juarez's successor, Diaz led a military coup which ejected Lerdo and established himself as dictator, remaining in power for forty-four years.

The dictatorship of Diaz was supported by the army generals, the clergy, foreign capitalists, the large landowners or *hacendados*, and a group of urban intellectuals known as the *cientificos*. The latter greatly influenced economic policy. Their leaders, like Diaz's finance minister Limantour, believed in the philosophy of economic liberalism. The *cientificos* gained great prestige in Latin America, and between 1891 and 1910 were the intellectual leaders of the Hispanic world. Economic liberalism continued to be the accepted doctrine in most of Latin America until the depression of 1929.

Economic liberalism was not, of course, of Latin American origin. It was borrowed from the Western nations, notably England. It was based on the classical economics of Smith, Ricardo, and Mill. According to their views, the countries of the world should function under conditions of free trade. Price of goods in this international free trade would reach a level depending upon the comparative costs of production in different nations. For example, if wool could be produced more cheaply in Uruguay than in Argentina, the price of wool, under free trade, would fall to levels where only Uruguay and not Argentina would be able to produce at a profit. Argentina, in its turn, would produce beef or grain, products in which it had an advantage in terms of costs over Uruguay. The resulting specialization of Uruguay on wool and Argentina on grain and beef would be advantageous in that the two countries would produce the products in which they were most efficient and at the lowest possible cost to the consumer. By producing wool, grain, and beef, moreover, instead of manufactured goods, Uruguay and Argentina would receive a higher economic return than if they had produced manufactured goods. Their standard of living would theoretically be no lower than that of manufacturing countries, assuming that the demand for their agricultural products was as high as the demand for manufactured products. In this ideal system of free world trade, production would be allocated among the nations according to their relative efficiencies.

The *cientificos* and Diaz supported not only free trade but, in addition, believed strongly in the use of foreign capital to speed up the process of economic development. Foreign capital, under these policies of free trade, free-exchange rates, and the free import and export of funds, came into Mexico to build railroads and public works. Argentina, also accepting free trade, received a great deal of capital. In these years, the free-trade economies of Latin America thrived, and large profits were made through the sale abroad of basic raw materials and food products.

Important also was the freedom attained by the landowning aristocracy through the general acceptance of a laissez-faire philosophy in domestic economic life. Landlords did not need to assume any great obligations toward agricultural labor. There was a free labor market as well as a free international market. The oversupply of labor easily resulted under these free conditions in the payment of substandard wages. Naturally this was beneficial to the landlords.

Thus freedom of foreign and domestic trade was highly acceptable to the *hacendados* who controlled the Latin American governments. As long as foreign capital was attracted, wages remained low, the proceeds from the sale of food and raw materials abroad remained high, and the cost of foreign manufactured goods remained low, economic liberalism was a profitable system. Not too well understood in these early days was the additional advantage that, to sell large quantities of food and raw material abroad, these nations had to have free trade to accept the goods of other nations in payment. The "planter" aristocracy of Latin America was thus just as enamored of free trade as the American planters had been before the Civil War. But unlike their counterparts in the United States, the "planters" in Latin America continued to control the governments. In Latin America there was no Civil War.

Latin American Mercantilism

The colonial period, however, had not only created and perpetuated feudalism, but had established a mercantilist system under the tutelage of the mother country. Trade relations, trade routes and prices had been rigidly controlled. High tariffs and trade restrictions hampered or prevented trade with any country except Spain. Some extremely ridiculous requirements proved very burdensome and thwarted development, such as the stricture that goods from Buenos Aires be shipped to Europe across the Andes via Peru. Much of the Spanish mercantilist trade restrictions were swept away by the revolutions, but the tradition of state control of economic life remained. The normal Latin American attitude was not that of free trade and economic liberalism. The policy of the free trading *cientificos,* although in keeping with the economic interests of the landowners, violated their traditions.

Thus economic liberalism, which was not in keeping with the political and cultural traditions of Latin America, imbued as it was with belief in state paternalism and mercantilist regulation, could continue only as long as the economic advantages continued. Great profits did continue from the sale of raw materials and food for many years and a good deal of foreign capital was attracted to Mexico, Argentina, and Uruguay. This was the situation until markets for food and raw materials became disrupted and less profitable after World War I and the Great Depression finally caused their collapse. Most Latin American countries were then faced with the necessity of abandoning liberal policies, and a new era of economic nationalism was ushered in. But Mexico and Uruguay moved in these new directions several decades ahead of the other nations.

Economic Nationalism Begins in Uruguay

The shift to economic nationalism began in Uruguay in 1904. Prior to this time, this tiny country of 2.7 million people was torn by severe internecine strife. Finally, the Blanco party of the landlords was defeated, and Batlle y Ordonez assumed control. For his first term in the presidency of four years, he was occupied in pacifying the country and introducing honesty into the bureaucracy. In his second term (1911–14) however, he began a really remarkable economic transformation that followed a middle course between socialism and capitalism and which was the first essentially nationalistic program to appear in Latin America.

President Batlle undertook to reorganize his country without land reform and through industrialization. In the latter half of the nineteenth century the progressive enclosure of the fields in the large estates or *latifundias* left the peons with a bare subsistence on the land. They could earn only a few pesos a month and lived in wretched hovels on starvation diets. Gradually more and more of the peons migrated to the city, mainly to Montevideo. The result of these migrations was the beginning of an urban proletariat with a restless revolutionary outlook. Combining with the governmental bureaucracy, they eventually triumphed over the landowners and established Batlle as president.

Even before Batlle y Ordonez became president, Uruguay had begun a policy of protectionism for local industry. Uruguay was especially anxious to protect the local manufacture of shoes and flour, and moderate tariffs had been enacted as early as 1875. In the latter part of the nineteenth century, as with other countries which were accepting economic liberalism, foreign capital had been welcome. Despite its small size, Uruguay had the third largest foreign capital investment in South America. But the foreign capital which was mostly English had gone into public utilities and railroads and not into domestic industry. Protective tariffs had to be adopted to promote this industry.

The program which Batlle introduced in his second term after 1911 consisted of the creation of state monopolies of insurance and electric power, the establishment of a central bank, construction of state railways, and a great increase in the tariffs to protect domestic industries. This program proved a workable compromise since it did not seriously disturb the land tenure status of the old ruling class while promoting industrialism through protective tariffs and state enterprise.[2]

The Mexican Revolution

Mexico pioneered along with Uruguay in the development of a new economic independence based on nationalism, socialism, and the simultaneous development of private business enterprise. Mexico differs from Uruguay in that these changes were achieved with less statism or rigidity in government direction. The new order began with the revolutions of 1910 to 1917. Great opposition had developed to the Diaz regime from the wretched rank and file of the army, the poor peasant farm population, the workers who were underpaid and wanted to organize unions, and the intellectuals who could not view the Diaz government with the cynicism of the *cientificos* who avowed democracy but supported dictatorship. Part of the revolutionary trend was also racial. Although a *mestizo* from Oaxaca, Diaz despised the Indians, and wanted a Mexico dominated by whites. He had turned his back on the goals of Juarez: the triumph of the Indian, the subjugation of the Church, the elimination of government graft and corruption, and the division of the land of the *haciendas* into small peasant holdings.

All the pent-up opposition and frustration was organized temporarily around the support of Francisco Madero, a small Messianic vegetarian of impeccable integrity, but with no political ability to carry out his ideals for the common man's welfare. After a little over a year in power, Madero's chief general, Huerta, seized the government and arrested his commander-in-chief. Madero was then shot on his way to prison. Although Huerta succeeded in restoring order, he was forced out of power by the landing of American marines in Vera Cruz in 1914. Wilson ordered the landing to protect the lives and property of Americans and to secure an apology for the arrest of some American marines in Tampico.

A period of utter chaos followed the exile of Huerta. Three leaders struggled for power, Carranza in the northeast, Villa in the northwest, and Zapata in the south. With the aid of

Obregon, his chief lieutenant, Carranza finally established a new government by promising land reforms and supporting the organization of labor. A constitutional convention met late in 1916 in Quertaro and drafted a revolutionary document. It continued a new doctrine of property which in effect gave the government the real ownership, with individual rights largely those of tenure and subject to removal and confiscation by the government at any time. There were also provisions for the eight-hour day, the end of child labor, employer responsibility for accidents and disease, and the right of collective bargaining. The Church was curtailed by making all marriages civil contracts and by placing education under the control of the state. Thus the revolution, finally consummated by the Constitution of 1917, supported organized labor and the peasants, and attacked the Church and the large landowners.

The Mexican revolution followed the movement away from colonialism and toward economic nationalism which had begun in Uruguay. It had great psychological influence because it symbolized the rise of the peasants against the landlords and the Church. It made reformers hopeful that the landed interests could be overthrown. As Mexico proceeded to industrialize through its own efforts, there was hope also that a higher standard of living and economic independence could be achieved by internally inspired political revolutions. The old Hispanic faith in the salutary role of the state was revived. Since Mexico was also to some extent a socialist worker's state, the belief in worker-supported socialism gained momentum in other parts of Latin America.

The Nature of the Old Latin America

We are now able to give a summary description of the older culture into which the disturbing influences of economic nationalism, socialism, communism, fascism, and modern capitalism entered, causing social revolution during and after World War II. Throughout most of Latin America a colonial one-product agriculture had continued to dominate economic life. Land ownership was highly concentrated in the hands of an agricultural aristocracy. This group, aided by the army, controlled most of the nations through dictatorships based on a semblance of democracy and supported by pro-democratic propaganda. The dictators ruled "in the interest of the people." A small amount of industrialism had developed due to both foreign and domestic investments. The rising industrialists and middle classes had thrown in their lot with the dictators, seeking economic subsidies from the state and protection from the wage demands of the working classes. Foreign investors also supported the dictators for similar reasons.

Underlying this external social structure were the less tangible elements of the old Latin American culture. They consisted of attitudes of status and subservience, faith in the patriotic national leader, faith in the paternalistic landlord or employer and fatalism concerning economic or social betterment. Mysticism and superstition were still widespread. Graft and corruption in government were expected and even envied.

But in conflict with the social structure and cultural attitudes supporting the status quo, the democratic ideals of the early revolutionary leaders were still revered, at least among the educated. Nationalism and the desire for economic betterment and independence had grown. The achievements of Uruguay and Mexico had aroused and stimulated the imagination of Latin American liberals.

After World War II, widespread knowledge of well-being in the rest of the world caused revolutionary elements in the old culture to grow and led also to the formation of modern revolutionary tendencies. A new Latin America began to emerge. It was the work of a variety of elements, the working classes, the new class of businessmen, farm peasant leaders, the intellectuals, and the university students. Although communism and fascism have been strong, the social revolution has centered around what has been termed the *economic policy revolution* supported by socialists and liberals. This new policy will be discussed in the next chapter.

References

1. Hubert Herring, *The History of Latin America*, A. Knopf, New York, 1960, p. 133.
2. Pedro C. Teichert, *Economic Policy Revolution and Industrialization in Latin America*, University of Mississippi, University, Miss., 1959, p. 60.

THREE

CAPITALISM VERSUS COMMUNISM IN LATIN AMERICA

AS WE HAVE SEEN, THE INTERNAL ATTACK ON THE OLD CULTURE OF Latin America began in Uruguay and Mexico. In both countries, power was taken away from the landlords, and the peasants, workers, and businessmen began to control governmental policy. In Mexico the great estates were broken up, and gradually the land was redistributed among the poor farmers. The primary reform in Uruguay, however, was not land redistribution but a combination of economic nationalism and moderate socialism. As the years went by after the Mexican Revolution, the Mexicans also moved in these directions and the peasants and workers lost power to a clique of liberal businessmen who combined socialism with capitalism and economic nationalism.

The Economic Policy Revolution

Thus Uruguay and Mexico by the time of World War II had adopted a new program for economic development which has been called by Professor Teichert the economic policy revolution.[1] It fostered a mixed economy, neither wholly socialist nor capitalist. Tariffs and exchange controls stimulated domestic manufacturing industries such as textiles, cement, shoes, clothing, and the processing of food products. There was economic planning by state financial institutions through the regulation of credit and exchange rates. Basic economic fields such as railroads, telephones, electric power, petroleum, banking, steel, cement, chemicals, and power development were taken over by the government. Social insurance was made comprehensive.

Until the depression of 1929, no other Latin American nations followed these policies to any great extent, but by 1932 many of the countries had turned at least to economic nationalism and social insurance. After World War II a new group of liberals gradually gained political power who represented businessmen, civil servants, workers and poor farmers. These new liberal governments adopted much of the economic policy revolution and were mainly democratic by 1960.

In fact, during the postwar period there was much cause for optimism. Latin America seemed to have a new and effective policy for economic development. Moreover, the majority of the governments were becoming democratic, and pro-Americanism was replacing anti-Yankeeism. Most important, Latin America was enjoying a great economic boom.

The Rise of Democracy

The political history of Latin America before 1960 had been an account of the careers of dictators who ruled in the interests of the *hacendados,* the army, foreign capitalists, and the Church while giving hypocritical lip service to democratic beliefs and institutions. A new dictator would be installed while thousands shouted "viva democracia!" Although several countries were noted for their democracy (Chile, Colombia, Costa Rica, Mexico, and Uruguay), most Latin American nations had dictatorships. Yet by 1960 democratic regimes controlled Venezuela under Betancourt, Colombia under Camargo, Chile under Alessandri, Argentina under Frondizi, and Brazil under Kubitschek.

The democratic leaders of these countries not only adopted much of the economic policy revolution, but were in favor of capitalism as the chief means of rapid economic growth. Although socialism continued to play an important role in these countries, capitalism was regarded as the mainstay of progress. The new liberals believed in mixed economies which were no more socialistic than those of England or Sweden. Unfortunately, however, they were more in favor of deficit spending than the socialized governments of Western Europe. Their radicalism, if it may be called that, followed these lines rather than the extremes of state ownership.

The new democratic leadership was also pro-American. Much of Latin American radicalism in the past had been anti-Yankee. We were charged with imperialist aggression, and *Tio Sam* was regarded as the chief obstacle to Latin American economic and political independence. In Mexico in 1928, American business property had been expropriated. Under Mateos, Aleman, and Camacho, however, Mexico's semidemocratic government welcomed American capital. The governments of Frondizi, Alessandri, Prado, Camargo, and Betancourt in the other countries were decidedly pro-American.

The Economic Boom

In the late forties, and especially the fifties, many of the Latin American nations made rapid economic progress. By 1950 most of Latin America was booming and the annual rate of growth of the gross national product was between 4 and 5 percent a year.[2] This exceeded the average rate of growth in the United States and most of Western Europe. In some countries, such as Brazil, Chile, Costa Rica, Mexico, Peru, and Venezuela, the rate of growth of the total gross product per year was above 5 percent. Argentina, however, suffering from the regime of Perón, hardly grew at all.

The boom in the fifties was mainly due to the increase in industrialism. Agriculture lagged behind, and in some cases went backwards. The basis for the industrial growth had been created after 1930 by protective tariffs and exchange control. But after World War II, two factors were especially important: (1) the great accumulation of foreign credits resulting from high prices of food products and raw materials during the war, and (2) the growth of American direct investment.

By 1957, however, optimism began to turn into pessimism. There were signs of slackening in the rate of growth and by 1958, the Latin American boom was over. The average rates of growth declined from 5 to 2 percent. In some countries, such as Argentina and Chile, the rate of growth had dwindled to nothing. In the former nation, per capita real income actually declined. Latin American terms of trade deteriorated and there were large trade deficits. Conditions became worse in 1959 and 1960 until Argentina, Brazil, Bolivia, Chile, Ecuador and Uruguay were in a critical economic condition from inflation, unemployment, and trade deficits.

The liberal democratic governments which were in power by 1960 in most of Latin America faced an acute economic crisis. They were on trial not only to meet this crisis effectively, but to prove that the economic policy revolution and American economic support were the right instruments with which to meet it. Capitalism and democracy were on trial and under circumstances that were unfair to both.

The liberals had inherited and advanced the economic policy revolution introduced by dictators such as Perón in Argentina, Vargas in Brazil and Jimenez in Venezuela. But by 1957 this policy had failed, and yet the new governments seemed to have no alternative except to go farther in these same directions. The new democratic leaders were blamed for the failure of the policies their dictatorial predecessors had introduced but had not effectively carried out.

Why the Economic Policy Revolution Failed

Opinions differ widely as to why the economic policy revolution failed to sustain the rate of economic growth which was the main cause of postwar optimism. The following factors, however, were involved: (1) Insufficient capital, both domestic and foreign. (2) Inability to curb inflation. (3) The small size of domestic markets and the lack of a Latin American common market. (4) The failure to carry out programs of land reform. (5) Political instability and lack of continuity. (6) "Political socialism," or the provision of aid to the lower income groups for the sake of holding political power, usually through inflationary spending. (7) Inability to get enough American capital because of anti-Yankeeism. (8) Communism, Perónism, and other political disruption. (9) Failure to remove illiteracy and to provide enough technical education for farmers, workers, engineers, and businessmen.

The failure can be largely summarized by saying that except for Mexico and Uruguay the whole scope of the policy revolution was never adopted by the dictators who introduced it. The Latin American nations enacted protective tariffs and exchange control, nationalized some fields such as mining, utilities, railroads and communication, undertook public works projects, often ill-advised, accepted some foreign capital, principally from the United States after World War II, and did a great deal of economic planning on paper. All these efforts were on the credit side of the ledger.

The debit side, however, was considerable. In most countries, domestic saving did not get under way. In the end, no underdeveloped nation can rely for most of its capital on foreign sources. It must begin rapidly to create its own capital. This is the prime economic need of Latin America.

In addition, the Latin American nations did not curb inflation. Many Latin American politicians and economists espoused deficit spending on the assumption that they should follow Keynesianism. Although Keynesian doctrines may be valid for large advanced countries with problems of *unemployment,* they are not applicable to small underdeveloped nations with problems of *underemployment.* When unused labor or capital exists, an increase in money purchasing power in a large advanced country leads to greater production and less unemployment. When there is a shortage of capital and labor, as in a poor country, an increase in money usually causes inflation and an even greater shortage of capital. Countries like Argentina, Brazil, and Chile were in no position to stimulate production through monetary methods. Classical economics which stresses savings, capital accumulation, and lower prices and costs was more appropriate.

Moreover, the growth of industrialism required a broader market. Little Uruguay, for example, was not well suited to the development of industrialism. Argentina was not much better prepared for it, but for different reasons. It lacked industrial raw materials and fuel. But a common unit including Argentina, Brazil, Chile, Paraguay, and Uruguay with wider markets and more industrial raw materials might have industrialized much more easily. Until recently, however, there has been no common market, and each country has attempted to improve itself economically in isolation. Tariffs against American and European goods were reasonable, but tariffs against each other were not.

Moreover, the failure to provide land reform or general agricultural reform in most of the Latin American countries has not only resulted in the continuation of rural poverty, but in failure to build a base in increased agrarian productivity for the rise in population, and the use of more labor in industry, commerce, and the service trades. Industrialism requires both a decrease in the proportion of labor devoted to agriculture and greater farm productivity. But in some Latin American countries a decline in the farm population meant a decline in the over-all volume of food production.

Finally, political instability and nationalism limited progress. Political instability hampers the inflow of foreign capital. It gives rise to changes in economic policy before any one policy can be carried out. It leads to destructive "political socialism" as in the regime of Perón. Ten years were spent in Argentina in a systematic inflationary attempt to create a fictitious prosperity which would benefit labor and the lower income groups, but the results were disastrous, and economic progress was set back for years. Also, exploitive dictatorships limited progress and milked the economies of Latin American nations after World War II. There were regimes such as those of Batista, Jimenez, and Trujillo. The economic policy revolution was seriously retarded by their avarice.

Thus the economic policy revolution which had developed in Uruguay and Mexico proved a failure when adopted by dictators in Argentina, Brazil, and Venezuela and by democratic governments in Chile between 1940 and 1957. It was a failure not because it was inherently unsound, but because it was not completely followed or was negated by inflation, lack of saving, anti-Americanism, lack of land reform, political socialism and political instability. The democratic governments of 1960 adhered to the policy and sought to correct the causes of its failure. But in addition to their extreme economic difficulties, they faced the rise of communism and the persistence of fascism.

The Threat of Fascism and Communism

Despite the growth of prosperity after 1950, fascism had become politically significant in Latin America. Perón controlled the government of Argentina until 1954, and even after his overthrow, Perónism remained a powerful political force. Frondizi was elected president by appealing to Perónists for support. Bolivia had come close to fascism under Estensorro. Vargas at times gave signs of establishing fascism in Brazil in his *Novo Estado,* and much earlier, Mexico had turned toward fascism under Calles, an admirer of Hitler.

Communism also had become politically significant. The communists in Argentina could command 100,000 votes. The communists in Brazil got ten percent of the vote in the presidential election in 1945. In both Brazil and Chile they were so strong and disruptive that the communist parties were outlawed. Communism was also strong in Cuba, Bolivia, Ecuador, Mexico, and Venezuela. In 1958, communist party membership in Latin America was estimated at 80,000 in Argentina, 50,000 in Brazil, 35,000 in Venezuela, 25,000 in Chile and 12,000 in Cuba.[3]

The threat of communism became acute, however, as a result of the revolutions in Guatemala and Cuba. In 1945 the middle classes and workers in Guatemala overthrew the pro-landlord government and adopted a constitution resembling the Mexican constitution of 1917. Recognition of the rights of labor and the redistribution of land were the principal objectives. The new regime in Guatemala, although radical, was not communist in the beginning. Gradually, however, the communists, not numbering over two thousand, infiltrated the key government positions and seized power under President Jacobo Arbenz in 1950. The communist Arbenz, operating under direct control by Moscow, was finally ousted in 1954. But the success of a small communist minority in Guatemala proved to the Latin Americans that communist revolution was a real possibility.

Further proof came with the Cuban revolution under Fidel Castro, leader of the student opposition to the dictator, Batista. The twenty-sixth of July movement began guerrilla warfare in 1958 and in 1959 forced Batista to resign and flee into exile. For six months it appeared that the Castro regime would merely duplicate the land reforms of the Mexican revolution, but Castro had early come under the influence of the communists, and with the removal of the moderate Urrutia as president, the communists gained full control. By 1960 Chinese and Soviet communists were virtually dictating the policies of Cuba from their respective capitals. It seemed that they intended to use Cuba as a base for the political and military conquest of Latin America.

Fascism or communism could seize power in several of the

countries if the high rates of growth of the fifties are not resumed. The democratic governments must restore prosperity
and growth to avoid this calamity, since the collapse of the
economic boom is a serious factor in the revolutionary crisis
in Latin America.

By 1961 the business and political prospects in many of the
countries were not much better. By 1962 a new flight of capital
had begun and the political situation was decidedly worse.
Perónism had led to the overthrow of Frondizi in Argentina,
and fear of leftist tendencies had caused the army and conservative political groups to force the resignation of Quadros in Brazil.
Communist disturbances continued to be severe in Chile and
Venezuela. In Ecuador, the government of Ibarra, which supported the United States, had been overturned by the communist infiltrated air force. Fear of communism under Haya de
la Torre had led the army in Peru to establish a dictatorship
in that country.

The communists in Latin America have advantages in their
attempt to capture these countries. The great poverty helps them.
Communism thrives in retarded and backward regions rather
than, as Marx believed, in the last stages of advanced capitalism.
Another advantage is the persistence of feudalism and statism
and the absence of a strong middle class. Yet another advantage
is the illiteracy and simple literal-mindedness of large parts of
the population. The poor peasant farm worker readily believes
the promises and lies of communist agents, and the communists
also can capitalize on the widespread hatred of the United
States, the anti-Yankeeism.

The Old Latin America Versus the New

We began our analysis of the crisis in Latin America by
pointing out that society changes as attitudes and values change.
Revolutionary change occurs as a result of some shock or jolt to
the old culture. In Latin America, knowledge of the welfare
of the western nations and the United States has provided a
jolt. The creation of a better life began and seemed to be making progress from 1940 to 1957, but then came the decline of
the boom and the spectacular rise of communism in Cuba under

Castro. These were additional jolts. The communists began to argue all over Latin America that only their way of life could ultimately benefit the people. They rejected the economic policy revolution as the program of dictators and democratic liberals alike. They charged that the "false" boom of the 1950s was the work of American capitalism. It could not lead to permanent progress for the masses, and was merely the result of imperialist penetration which would only enrich the foreign capitalists.

The difficulty Latin America is having in its effort to promote economic development and independence lies in the clash between the old culture and the new. The economic policies of Uruguay and Mexico were fundamentally sound. But they could not be carried out fully either by the dictators or the democratic governments that succeeded them because of the opposition of the old culture.

The old culture has a social structure based on feudalistic, one-crop agriculture and it has been maintained for years through the political power of the landlords and the military. These groups resisted the breakup of the large estates, the increase of education and the rapid industrialization of Latin America. Although the dictators, Perón and Vargas, and the democratic governments of Chile made progress toward industrialization, the full development of the new policies proved arduous because of the continuing power of the landlords. To appease organized labor and the unemployed farm workers without dispossessing the landlords, all three countries resorted to elaborate public works and social security programs which could only be financed by inflation.

Not only the political power of the landlords, but also the feudalistic desire for a great leader made democracy and the rule of the middle class difficult. With the absence of a strong middle class, real democracy was hard if not impossible to achieve. Throughout the world, democracy rests on the strength of the middle class. It is the feudal peasant psychology of the lower classes in Latin America which has made them seek a great man, a demagogue, who will promise great progress quickly and in the meantime give quick "evidence" of progress through imposing public works, higher wages in inflated currency, and comprehensive social security systems that cannot be supported on the low national incomes now prevailing in most of the countries.

Thus Latin America is in much the same position as Russia was in 1917. There a shock had been given to the old culture by a great war. The people demanded immediate and rapid change. But the country was still largely feudal and agrarian. Industry had not grown very much. The middle class was small and weak and there were no strong, well-ingrained traditions of democracy. Instead there was suspicion and hatred of Western capitalism, and vigorous nationalism and pro-Slavism. Russia felt that it had to progress by itself and in its own way. The people demanded betterment and a new culture, but they could not accept Western capitalist industrialism for the very reason that the change was required, the old Russian agrarian feudalism. Somehow the leaders for change had to promote change within the fabric of feudalism. This is what Lenin did. His totalitarian undemocratic communism substituted a new group of lords for the tsar and his nobles.

In Latin America the situation is similar. Economic progress could not be made between 1940 and 1957 except under dictators. The failure of the dictators has led to a period of democratic government, but the power of the current liberal democrats is tenuous indeed. Because of its old culture, the natural tendency of Latin America is either to turn again to military dictators of the old type or to communist dictators of the new type. Russia has set up Castro on his island as an alternative people's dictator. In effect, the Russians say, "Look at Castro! He is the dictator who is really *latino* and will aid the people. Since you want a leader, this is your type of leader, *un verdarero lider del pueblo.*"

In view of these similarities between Latin America and Russia, one might well ask, why has democracy triumphed in recent years? There are several reasons. (1) Latin America has advanced farther toward industrialism than Russia had in 1917. (2) In some countries the middle classes and businessmen are strong. (3) There is a democratic ideology in Latin America, superficial though it may be. (4) Western European immigration has strongly affected some of the countries. (5) The hated United States exercises a powerful though resisted influence.

But the triumph of democracy may be short-lived. The survival of the liberal democrats depends upon their ability to solve the economic problems of Latin America, and the extent to which they can obtain aid from the United States. What has our policy been?

American Anti-crisis Policy

Fortunately our Federal government became aroused to the existence of a serious crisis in Latin America after 1958. It took the communist revolutions in Cuba and Guatemala to make us fully aware of it. To meet the crisis and thwart communism, the United States followed three policies: (1) Armed threats and military assistance. (2) Attempts to unite the Western Hemisphere nations against both communism and fascism through the Organization of American States as in the Declaration of San José in 1960 and the conference at Punta del Este in 1961. (3) Loans through the Export-Import Bank, support of the Inter-American Development Bank, and the program of the Alliance for Progress implemented by the Charter of Punta del Este and based on the Act of Bogota of 1960.

Here we are concerned primarily with economic policy, and we shall attempt only to outline briefly the history and nature of the Alliance for Progress. This American economic answer to underdevelopment in Latin America and the threat of communism did not begin with President Kennedy's speech of March 13, 1961. If any one person can be regarded as the father of the program, it was President Kubitschek, who proposed it in its original form as Operation Pan-America. Further delineation was provided in a meeting of the Organization of American States in Bogota in September, 1960. The Act of Bogota, signed by nineteen members of OAS,[4] declared (1) that the "preservation and strengthening of free and democratic institutions . . . requires the acceleration of social and economic progress in Latin America adequate to meet the legitimate aspirations of the peoples of the Americas for a better life . . ." (2) that economic development programs "may have a delayed effect on social welfare, and that accordingly early measures are needed to cope with social needs," (3) that "social progress will require maximum self-help efforts," and (4) that it is advisable to launch a program for social development which also promotes productivity and strengthens economic development. Having stated these principles, the nineteen nations drew up a list of measures for the improvement of conditions of rural living and land use, housing and community facilities, educational systems, public health, and domestic resources. They welcomed the decision of the United States to establish a special inter-American fund for social development to be administered by the Inter-American Development Bank. In addition, they proposed measures for economic development and multilateral cooperation.

The Alliance for Progress

The Alliance for Progress program proposed by President Kennedy in his speech on March 13, 1961 to Latin American representatives at the White House was the major implementation of the Act of Bogota. At that time the late President said, "If we are to meet a problem so staggering in its dimensions, our approach must itself be equally bold, an approach consistent with the majestic concept of Operation Pan America. Therefore, I have called on all the people of this hemisphere to join in a new Alliance for Progress . . . a vast cooperative effort, unparalleled in magnitude and nobility of purpose, to satisfy the basic needs of the American people for homes, work and land, health and schools . . ." To carry out the program, President Kennedy proposed that the United States grant $20 billion over a period of ten years according to plans worked out by the cooperating nations.

In August, 1961 a special meeting of the Inter-American Economic and Social Council of OAS was held at Punta del Este in Uruguay to discuss the ways of carrying out the Alliance for Progress program. The result was the Charter of Punta del Este which outlined twelve objectives:

1. Per capita growth must increase by at least 2.5 percent a year.
2. Incomes and standards of living must be raised.
3. Economies must be diversified and commodity prices stabilized.
4. Great industrialization.
5. Greater agricultural productivity.
6. Comprehensive agrarian and land reforms.
7. The elimination of illiteracy.
8. The increase of life expectancy.
9. An increase of low-cost housing.

10. Avoidance of inflation.
11. Economic integration of Latin American countries.
12. Prevention of the ill effects of excessive exchange fluctuations on national earnings.

In the first year of the Alliance for Progress, Congress appropriated $1 billion, and in the spring of 1962, Kennedy recommended an appropriation of $3 billion for 1963 which was subsequently cut back by Congress 20 percent. The administration of the program was placed in the newly organized Administration for International Aid (AID), the successor of ICA. The Alliance for Progress part of AID was headed by Teodoro Moscoso, a Puerto Rican who had been ambassador to Venezuela, and a prominent figure in the Puerto Rican economic development program.

It is not surprising that in its first year the Alliance for Progress encountered serious difficulties. The democratic governments behind the program were in a shaky political position. The program was attacked both in the United States and in Latin America. In the United States, Congressmen became discontented with lack of progress made in land and tax reform. In Latin America, nationalists and communists attacked the program as destructive of national independence, and as a new form of "Yankee imperialism." The chief concern of most Latin American experts was over the ability of Latin American liberals to make the needed reforms for social development and to prevent economic development from eclipsing social development and unduly enriching the top-income groups. The problem was, as Kennedy put it, to see that the money reached "the man in the street." Without this result the whole program could become a political boomerang, destroying the prestige of both the democratic governments and the United States.

The success of the American anticommunist and crisis policies thus depends heavily upon the success of the democratic governments. Can they, through cooperative planning with the United States (1) promote economic development at the rate of at least 2.5 percent a year, (2) simultaneously promote social development, and (3) remain in power? The crisis in Latin America came from the demand of the common man for betterment, the failure of the economic policy revolution to accelerate or sustain economic growth and simultaneously promote social development, and the disappointing collapse of the post-World War II boom. Economic aid from the United States may tend to "prime the pump." But it cannot solve the economic problems of Latin America by itself. They must be solved by a new attempt to make the economic policy revolution work by fuller and more conscientious use of its features.

The twelve objectives of the Alliance for Progress accepted at Punta del Este constitute an enlarged and complete version of the economic policy revolution, which originated in Uruguay and Mexico. The postwar Latin American dictators accepted only part of it, and were ineffective in carrying it out for reasons we have described. The succeeding democratic governments inherited the failures of the dictators, the economic crisis, and the threat of communism. The United States, through the Alliance for Progress, has entered the Latin American political arena literally to force through economic aid (or bribery) the full adoption of the economic policy revolution. Will this American effort succeed? Can we force progress on Latin America? Probably not. The real hope lies in the liberal and mixed capitalist-nationalist-socialist leaders in Latin America itself.

References

1. Cf. Pedro C. Teichert, *Economic Policy Revolution and Industrialization in Latin America*, University of Mississippi, University, Miss., 1959.

2. The Economic Commission for Latin America.

3. U. S. Senate subcommittee report, 1959.

4. Cuba voted no, and the Dominican Republic was not represented.

II

The Economic Development
of Latin America

THE ECONOMIC PROBLEMS
OF LATIN AMERICA

RECENT VISITORS TO LATIN AMERICA HAVE BEEN SURPRISED TO find there a great number of socially minded, well-educated and forward-looking men. These "new" men have an excellent grasp of the social and economic problems confronting their countries and have made many constructive proposals for their solution. Among the men in this new liberal group cited as examples by Adlai Stevenson and William Benton after their two tours of Latin America are Jose Figueres, the great Costa Rican liberal; Crisologe Larralde, the leader of the People's Radicals in Argentina; Alberto Lleras Camargo, the former president of Colombia; Lopez Mateos, the president of Mexico and Raoul Prebisch, Latin America's leading economist. Many others could be mentioned. Many are not politicians or professional men, but progressive businessmen.

In our opinion, the future of Latin America rests largely in the hands of this new group. If they can gain political power and retain it, Latin America will progress rapidly. But they are faced by both rightist and leftist opposition. On the right are the army, the large landowners and reactionary or monopolistic businessmen, and on the left, Perónists, Fidelistas and other kinds of fascists and communists.

The "new" men can provide constructive leadership because they have a greater understanding of Latin America's problems than any other group. Although they know more than others, however, it appears that their knowledge is not very well organized. It can only be translated into constructive effort if it is based on some sound economic theory which is pertinent to the solution of their national problems.

We insist, therefore, that without a basic economic theory for Latin America the Latin American liberals who gained polit-

41

ical power in Argentina, Guatemala, Colombia, Honduras, Venezuela, and the Dominican Republic after 1956 and who already had power in Mexico, Costa Rica, Uruguay, and Chile will ultimately fail. The liberals, as we have seen, originated the economic policy revolution. But this policy revolution failed presumably because it was not adopted in its entirety. It may have failed, however, *because it was not founded on a clear and well-defined economic theory*. Latin America today urgently needs such a theory. Not only does Latin America need it, but the United States as well. We cannot aid Latin America effectively in its struggle "to get into the sun" without such a theory. The lack of it is the major weakness in our Latin American foreign policy.

We are not contending, however, that the economic policy revolution and the Alliance for Progress were steps in the wrong direction. But at this stage the analysis of Latin America's problems needs to be synthesized, made more explicit, and given a sound theoretical foundation. To put it another way, Latin America now needs "to pull its best thought together."

But how can this be done? The first steps consist of clarifying the major elements in economic development and then looking at the economic problems of Latin America in terms of these elements. We need to re-examine, first, the age-old question: What makes a poor nation begin to grow richer? Then, we must examine Latin America's problems to see why the wrong answers are being given to this question.

The Elements in Economic Development

1. THE CLASSICAL ANSWER: CAPITAL ACCUMULATION

Most of the basic questions about economic development were first raised years ago by the classicists—Smith, Ricardo, Malthus, and Mill. These men divided the factors affecting development into the elements described by us in Chapter 1: labor, resources, capital and technology. The wealth of a nation depended on its population, its land, its capital and the extent of the division of labor (the earliest conception of technology). But of these four elements, the classicists stressed *capital*.

The classicists thought that the accumulation of capital was primarily responsible for the level of wages and national wealth. Adam Smith made this break with earlier thinking which stressed the importance of land. Smith was the first great advocate of industrialism as the main instrument of progress. Industrialism grew through the following steps: income was saved, savings were invested in man-made equipment or capital, the growth of invested capital increased production, and increased production led to higher wages and national wealth.

But two of the leading classicists, Ricardo and Malthus, were pessimistic. They were both concerned over the tendency of population to grow and offset all of the advantages gained from increased production. Malthus saw wages constantly returning to subsistence levels because population grew at a rate faster than the means of subsistence.

Fortunately for economic progress, the pessimism of these classicists was unfounded. Land was not fixed. Its productivity could be increased by better farming methods and fertilizer. Tremendous quantities of new land were put into use outside Europe. Wages rose above subsistence. But the classicists, although their assumptions were sometimes erroneous, provided invaluable economic insights. They called attention to two fundamentals: poor countries are scarcity economies, and the only way out of scarcity is more production through saving and investment.

For Latin America today, the classical view of economic effort as a life and death struggle against the "niggardliness of nature," Adam Smith's term for scarcity, is still appropriate. Although Latin Americans can aspire ultimately to an economy of abundance, this must be achieved largely "the hard way," through saving and capital accumulation. Short cuts through inflation and expensive social security systems will only retard progress. Even foreign aid and foreign loans can only "get the ball rolling." No matter how much rich countries aid poor countries, it can never be enough. They must somehow "tighten their belts" and begin rapid and substantial *domestic* capital accumulation.

2. POPULATION GROWTH

The second concern of the classicists was over the growth of population. As we have noted, Ricardo and Malthus saw it causing economic stagnation and the eternal poverty of the lower classes. Over 150 years after Malthus and Ricardo wrote, we are still faced with the evil of population pressure. The population of two-thirds of the world is increasing at an excessive rate. To be sure, wages have not been forced down to subsistence in the advanced third of the world. But the gloomy predictions of Malthus have not come true in these areas only because the rate of capital accumulation has exceeded the rate of population growth. The Malthusian theory of population is still true as a form of economic analysis. No nation can advance above subsistence for most of its people unless the means of subsistence grow faster than population. This lesson of classical economics is still valid.

But the lesson has not been learned in China, India, Indonesia, and most of Africa and Asia. It has also not been learned in Chile, Haiti, El Salvador, Cuba, Puerto Rico, and other parts of Latin America. Even among Latin American intellectuals there is much confusion about the matter. Religious and cultural attitudes lead to prejudice in favor of large families. Intellectuals rationalize concerning the economic advantages of population growth. They argue that it is a stimulant rather than a depressant. But it can only stimulate growth in a nation which has begun to increase its capital and production rapidly. This stimulating effect operated in the United States because we were growing rapidly and were resource-rich. But Chile, Colombia, Cuba, El Salvador, Costa Rica, Haiti, and even Argentina should heed the teachings of Malthus, who postulated an optimum population in relation to capital and resources. Most Latin American countries have not reached the optimum.

3. ECONOMIC INCENTIVE

The classicists pioneered also in stressing the need for economic incentive. If an increase in the standard of living depends on an increase in production, and an increase in production depends on the increase in capital and its investment, there must be incentives both to save and to invest. Let us consider saving first. Capital cannot be accumulated without saving. What makes people save? There are both negative and positive motives. We save to take care of the "rainy day" and to have "substance" in our old age. We are afraid of "want." But we also save to be better off and to obtain some of the luxuries of life. None of the reasons for saving can motivate us, however, unless our objectives can be achieved. If, for example, we find that our life savings are likely to be wiped out by inflation, we will spend today and forget tomorrow. In Latin America, inflation has been huge and chronic in about half the nations.

Counterbalancing this negative condition, however, are the high rates of interest and profits prevailing in most of the countries. If one does save and invest, he gets a high rate of return on his capital. But these high rates of return are often wiped out along with the principal unless people are willing to put their savings into land and buildings or into individually owned and operated business enterprises.

Far too large a proportion of the Latin Americans who save put their money into real estate. There are two reasons for this. On the one hand, it seems, and probably is for the most part, safer. On the other hand, there is a prejudice in favor of land ownership which is a vestige of feudalism. Land ownership is honorable; trade or business enterprise, vulgar. Thus economic incentives are limited. Earning money from capital is to many only good when it is earned from agriculture or real estate. For a thriving economic system, economic incentives must be broader. In the England of the classicists, feudalism had broken down. Trade and business had become honorable.

Strong economic incentive in a poor country also requires a relatively low level of wages. Low wages, however, are not merely low money wages. What is needed is low labor costs. For each dollar of wages the output of labor must be high. In poor countries wages may seem very low. But in terms of output they are very high. When dictatorships seize power and raise wages both directly and indirectly through expensive social security systems as in the case of Perón in Argentina, the already high labor costs become excessive. Business stagnates. In a poor country it is unfortunate but true that wages must be kept low. We are inclined to think of the United States as a high-wage country. In the days of our most rapid development, however, wages were low in proportion to labor productivity. From this fact came high profits, the prime incentive needed for rapid advancement.

4. THE ENTREPRENEURIAL OR MIDDLE CLASS

Another significant factor in economic development, early recognized by the classicists, was the role of the businessman, the undertaker, or *entrepreneur*. The development of an advanced economic life requires the organization of labor, land, and capital in profitable and productive combinations. Under capitalism, an entrepreneurial class must perform these functions. If poor countries remain capitalist, there is no substitute for the entrepreneurial class. It must be large, optimistic, intelligent, energetic, enterprising, and imaginative. It must be richly rewarded for its efforts and not frustrated by excessive and unintelligent government regulations. Nor should it have an inferior status in the social hierarchy or be corrupted by the graft, laziness, and inefficiency of government bureaucracy.

The difficulty with most poor countries is the absence, small size, or corruption of the entrepreneurs. The lack of resources or capital is less serious than the lack of good businessmen. Countries like Costa Rica, Mexico, and Puerto Rico have revealed that the development of a smart entrepreneurial class has gone far toward offsetting the lack of capital and resources. The enterprising businessman gets the capital.

Not the least function of the entrepreneur is what economists call innovation. The scientist in the laboratory discovers basic truths about nature. This we call "pure" science. The inventor applies pure science to the satisfaction of human wants. In the nineteenth century, invention was largely the work of individuals. Today it is mainly a group enterprise, and research staffs of large corporations and governments are supplying the leading inventions. Once a new product is invented it should be produced, and thus become a means of satisfying wants. This is innovation. Some economists, notably Schumpeter, have visualized capitalism as growing mainly through waves of innovations.

In some countries in Latin America the small entrepreneurial class has been imaginative and there has been a considerable amount of innovation. This is true especially in Brazil, Mexico, and Puerto Rico. In many of the other countries, Latin American business has been extremely conservative. The conservatism of the landlords spreads over into the business classes. Innovation, such as develops, is usually the work of American or other foreign businessmen. When this "enterprise" is revealed, it is often resented by domestic businessmen. Even the higher wages and fringe benefits accruing to domestic labor from the innovations and modernization introduced by foreigners, especially Americans, is resented.

5. ACCEPTANCE OF CAPITALISM

No progress can be made in any socioeconomic system unless the system is accepted. With one foot still in feudalism, Latin America has great difficulty in stepping over completely into capitalism. As we have pointed out earlier, it would be easier culturally for Latin America to turn fascist or communist. Latin Americans must make up their minds whether they have faith in capitalism as the primary means of advancing their standard of living. If they have faith in capitalism, they must provide for capitalist incentives, limit the role of the state in economic life, and place production and productivity ahead of social security or economic equality as national goals. They must limit legalized monopoly, and not go to extremes in government subsidies to industry and agriculture. They must not embark upon uneconomic or unproductive public works, such as elaborate public buildings and housing projects, or new ultramodern capitals like Brasilia located in sparsely populated areas.

It is possible and even desirable for Latin America to develop mixed economies in which there is a large degree of socialism. But the problem here is twofold: faith in capitalism and the maintenance of balance. If the growth of socialism in Latin America destroys capitalism, either intentionally or not, economic growth will be seriously retarded. Capitalism is the most efficient means of rapid economic growth. Rapid growth in the advanced countries has been due to capitalism. Yet there is great ambivalence in Latin America about capitalism and many are inclined to believe that socialist or communist methods will speed progress. But balance must be maintained. A combination of capitalism, socialism, and economic nationalism will speed progress; socialism or communism by themselves will lead to stultification. They will retard Latin American growth for many years. This is happening right now in Cuba and Bolivia.

Related to faith in capitalism is capitalistic optimism. The depression of 1929 temporarily destroyed this optimism in the United States. But prior to the depression, Americans were not pessimistic or cynical. They believed that things would get better and better *under capitalism*. Even in the worst days of the depression, Americans did not give up in favor of socialism. One essential to Latin American progress is this capitalistic optimism.

6. ECONOMIC BALANCE

Another element in growth is balance. One part of an economy must not grow at the expense of another part. For example, it will be fatal to Latin American industry if it grows at the expense of agriculture, since the former is based on the latter. You cannot get a supply of industrial labor without shifting workers from the farm to the city, but you cannot shift labor from farming into industry unless farm productivity grows. The remaining farm workers must be able to feed the departing farm workers and themselves as well. In addition, there must be a balance between production for export and production for domestic consumption. As we shall see, these two types of unbalance are seriously retarding Latin America. Some countries have developed industry at the expense of agriculture. Falling short of that, other countries have developed industry and merely neglected agriculture. Still others have neglected industry for agriculture. Most of the countries have encouraged export farming or raw material production to the neglect of domestic production.

7. THE ROLE OF GOVERNMENT

For rapid advancement, poor countries should encourage capitalism. To do this the state must maintain order and protect property rights. It should also prevent extreme inflation and avoid high taxes on profits or business enterprise. It must encourage business by improving transportation, removing illiteracy, maintaining sanitation, and providing a sound currency and banking system. But it is reasonable to assume that in countries which are economically far behind, the role of the state should be greater than in more advanced nations. In underdeveloped countries some socialism is appropriate because it provides planning to remedy unbalance and government enterprise to fill in gaps in production that private enterprise has not yet filled and cannot fill for some time. But the ultimate objectives should be capitalistic. There should be a "capitalistic socialism" which will aim primarily at greater industry and productivity rather than economic equality and social security. The latter are desirable aims, but they should be secondary to greater production and an overall higher standard of living. Put another way, the role of government should be to speed up growth, not to create an economic utopia.

The ends, moreover, should be primarily materialistic, not spiritualistic. As the Castro regime progressed in Cuba, it became utopian. The Revolution of July 26 became an end in itself. As beans and rice got short in supply, Castro harangued the people to defend the revolution, and in doing this he was asking his people to exchange material for spiritual goals. It is conceivable that the Cuban people, or a part of it, could go on for years happy with spiritual gains while they eat less, their automobiles fall apart, and their houses collapse over their heads. But this is not the kind of "progress" we should advocate in Latin America. Government should promote material as well as spiritual goals. Too much emphasis on equality, the rights of man and cradle-to-the-grave social security will destroy Latin America. In the end, it will lead to both spiritual and economic bankruptcy.

The Specific Economic Problems of Latin America

From our discussion it is apparent that the main problem of Latin America is economic growth. The Latin American nations are poor, and no amount of social or spiritual improvement will compensate for the basic poverty. Poor nations become richer through changes in resources, capital, population, and technology. There are seven simple elements in the growth of the wealth of nations: capital accumulation, optimum population, adequate economic incentives, a strong and efficient entrepreneurial middle class, the acceptance of capitalism, economic balance in growth, and government policies that encourage private as well as public enterprise. Most of the specific economic problems of Latin America are related to these various elements. We must now survey these problems briefly before we can begin to see the kind of development theory needed in Latin America for liberal and effective economic policies. What are the problems which a development theory could be used to solve?

1. Problems of Population and of the Labor Force. These problems are partly quantitative and qualitative. In countries like Bolivia, Haiti, Puerto Rico, Cuba, and Brazil population has been, or is now, too great for an optimum relationship to capital, technology, or resources. In some countries also, population tends to grow at a rate which offsets the advantages gained from increased production. In Mexico and Colombia economists now watch the relative growth rates of population and production and are optimistic only when the latter more than offsets the former. There is a great race going on in Latin America between population and production. In Mexico and Colombia production has been winning. In Chile, Haiti, and El Salvador population is winning.

Population must not only be of the right quantity but also of the right quality. For efficiency and rapid economic development, the labor force, or working part of the population, must become larger, healthier, better educated, and occupationally trained to suit the growing industrial needs. Various qualitative labor problems plague Latin American nations. In most of the countries, the labor force is inadequate because of poor health, lack of education, and lack of industrial or professional training. But in some countries, notably Argentina and Chile, excesses of technically trained workers have developed because the rate of industrialization is not rapid enough to absorb them. Since the unemployed technical men emigrate, these countries have been educating technicians for the benefit of others. They can ill afford to aid other nations in this way.

An effective labor force is not only one that is well trained, but one that has attitudes and habits conducive to high productivity. Here we have another Latin American labor problem. It is probably true that Latin American workers will not work as long or as hard as labor in other countries, and that there is a considerable amount of absenteeism. Observance of Latin American labor has led many Americans even to conclude that Latin Americans are indolent by nature. If the rate of productivity is low, however, the causes are probably cultural rather than the "inheritance" of laziness.

Latin American labor has been subject to a psychological and cultural environment which is not conducive to great effort on the job. We all work either because of wage incentives or for philosophical and moral reasons. If earnings are very low and there are few goods that we can buy, leisure—even with greater poverty—has its attractions. Thus in Latin America higher wages might induce people to work harder, but the scarcity of consumer's goods or the lack of specific knowledge of what a higher standard of living could mean make higher wages a meaningless lure and a leisurely life more attractive. The Latin American is not subject like the North American to high-pressure advertising. Although Latin Americans have in recent years begun to demand a better way of life, they often seek it through political reforms or revolutionary means rather than through harder work.

2. *Philosophical and Moral Background.* Latin Americans are by nature not only unsuited to vigorous work, but to business enterprise as well. Latin Americans have been strongly influenced by feudalism and Catholicism rather than by individualism and Calvinism. The semifeudalistic system established by the Portuguese and Spaniards made work a mark of social and racial inferiority. The foreign conquerors lived in idleness on the labor of Indian peons and Negro slaves. Anyone who worked was inferior. The feudalistic degradation of work has been carried over into modern times. The ideal life has been that of the indolent landowners on the great hacienda. Catholicism also contributed to these views by stressing grace rather than hard work as the means to salvation. Under Calvinism, hard work, saving, and business triumphs were religious as well as economic virtues.

The population and labor force problems of Latin America are not unsolvable, but when one realizes all that the solution entails it becomes apparent that many years will be required for a complete solution. Great improvements are needed in health, education, and housing. There is need for extensive industrial, technical, and professional training. The attitudes and habits related to work must be adapted to the requirements of an industrialized economy. The general public needs to become aware of the specific ways in which a better economic life can be achieved, both through production and consumption. It must realize also the effects of too rapid an increase in population on the standard of living. Many of these necessary changes may come about naturally, however, as a result of an increase in the standard of living and the growth of industrialism.

3. *The Problem of Technology.* In addition to labor and population problems, Latin America has a problem of technology. The need for new technology exists in every phase of economic life. It is especially great in agriculture, construction, road building, communications, and the distribution and marketing of goods. Fortunately, Latin Americans do not have to invent

the new methods; they can borrow them. But borrowing modern technology is not enough, and the rate at which it is introduced is a problem in itself. For example, Latin Americans do not need as modern a telephone system as we have, at least not in all the countries. But how rapid should the modernization be in view of other pressing needs and the scarce means of meeting them? Modern technology, moreover, to be borrowed must be used. To educate Mexican or Guatemalan farmers in the most modern methods of farming would do no good unless they are willing to adopt the new methods and have the capital and equipment to use them. Traditionalism, as well as lack of capital, often stands in the way of use.

Apart from lack of capital, there are three other obstacles to the introduction of new technology. The first of these is lack of education. Adoption of new industrial methods requires an enormous amount of education on various levels. A basic requirement is literacy, and in some of the nations the illiteracy rate is over 50 percent. Also, large numbers of skilled workers, technicians, engineers, and professional men must be trained. A second obstacle is antiforeignism, especially anti-Americanism. For years Mexican oil was undeveloped partly because of opposition to the use of American engineers when none had yet been trained at home. The same situation exists in Argentina and Brazil. In the present stage of industrialism many Latin American countries will have to use foreign engineers and businessmen. Refusal to do so will retard technological advancement. A third obstacle is the social structure. The slowness with which agriculture has been modernized is partly due to the opposition of the landowning class. Modernization means in many cases the removal of the old wage system, the breaking up of large estates, the cultivation of uncultivated areas, and agricultural diversification. Even if the large landowners could be sure of higher returns from these changes, they would fear the social and political results.

The introduction of modern methods in agriculture is in many instances linked to land reform. Chile is a good example. There the landowners have refused to allow the large estates to be broken up because they fear loss of political power through any marked improvement in the status of the poor farm workers. Failure to break up the estates has retarded the use of modern methods because the large landowners will not introduce them

except when they are producing crops for export, and modernization is needed to meet foreign competition. The landowners
have also opposed the improvement of education and the removal of illiteracy in line with their policy of keeping the farm
worker down.

4. Natural Resources. In addition to modern technology and
a good labor force, economic development requires natural re-
souces. A superficial examination of Latin America is likely to be
misleading as to its richness in this respect. From a natural standpoint, Latin America is an area of superlatives. In Chile lies the
world's greatest supply of nitrates. The oil resources of Venezuela
are among the richest in the world. It is believed that the greatest
deposits of iron ore in the world are in Brazil and there are also
large deposits in Venezuela. The Argentine Pampa is one of the
greatest grain and cattle-raising areas in the world.

With such natural advantages as these, it would seem that
South America should develop into one of the greatest of the
world's industrial areas, but there are drawbacks. We have already indicated the drawbacks involved in the backwardness and
deficiency of the labor force and in the lack of technology. We
have touched also very briefly on the way in which Latin American culture and institutions serve as impediments. But from the
standpoint of resources there is another great problem. For the
growth of industrialism, resources and labor must be properly
located. In Latin America, unfortunately, juxtaposition of the
labor force and resources is often lacking. Brazil does not have
the coal for a great steel industry, although some steel is produced there. Chilean nitrates are a long way from the market
for them and synthetic nitrates have largely been substituted.
The petroleum of Venezuela is far from the places where it is
being used. Or, to put it another way, these countries have not
developed the standard of living or industrialism which would
create a great market for the resources at home. Much of the
dependence of Latin American countries on other nations can
be attributed to the fact that both resources and agricultural
products cannot be amply used due to lack of industrialism. As
a result, their economies are to some degree *exclaves,* which consist merely of external parts of other economies in foreign
countries.

5. Transportation. The bad location of South American resources could be remedied to some extent by improved trans-

portation. But the problems of transportation are also serious. The Andes mountains greatly impede east-west commerce. Very few passes exist through this formidable land barrier. The rivers of the continent flow eastward for the most part, and not north and south to connect a land area which runs mainly north and south. Contrast this with the great chain of the Ohio, Missouri, and Mississippi Rivers which has played such a crucial role in our own history. Moreover, the railroad building of Latin America has been inadequate in most countries. Similarly, roads are lacking all over the continent. Today, air lines have done much to supply the needs of transportation and trade where roads are poor or nonexistent. This is especially true on the west coast, and in the northern countries of Venezuela and Colombia. But airlines cannot take the place of roads and railroads entirely.

6. *Land-man Distribution Ratio.* There is a problem also of the bad location or improper distribution of people on the land. Central and South America present some of the world's most extreme land-man ratios. In island regions such as Cuba, Haiti, and Puerto Rico, population is very dense and exceeds the resource potentialities of the area. In Haiti, for example, in 1960 there were 327.1 persons per square mile. How is this excessive population to be relocated or industry developed locally that will be sufficiently productive to raise the standard of living? Puerto Rico and Cuba also have large land-man ratios. Puerto Ricans can emigrate to the continental United States, but this creates many problems of its own, both cultural and economic. The Puerto Ricans, coming from a one-product agriculture, cannot be assimilated easily into either American agriculture or industry.

There are great urban clusters of population as well as areas of great density. The cities of Latin America are among the largest in the world. Buenos Aires, Mexico City, Rio de Janeiro and São Paulo have over three million people. Although there is much industry in the Latin American cities, they have attracted a large number of persons who live rather poorly from occasional employment and government relief. Their splendidly built main streets often hide great slum areas around the periphery and in the "old" city. Most of them are overgrown and unduly large. There is not a sufficiently large underlying economic base to support their large populations. As a result, many of the people in the cities live in poverty and considerable idleness and are ripe for social revolution.

In contrast to the overpopulated islands and the overgrown cities, there are large areas of Latin America which are underpopulated. There are many reasons for this. Feudal agriculture or primitive subsistence farming cannot support a large population. Productivity is low because of lack of irrigation, exhaustion of the soil, and the need for reforestation in some areas and clearing in others. Lack of means to transport produce is another factor.

Thus over-all size is not always the main population problem in Latin America. There is great need for regions which can be developed for modern agriculture, and poor farmers and the excess city population should be transferred to these regions. When population began to accumulate in our country in New England, along the seaboard, and in Eastern cities, there were great agricultural areas to the Middle and Far West to which Americans migrated. They took up new land and started new farms and factories. For decades there was no lack of space. But it was not only the space. The land was good. It was made accessible by clearing, by roads, and by railroads, and the use of rivers. In South and Central America there are few "development areas" that would correspond to the American frontier. There are really only four—the highlands of Costa Rica, the central valley of Chile, the highlands of Aritioquia in Colombia, and the three southern states in Brazil. It is often said that it spite of the great land mass of Central and South America, Latin Americans are land poor. However, good land is scarce partly because of failure to open up areas for development such as we created in the Middle and Far West. South America needs pioneers.

7. *Problems of Land Tenure and Monoculture.* Change in land tenure is one of the oldest problems of Latin America. It has been discussed for years. In most Latin American countries land is still held in large estates. The typical situation is one in which the large *estancias* are devoted to one type of produce, mainly for export, and farmed by cheap labor. Farm workers are largely tenants who are poor and frequently in debt. Large parts of the *estancias* are left idle when the market for the main product does not warrant full production. Agricultural credit is limited or supplied only to the owners of large estates through

government banks. The large landowners have often controlled the government and made credit available to themselves. Very often heavy borrowing by landowners has been due to extravagance and a tendency to live beyond their means. The land has not been heavily taxed and sometimes not taxed at all. Most governmental revenues have been derived from customs duties and sales taxes. When debt burdens grow, deficit spending is encouraged to provide additional bank loans and to create inflation which makes debts easier to pay.

Granted this situation, the natural inclination of land reformers has been to advocate the breaking up of the large estates into smaller tracts for distribution to the landless peasant or peon population. Where this has been undertaken, the results have not been very satisfactory since the poor state of the soil and the inefficiency of independent farmers has made the small farms uneconomical and incapable of supporting their small owners. The newer solutions are to force, through taxation, the full use of the land on the estates, and the introduction of modern methods and machinery. Increasingly also, industrialism has been advocated as a way out by drawing off unused and underemployed labor. Mexico, which first sought solution through the division of landed estates into small holdings, finally turned to industrialism as the main means of employing the poor and landless.

An additional problem on the large estates has been the development of exploitive and onerous systems of sharecropping and tenancy. Land has also been held merely for land-value speculation rather than for full or efficient cultivation. In some cases there is excessive investment of savings and profits on the land rather than in more productive business ventures. In some countries the lack of capital available for business has been due in part to the concentration of investment in unprofitable, but more socially respectable agriculture.

8. Monoculture and Dependence on Exports. A great price and marketing problem associated with large estates is that of monoculture and the resulting unbalanced dependence upon exports. Without either industrialization or diversified self-sufficient agriculture, Latin American economies have in the past been unduly one-crop economies. Only the slightest reflection brings to mind the various one-crop economies, the coffee economy of Brazil, the banana economies of Central America and Ecuador, the wool and meat economies of Argentina and Uruguay, and the sugar economies of Puerto Rico, Cuba, and the Dominican Republic. The disadvantages of centering an economy around one-crop agriculture are obvious. A depression in the foreign market for one crop depresses the whole domestic economy, since it is so dependent upon the spending resulting from the sale of the one crop. Agricultural prices, moreover, tend to lag behind industrial prices, with the result that the agriculturally oriented nation tends to sell its products cheaply and to buy dear industrial products with the income from the one-crop agriculture. Finally, the economy becomes frozen, or rigidly based upon the single crop, revealing neither economic balance nor the ability to grow or become industrialized.

9. *Agricultural Labor Force.* One basic index of the development of any country is the percentage of the labor force devoted to agriculture in contrast to manufacturing, construction, trade, and service. As a nation advances economically, the amount of labor devoted to agriculture declines in favor of other occupations. Ultimately manufacturing and mining decline and the service and trade elements absorb more and more labor. If this index can be taken as a measure of underdevelopment, the degree of it and the recent progress can be found in the following data of the percentage distribution of the labor force in 1945 and 1955.[1]

	1945	1955
Agriculture	56.2	50.7
Manufacturing and Mining	15.1	15.7
Construction	3.1	3.7
Services	23.2	27.6
Not specified	2.3	2.4

10. *Capital Investment.* Fundamental to the growth of the economy and its industrialization is the investment of capital. The rate of Latin American industrialization depends mainly upon the investment rate. Between 1948 and 1957, largely due to lack of capital, the growth of industrial production was only 40 percent in Latin America in contrast to 75 percent in Europe and 150 percent in Asia and the Middle East.

11. *Problem of Inflation.* Working against the rapid development of Latin American countries is the critical and persistent

problem of inflation. In Latin America it is seldom confined, if it begins, to a price rise of 5 or 10 percent. It is usually of the extreme variety, and capital investment and normal economic progress are disturbed in a number of ways. Inflation as we have seen, discourages saving, the basis of capital formation. It encourages speculation which is a disruptive and unproductive economic activity. Inflation also discourages foreign investments, especially when it results in blocked currency and the remittance of profits is prohibited. Inflation may cause political instability which is yet another deterrent to steady economic growth. In countries where large sections of the population have relatively fixed incomes such as government employees and teachers, inflation causes much hardship and political unrest. Small business also is injured. Interest rates on funds available for private business may rise so high that borrowing is seriously discouraged. Instead of investing in ordinary business activities, those with capital use their funds for various kinds of speculation. The supply of loan capital may dry up completely.

The inflation picture is a technical and complicated one which will be discussed more fully later. There are a number of factors affecting the degree of inflation or the ability to hold the line against further price rises. One factor consists of budget deficits. Some countries, such as Brazil, have not only failed to balance their budgets but have favored deficit spending to promote public works and such projects as the new national capital, Brasilia. The falling off of exports and the development of unfavorable trade balances is another factor. Unfavorable balances lead to an outflow of gold and to shortages of dollar exchange. Currency depreciation may follow as well as further deficits due to declining tax receipts.

Conclusions

The social revolution in Latin America arises, as we have seen, out of the problems of economic development. Economic development requires capital accumulation, the acceptance of capitalism, proper economic balance, effective incentives, an optimum population, a strong entrepreneurial class and government policies that promote private as well as public enterprise. The specific economic problems we have described reveal that in many respects these basic elements for growth are lacking in Latin America. Population grows too rapidly. Institutions and attitudes derived from feudalism are inimical to capitalism. Technology is antiquated. Natural resources are insufficient and inadequately utilized. Transportation is deficient. People are improperly distributed on the land and crowded into big top-heavy sities. Land ownership is concentrated in the hands of a few great landlords who perpetuate the system of large inefficient *estancias*. There is the perplexing problem of reducing monoculture. There is insufficient industrialization. The Latin American nations lack capital and are not accumulating domestic capital rapidly enough. Finally, there is the chronic evil of inflation.

Facing these problems early, Uruguay and Mexico developed a set of policies combining economic nationalism with moderate socialism and private enterprise. The main object was rapid industrialization. After 1930, most countries adopted parts of this program, the economic policy revolution. Except in Mexico, the policy revolution failed. The dictators that adopted it did not fully understand or follow it. After 1955, dictators began to fall and were succeeded by democratic liberals. These "new" men inherited both the policy revolution and an economic crisis. They are now struggling to maintain their political power.

The hope of Latin America lies in these "new" men whose understanding of the problems of this area exceeds that of any other group. But their understanding requires coordination through the formulation of a new theory of development for Latin America. Such a theory rests on the elements outlined in this chapter. With these elements as background, we will now examine some of the leading theories of underdevelopment, theories that undertake to explain why it exists and how development can be induced. We shall then derive from the underdevelopment theories a theory of our own. Acceptance of this theory would start Latin America rapidly along the road toward a higher standard of living and the solution of the crisis of the social revolution. It could defeat communism.

References

1. *United Nations Bulletin for Latin America*, Santiago, Chile, February, 1957.

FIVE

WHY ARE NATIONS
UNDERDEVELOPED?

IT IS APPARENT THAT LARGE PARTS OF THE WORLD ARE "UNDER-developed," but this may have a variety of meanings. Some regard underdevelopment as low per capita income in contrast to income in the United States, Canada, Sweden, and Australia. Others contend that a country is only underdeveloped when its government regards development as a national problem, or announces goals or policies of development. Still others consider a country underdeveloped when it lacks modern technology or has little industrialization. Perhaps it is best to classify a country as underdeveloped, however, because it has not one, but a number of characteristics which indicate lack of advancement. Among the characteristics associated with underdevelopment are the following:[1]

1. A high proportion of labor in agriculture to the total labor force (60 to 90 percent).
2. Underemployment or disguised unemployment.
3. Little capital per capita.
4. Low per capita income and savings.
5. Little industrialization.
6. Concern mainly with primary industries such as agriculture or mining.
7. Backward technology.
8. Poor credit, transportation, communication and marketing facilities.
9. High fertility and rapid population growth.
10. Poor general and technical education.

In Latin America, most of the nations have all of these characteristics. Argentina, Brazil, Chile, Colombia, Mexico, Uruguay, and Venezuela reveal the greatest degree of advancement. But in these countries also there is underemployment, little capital per capita, little industrialization relatively to the United States and the Western European nations, concern with primary industries, backward technology, and inadequate credit, marketing, and transportation. Except for Venezuela, Argentina, Chile, Puerto Rico, and Uruguay, per capita income is also very low. Moreover, all these countries are underdeveloped in the sense that a development problem is recognized, and the governments have plans and goals for development.

Having classified most of Africa, eastern Europe, Asia, and Latin America with three-quarters of the world's population as underdeveloped, economists can become exceedingly discouraged. The situation in most of the countries is difficult indeed. There is excessive population growth, lack of resources and capital, low or nonexistent saving, poor technology, and lack of economic incentives. When added to these difficulties are the retarding influences of nationalism, antiforeignism, premature welfare-statism, restrictive trade unionism, communism, antimaterialism, the philosophy of graft and the squeeze, the undivided large family system, the lack of experience with capitalist economic institutions, and the low level of education, the situation can seem hopeless. Yet, despite these tremendous obstacles, there *is* hope. Rapid development *is* occurring. The preliminary step in promoting development, however, is the discovery of a theory which will apply to the underdeveloped countries involved. As we stated in the last chapter, our object is to provide such a theory for Latin America. It must be based on the underlying causes of low production.

Causes of Underdevelopment

1. TROPICAL CLIMATE

One explanation for low production is tropical climate. We find that many of the underdeveloped areas of the world are tropical. The conditions prevailing in the tropics retard agriculture, which is the original economic base from which an advanced economy develops. Among the deterring factors in tropical areas are the poor quality of the soil which, when cleared, often proves unfertile, and does not revert to the great productivity of the jungle. There is greater susceptibility to weeds and plant disease. The tropics are also unfavorable for the growth of livestock and the production of milk. Much has been said also about the adverse effects of tropical climate on the productivity of people. Undoubtedly, geographical conditions have played a part in the underdevelopment of many nations including those in northern and central Latin America. But slow development cannot be attributed to tropical climate alone.

2. SOCIAL DUALISM

Far more important than climate is sociological or cultural dualism. The underdeveloped countries have, for the most part, lived under social systems which not only retarded material advancement, but set almost insuperable obstacles to it. Such material growth as has occurred is due to the "invasion" of capitalism. But the intrusion of Western capitalist culture has been resisted, and according to the Dutch economist, J. H. Boeke, sometimes causes cultural disintegration.[2]

The cultural block to economic advancement can seem insurmountable, especially in such regions as Indonesia and parts of Africa. The cultural barrier is great also in Latin America. As we have pointed out earlier, there are vestiges of feudalism, attitudes toward work and business enterprise, and the vested interests of large landowners to cope with. But Latin America has been "invaded" by capitalism in one form or another since colonial days and the cultural resistance to material progress is by no means insurmountable. This is especially true since the development of the social revolution after World War II. Dr. Boeke, however, after many years in Indonesia became defeatist. He saw the Dutch "ethical policy" which sought to raise the economic level of Indonesians fail. The culture of the east provided no profit motive, no desire to work beyond a minimum amount, no demand for more than a small quantity of primitive consumer goods. It caused overpopulation, persistence in confining agriculture to rice growing, and much absenteeism. Boeke attempted to apply neoclassical marginal productivity economics to Indonesia and found that only a negligible number of Indonesians would accept this western form of thought.

Although sociological dualism undoubtedly retards economic growth, especially when persistence in a culture is supported by nationalist and antiforeign sentiments, it could be broken down if we understood more clearly the nature of the psychological and cultural factors in economic development. An attempt has been made by Professor Everett Hagen to introduce these elements into a theory of development.[3] He believes that capital formation, as such, does not lead to economic progress. It is only when the investment of capital is accompanied by improvements in technology that progress occurs. Changes in the psychology and institutions of a people are required if this is to happen. But what will cause a change in these noneconomic factors? He believes that five forces may bring about a change: (1) a gradual increase in technical knowledge, (2) tensions or conflicts in the upper social classes, (3) pressure from the outside that threatens the existing social structure, (4) new economic opportunities offered by the outside world, and (5) the imposition of a new economic and social system by an imperialist government through force.

These five factors did not lead Professor Hagen to be optimistic about rapid development in backward regions. The gradual increase in technical knowledge would be too slow, the elite might not be threatened by the outside world, and the new nationalism prevents imperialist domination. Modern technology could not be imported readily because of resistance to it, and the lack of trained men to use it. As a result, Hagen reverted to a theory of entrepreneurship not unlike that of Schumpeter. An entrepreneurial class must be developed as the force initiating the transition to modern economic methods. The entrepreneurial group, he thought, should come from the lower ranks of the elite, and feel frustrated in its desire for higher social status. It should find that it could achieve higher status against the "social blockage" of the upper elite by enterprise and the accumulation of wealth. If this entrepreneurial group could achieve status through modern business methods, it would revolutionize the society involved, and start it toward rapid economic progress. It would be the carrier and disseminator of new technology. Apart from the revolutionary action of such a group, there seemed to Hagen to be no other way of modernizing the economy except the slow process of a gradual change in attitudes through education.

3. THE POPULATION EXPLOSION

Since the beginning of the nineteenth century, the population of the peripheral regions of the world has increased at a rapid rate. At present, some parts of the world are increasing at a rate of 3 percent a year, which is regarded as the biological maximum.

The reasons for the great growth are various, but they are primarily concerned with the decline in mortality rates. Colonialism has played its part through spreading preventive medicine and sanitation. But whatever the reasons for great growth, some regard it as a potential "shock" which will cause a breakdown of the social institutions retarding production growth. In other words, population pressure will provide both the need for and cause of economic change.

This thesis, along with the entrepreneurial thesis, supplies another possible means of breaking down the institutional barriers to economic change. But it would have no validity except as an explanation of the beginning of change unless it can be assumed that population pressure will continue for some time. It is well known that as the standard of living rises or as people become more urbanized, the rate of population growth declines. As a cause of progress it would be reduced by progress. As people become better off, they would have fewer children and thus less incentive to become better off. Professor Hagen, for example, believes that this "standard of living effect" should negate the effects of population pressure. But, as has been pointed out by those studying advancement in backward regions, the dualistic character of these regions, part urban and advanced and part rural and backward, causes a rise in the standard of living and a decline in the rate of population growth only in the advanced urban regions. Population pressure may continue in the rural areas and create a continued need for economic advancement. It may be concluded that economists by no means agree as to whether population pressure is an effective shock treatment for stagnant economies or that it will continue to have stimulating effects if these in fact exist. Also, the rise in population can destroy all of the advantage of greater production to a country, if the supposed standard of living effect does not take place. This has been true in many of the Latin American countries.

4. TECHNOLOGICAL DUALISM

A variant of the population pressure thesis is that population growth would stimulate over-all economic growth if technological improvements were made as a result of it in agriculture or at least in that part of the agriculture of a backward region providing food for domestic consumption. But usually this does not happen. All underdeveloped countries are characterized by marked technological dualism. There is an advanced or relatively advanced urban sector where the standard of living is high and production is industrialized. Coexisting with it is a backward rural and handicraft village sector. Population pressure leads to more employment in the former, but not in the latter. The reason is that modern technology is not applied to agriculture.

Thus the question naturally arises, why is industrialism not carried over into agriculture? The explanation lies in the fact that where good arable land is very scarce, as is the case in most underdeveloped regions such as Latin America, it pays to use labor more intensively on the land. It does not pay to use machinery which saves labor. Unless the amount of good land is increased or the size of farms increased, to use modern machinery and technology is not profitable. Rates of profit are much higher when labor is used because it is abundant and cheap. It does not pay to substitute machinery for cheap labor. In fact, the intensity in the use of labor is carried to the point where more labor has no marginal productivity and unemployment or underemployment occurs.

Why then is there not a movement of the unemployed labor into the cities? We have noted that in Latin America this does occur. The unemployed or underemployed peasant with courage or ambition deserts the farm for the city. But there he lives in the wretched slums that surround the cities and he is likely to suffer continued unemployment since the labor-saving machinery in the city makes the use of more labor unnecessary. There is no demand for more production. The backward farm sector does not create a demand for more goods from the cities, and thus more industrialization and employment in the cities.

The division of underdeveloped countries in this dualistic way into advanced and backward technological sectors can be found all over the world. It is an evidence of economic stagnation. When the agricultural sector shows no sign of technological change or industrialization, it can be concluded that the economy as a whole is not advancing. It is in a rigid condition induced by dependence on the more advanced foreign economies which stagnate it by confining industrialization largely to production for export and by providing no incentive for rural and domestic economic advancement. As Professor Higgins says, "industrialization without an agricultural revolution brought the underdeveloped countries where they are."[4]

5. THE BACKWASH OF INTERNATIONAL TRADE

The stultifying technological dualism that we have described is part of a vicious circle which may be attributed to colonialism in the first instance, and then to the peripheral status of unadvanced countries after they achieve their political independence. This status causes emphasis on international trade. Nations of the periphery are suppliers of raw materials and food products to the economic centers such as the United States, England, and West Germany. As exporters of raw materials and food, they suffer from a number of disadvantages. Among these are the following: (1) The prices of their products fluctuate widely, causing wide changes in national income, and severe depressions which interrupt economic growth. (2) The prices at which the products are sold fall relatively to the prices of machinery and industrial products which must be bought to further industrialization and economic advancement in the peripheral countries. In other words, the terms of trade of the unadvanced nations decline.[5] (3) Finally, there are the so-called backwash effects of trade.

The growth of foreign trade would seem to be an advantage to an unadvanced country. It enables it to buy the machinery and other capital goods needed for industrialization. But the expansion of trade has had its disadvantages. Adverse effects called "backwash from trade" result from trade expansion. The economy grows in an unbalanced fashion. Export trade increases at the expense of production for the domestic market. The expansion of local production of consumer goods is one of the main aspects of economic growth and, as a result of the emphasis on foreign trade, capital and the best local labor are diverted from domestic to foreign production. Because of the preponderant attractions of foreign trade, the nation never rises above peripheral or colonial status. There is a vicious circle here. The growth of foreign trade provides the greater import capacity needed for more foreign capital goods with which to advance industrialization and the domestic production of consumer goods, but the growth of foreign trade stifles the domestic trade to which the imported capital may be supplied. As Higgins points out, "some economists have gone so far as to argue that international trade, far from encouraging growth of underdeveloped countries, has actually retarded it by accentuating the dualistic nature of the economy."[6] Among the economists taking this position are Hla Myint and Gunnar Myrdal.

These are the backwash or adverse effects of foreign trade. The opposite, or favorable "spread" effects, sometimes occur, and in varying degrees. Ideally, an underdeveloped nation should through increased foreign trade (1) obtain greater import capacity, (2) use this greater import capacity to obtain capital goods for investment in domestic industry, and (3) enjoy a multiplication of income from increased domestic investment. But none of these favorable "spread" effects may occur. The increase of trade may not result in increased import capacity because of the declining terms of trade. If there is increased import capacity, the resulting imports of capital goods may be applied almost entirely to foreign trade agriculture, or mining. If this occurs, the multiplication of income from investment may not result in greater domestic income because there is no greater *domestic* investment. The increased income will be invested abroad, or fall into the hands of those already growing rich from foreign trade, or be absorbed by foreign countries due to further declines in the terms of trade. But in any case the failure of over-all economic development to occur is explained. The economy remains dualistic and stagnant because of overemphasis on foreign trade.

The oversupply of labor in proportion to land and capital also contributes to this stagnant situation. In the early days of the development of the United States, not only were we less dependent on foreign trade than underdeveloped countries such as Brazil and Colombia, but there was a shortage of labor and a plentiful supply of land. Where the labor supply is great, as in Latin American countries, it only pays to apply the capital to the flourishing export sector of the economy. Application of capital to further production in domestic agriculture soon results in diminishing returns due to the shortage of land and the absence of a market for domestic produce. Even employment of capital in domestic industry cannot raise the standard of living of a backward country or greatly reduce unemployment or underemployment unless productivity per man-day of labor is increased in domestic agriculture. Industrial production can benefit only the upper income groups or foreign trade unless production increases in domestic agriculture. And this cannot occur to any great extent as long as the oversupply of labor makes application of machinery unprofitable.[7]

6. THE LACK OF BALANCED GROWTH

Another explanation of underdevelopment stresses the need for balance between the parts of an economy. If one part grows when other parts are not growing, the demand for the products of the growing part is limited, and growth is retarded or soon ended. Growth must also not only be simultaneous between all parts of an economy, but between the social as well as the economic aspects. This is a modern version of the old concept of Adam Smith that the division of labor is limited by the extent of the market. It might be expressed "that the development of an industry is limited by the extent of the market for its products which is, in barter terms, the production of other products."

Two economists are associated with this view of the matter, Paul N. Rosenstein-Rodan and Ragnar Nurkse. The former conceived of three "indivisibilities," the indivisibility of production, of demand, and of the supply of saving.[8] Briefly stated, balanced growth is required for any considerable growth. Investment in one industry must be accompanied by investment in other industries, and investment in "social overhead capital" must precede most economic investment. Before much investment can occur, there must be roads, water supplies, power, communications, housing, sanitation, and education. The simultaneous investment in different industries and in social capital will create the second indivisibility, consisting of complementary demand. For growth in one industry, Say's Law must be brought into operation through production (and, hence, demand) in other industries. Finally, savings must grow to equal the growth of investment. This is the third indivisibility without which growth will collapse through decisions not to invest more because of lack of loan capital or too much inflation.

Ragnar Nurkse argued for balanced growth along the same lines. He believed in the need for a "wave of capital investment." This should occur in a wide number of industries. The capacity to invest is based on the capacity to buy. As he put it, "Even though in economically backward areas Say's Law may be valid in the sense that there is no deflationary gap, it is never valid in the sense that the output of any single industry . . . can create its own demand."[9] The only way out of the difficulty of lack of markets is the application of capital on a wide front in many different industries at the same time.

7. THE LACK OF A "BIG PUSH" OR "TAKE-OFF"

The views of Rosenstein-Rodan and Nurkse lead to the conclusion that there must be a "big push." In other words, a small amount of investment, especially if it is confined to one or two industries, will not result in any appreciable economic progress. There must be a "minimal investment effort." But in most underdeveloped countries, investment is not great enough to cause any sizable or sustained growth. In Latin America from 1947 to 1957 there were about $25 billion of foreign and net domestic investment. This came near the minimum level needed for a big push. But there was little diversification in some of the countries. Only in Brazil and Mexico did the diversification approach the needed "wide level." In addition, social investment did not occur rapidly enough. Latin American economies tried to grow and industrialize without adequate schools, housing, transportation, and communications.

Similar in some ways to the big push concept is the theory of the "take-off into sustained growth." With small amounts of investment and saving, a nation may remain for years in a stagnant condition. Growth, if it occurs, is only at very slow rates. But the history of development reveals that at some point a nation begins to grow rapidly and to sustain this growth. Professor Walt Rostow, an economic historian who advised the Kennedy Administration, undertook some years ago to analyze the take-off process. The rate of net investment, he found, had to rise above 10 percent, one or more substantial manufacturing industries had to develop, and an institutional and political structure had to be built which would encourage and exploit the tendency toward expansion.[10] Rostow examined the history of thirteen countries, and isolated the periods of take-off. He explained the appearance of these periods by long prior evolution of "preconditions" conducive to growth. But when "take-off" began, there was in effect a "big push." Investment became sizable and diverse and was backed up by a high rate of domestic saving. It would seem that the take-off theory adds little to the big push theory except the point that through some means the rate of saving must begin in the take-off to exceed 10 percent. In Latin American countries, it should probably range from 15 to 20 percent for a take-off, since some of the countries have reached the 10 percent level without inducing self-sustained growth.

The Probable Causes of Underdevelopment in Latin America

In the light of these theories of underdevelopment, how is the lack of advancement in Latin America to be explained? Is it due to tropical climate, overpopulation, social and technological dualism, the backwash of foreign trade, lack of balanced growth, or lack of a "big push" or "take-off"? Obviously, none of these factors alone explains the underdevelopment. Climate, no doubt, has made efficient and diversified agriculture difficult in Central America and northern South America. It partly explains the shortage of good land. But modern agricultural science could be employed to offset the effect of diseases, to provide fertilizers, and to increase the productivity of the land. It is doubtful whether tropical climate has been a crucial cause of the backwardness.

There is little doubt, however, as to the effect of too-rapid population growth. The population explosion in Latin America is not a stimulating, but a retarding, influence. It absorbs the results of increased production, and limits the growth in per capita income. In fact, it is doubtful whether an increase in population can shock an economy into growth unless it is already well advanced, or there is a shortage of labor in proportion to land and capital. At any rate, the failure of Latin American economies to grow rapidly cannot be attributed to a low rate of population growth.

Thus, the causes of underdevelopment must be found elsewhere. Among the valid retarding influences are social and technological dualism. As we have pointed out earlier, Latin America is held back by the vestiges of feudalism. The land-owning class has retarded progress by insistence on the *status quo*. This means old agricultural methods, leaving land idle, limitation of commerce and industry, dependence on foreign trade and monoculture, and resistance to social progress through imposing higher taxes to better education, health, and housing and to extend road and transportation systems. Added to the stultifying policies of the *hacendados* are the vestiges of feudal attitudes, and attitudes growing out of underdevelopment itself. There is insufficient incentive to work or engage in business enterprise. Work and enterprise are still derogated. Economic advancement is not sought through economic individualism, but through the paternalism of the state. There is also no great mass demand for consumer goods.

In addition, the growing nationalism has led to antiforeignism. This discourages much-needed investment of foreign capital. The antiforeignism not only shuts out foreign capital, but foreign technicians as well. The failure of Brazil to develop her oil resources can be attributed to these political causes. The nationalism of Great Britain, France, Germany, and the United States fortunately did not lead these countries to refuse or discourage foreign investment and the use of foreign technicians. Antiforeignism need not be linked to nationalism, but when this is the case, as in Latin America, growth can be seriously retarded.

Economic underdevelopment in Latin America can also be explained by the history of such a country as Japan. Where a large group of technically minded business enterprisers develops as in Japan, the rate of growth rises. The entrepreneurial class is the developer and spreader of modern capitalist technology. Japan's large population and lack of agricultural resources did not result in stultification largely because of the early appearance of an entrepreneurial class with a passion for modern machinery. It is ironical that Japan, with the setback of losing in World War II, and with resource handicaps greater than those of most Latin American countries, has actually begun to provide Latin Americans with many of the inexpensive manufactured goods which they could so easily produce for themselves.

Apart from social dualism, other leading causes of Latin American underdevelopment are unbalanced economy, the lack of a big push or take-off, the backwash effects of foreign trade and the declining terms of trade. They have caused the continuation of unproductive agriculture and the underemployment of labor.

References

1. Cf. Benjamin Higgins, *Economic Development*, W. W. Norton, New York, 1959.

2. Cf. J. H. Boeke, *Economics and Economic Policy of Dual Societies*, Institute of Pacific Relations, New York, 1953, p. 20.

3. Everett H. Hagen, "An Analytical Model of the Transition to Economic Growth," M.I.T., C.I.S. (Document C/57–12).

4. Higgins, *op. cit.*, p. 343.

5. Dr. Raoul Prebisch is the economist most noted for the "declining terms of trade" thesis, but there is a dispute over the validity of the assumption that the terms of trade of the primary producers decline. We believe that they do, but we will present the opposite view later.

6. Higgins, *op. cit.*, p. 345.

7. Cf. W. Arthur Lewis, "Economic Development with Unlimited Supplies of Labour," The Manchester School of Economic and Social Studies, May, 1954.

8. P. N. Rosenstein-Rodan, Notes on the Theory of the "Big Push," M.I.T., C.I.S., March, 1957.

9. Cf. Ragnar Nurkse, *Problems of Capital Formation in Underdeveloped Countries*, Oxford, 1953.

10. W. W. Rostow, "The Take-off into Self-sustained Growth," *The Economic Journal*, March, 1956.

SIX

AN ECONOMIC THEORY FOR
LATIN AMERICA

LATIN AMERICA URGENTLY NEEDS A SOUND THEORY OF ECONOMIC development. Lacking such a theory, there is no means of determining wise policy except random experimentation. Billions of dollars can be wasted in this way and the rate of development retarded. Fortunately it is now possible to formulate a sound economic theory for Latin America because of recent progress made in the analysis of development.

It must be emphasized at the outset, however, that no theory can be accepted which assumes that Latin America will develop entirely along lines of free enterprise. American businessmen seem to hope for an even greater degree of free enterprise in Latin America than we have in the United States. But the Latin American nations are mixed economies. A greater degree of socialism, government planning, and economic nationalism prevails than in the United States. Moreover, private enterprise is under greater restrictions from tariffs, exchange quotas, and other control devices than in our country. Most of the countries combine state socialism with private enterprise, and the latter is often monopolistic.

It must be understood also that Latin America is likely to move even farther away from free enterprise in the years to come. It is impossible for us to reverse this trend except in minor ways. Perhaps we can convince some of the countries that it would be more efficient to return part of the public utilities, transportation systems, and other government enterprises to private hands. It is also possible that the growth of American direct investments will increase the proportion of private to public enterprise. But no economic theory that assumes a complete return to private enterprise will work in Latin America. *Laissez-faire* is dead. It died with the *cientificos* of Mexico.

Moreover, if communism is to be prevented, a strong argument can be made for the paramount economic role of government in Latin America. The nations are very far behind, and the gradual evolution of industrialism will not satisfy the strong current desire for rapid improvement. A "big push" is needed. If it does not come through semicapitalist institutions, the people will turn to communism. But a big push requires government planning and control. Also, large-scale public investment, especially for the development of social overhead capital, is required. Even if a fully free-market system existed, it could not be relied on to create and coordinate the much needed "big push," or to attract capital into all the fields where it is needed.

The Prebisch Thesis

No theory as to the problems of Latin American economy makes greater sense than the Prebisch theory. With some modifications, enlargements, and qualifications, it can serve as *the* economic theory for Latin America. The Prebisch thesis must, therefore, be described and analyzed.

Dr. Prebisch begins with the assumption that the nineteenth century developed a "schema" consisting of the international division of labor between the center or centers and the periphery.[1] The center was to produce manufactured goods, and the periphery, raw materials and food. But by the twentieth century, as a result of the two world wars and the great depression, Latin America wanted to break the "schema." It desired industrialization and no longer was willing to accept a colonial, raw-material and food-producing status. Latin American economists, notably Dr. Prebisch, deny that Latin American nations would lose by industrialization even though their industrial production might be less efficient than that of the nations in the center. The growth of domestic industry is not incompatible with the further expansion and increasing efficiency of primary production in food and raw materials. Thus the standard of living could be raised through industrialization, and without a decline in the volume and efficiency of primary production.

The real problem of Latin America is how to develop industrialism on a large scale. Prebisch contends that the periphery is at a great disadvantage in promoting industrialism. Latin American incomes are low and there is only limited ability to save and invest.

In addition, Prebisch points to two other serious difficulties. These arise from the great dependency on foreign trade. First, the terms of trade have a long-run tendency to decline. In other words, the prices at which Latin America sells primary products do not keep pace with the prices of the manufactured products it has to buy. But its industrialization depends on the purchase of machinery and other capital goods through the import capacity created by its exports. Second, the demand for the primary products sold by Latin America (mainly to the United States) is inelastic. The rate at which the imports by the United States of Latin American products has been growing has declined until it now increases annually only 3 percent or less. This rate of increase in the demand for Latin American goods does not create enough import capacity to supply Latin America with the increase in capital goods it needs for rapid economic development.

Dr. Prebisch contends that industrialization and industrial advancement in the centers, the United States, Great Britain, and West Germany, should, through greater efficiency, have resulted in increasing rather than decreasing the terms of trade. In other words, manufactured goods should have become cheaper relatively to primary goods. But the reverse has been true, due to monopolistic price control and high wages in the centers, especially the United States. Even the greater product due to increases in efficiency in agriculture and mining in Latin America has been more than absorbed by the higher relative prices that had to be paid for manufactured goods. The economist's way of stating this is that the incomes of the productive factors—land, labor, and capital—in the centers are relatively more than their marginal productivity, and those in the periphery are less than their marginal productivity.

For some time, however, the declining terms of trade argument has been under attack in terms of both fact and theory. Before and during World War II, the terms of trade improved. But after World War II they again began to decline. Colin Clark and Arthur Lewis, however, by departing from the strict use of commodity terms of trade, have challenged the Prebisch thesis. They show that in terms of the relative demand and rates of production of industrial and primary products, it is conceivable that the terms of trade may rise instead of fall. Professor Gottfried Haberler of Harvard University also attacks the thesis. He contends that those who believe in declining terms of trade are guilty of overgeneralization and "reckless" predictions of future export and import price trends. Subsequent to Dr. Haberler's analysis, however, M. K. Atallah made an exhaustive theoretical analysis of the thesis through the use of mathematical models, and concluded that it could be, and probably was valid.[2] We accept this conclusion.

If we can grant that industrialization is desirable for Latin America, and that it is seriously limited (1) by low incomes which make it difficult to save and create capital domestically, (2) by the declining terms of trade which make it impossible to import enough capital for rapid development and (3) by the inelasticity in the demand for Latin American exports, what are the ways out of this stagnant situation? Dr. Prebisch considers three possibilities: (1) forced saving or some method of inducing a greater amount of domestic capital accumulation, (2) greater efforts to increase the volume of exports and efficiency in primary goods production, and (3) foreign loans and aid. Of the three alternatives, he chooses the last. Austerity or forced saving is not only a very strenuous and difficult policy to follow, but one which he thinks is not politically feasible. An increase in the volume of exports may only reduce prices without increasing the gross income and hence the import capacity derived from foreign trade. It may increase the backwash effects on domestic industry. In the past, increased productivity in primary production has been absorbed by the rise in prices of manufactured goods purchased abroad, leaving the primary producers without any gain from their increased productivity.

Since the only country which can provide a large amount of loans and aid to Latin America is the United States, the Prebisch thesis amounts to a support of closer hemispheric ties, the reduction or elimination of anti-Yankeeism, and acceptance of the Alliance for Progress. It is the economics behind the policies of the liberal governments that existed under Betancourt in Venezuela, Camargo in Colombia, Alessandri in Chile, and Mateos in Mexico.

The Enlargement of the Thesis

As thus far developed, the Prebisch thesis can serve only as the core for a Latin American economic development theory. It is not a well-rounded body of ideas, and has no historical orientation. It needs enlargement, but it does make the fundamental points that Latin America is unable to develop so long as it relies on foreign trade exclusively, and that the vicious circle of poverty cannot be broken in a hurry by forced saving and domestic capital accumulation alone. It also strongly defends industrialization as the only means to a much higher standard of living. It abandons the classical notion that peripheral nations benefit from the international division of labor. Thus the economic disease of Latin America has been partly diagnosed. Dr. Prebisch provides also part of the cure—the expansion of foreign loans and aid. But the thesis requires (1) a broader diagnosis, and (2) a broader curative prescription.

To broaden the diagnosis, the following causes of underdevelopment must be added: (1) The lack of disease control in tropical countries for plants, animals, and humans. (2) The population explosion. (3) The political influence of the *hacendados* and the army. (4) Antiforeignism, which results in the refusal to accept foreign capital and technicians needed for the development of resources. (5) Lack of education. (6) The persistence of antiwork and antibusiness attitudes. (7) The failure to encourage the development of the entrepreneurial classes. (8) The failure to plan for diversified and balanced agricultural and industrial growth. (9) Failure to undertake austerity programming when it is politically feasible—i.e., forced saving and balanced budgets. (10) Failure to curb the foreign investment of capital by nationals. (11) Failure to curb inflation. (12) In general, failure to follow fully or consistently the economic policy revolution.

The inclusion of these additional diagnostic elements, which are partly cultural and political as well as economic, is necessary if any broad cure is to be recommended. Foreign loans and aid can fail to bring rapid growth unless these elements are sufficiently taken into account. An attempt is made below to outline a broad prescription for Latin American development including these elements.

A Latin American Economic Theory and
Development Program

1. THE GENERAL ECONOMIC FRAMEWORK OF
DEVELOPMENT

The economies of Latin America must rapidly industrialize. In order to do this, there are three essentials: (1) capital investment, (2) protective tariffs or exchange controls, and (3) domestic markets. Capital investment is dependent primarily on domestic saving and only secondarily on foreign loans and aid. It is undesirable for Latin American nations to rely wholly on either. Huge foreign loans and aid discourage self-reliance and the growth of the domestic saving and investment upon which economic take-off must ultimately depend. Contrariwise, reliance unduly on capital independence retards growth to the point where a take-off may never be reached or is postponed for many years.

Capital investment must be great enough to provide the "big push." But in terms of Latin American conditions, how great is that? No one, of course, can answer the question with assurance. But it would seem that for rapid progress, the gross domestic investment should be 20 to 30 percent of the annual gross national product. Assuming a national product for Latin America of about $80 billion at 1960 prices, the annual gross domestic investment should amount to $16 to $24 billion. With foreign direct investment of only $1 billion, and Alliance for Progress aid of only $2 billion, the amount of domestic investment would have to be at least $12 or $13 billion a year. A considerable austerity program would be required to reach or sustain this level. Austerity must be imposed through balanced budgets, higher taxes, and restrictions on wage increases if the rate of domestic saving is to rise by this amount. Also, inflation must be curbed and political stability maintained to attract more foreign capital. It is not likely, however, that United States direct investments or foreign aid combined will rise much above $3 billion a year. A part of the domestic investment can be obtained from the earnings of foreign trade, but as Latin

America industrializes there will have to be less rather than more reliance on capital from foreign trade.

To promote economic development and the effective use of capital, there must be careful economic planning. The growth of each industry must be projected, and the interrelations between industries as they grow anticipated. Plans must be made for the development of power and energy resources. The growth of the social overhead must proceed in proper coordination with the growth of industry and commerce. There must be both balance and wide diversification. Even an investment of $30 billion a year would fail to produce great industrial growth if it were devoted to unneeded public works or exaggerated social security programs, or if it were concentrated in export industries, or in too few industries of any kind.

The assertion that Latin American progress depends on government planning is based on sound economic theory. Rapid development in underdeveloped countries cannot occur unless there is balanced development. As Nurkse has pointed out, progress in a variety of industries is needed even to create the market on which the development of any individual industry depends. Unfortunately, American business does not always realize that a program of government planning which might injure business at home may be an absolute essential in an underdeveloped country. We should not fear economic planning in Latin America, but promote it. It is an essential part of the Alliance for Progress.[3]

Effective planning requires economic control. The control devices in Latin American planning are tariffs, exchange control, taxes, and government enterprise. Latin American nations need to increase protection in the industries that they are attempting to establish or increase locally. We should not want a free-trade Latin America. The one exception is interregional trade. Where the Latin American Common Markets can be used to create within Latin America the demand needed for industrialization, they should be extended and the tariffs between the participating nations further reduced.

Exchange control should be continued where it can be used effectively as a substitute for tariff protection. This feature of the economic policy revolution was used with much success in Uruguay. Because of the graft and inequities involved in exchange control, the current tendency in Latin America is to do away with it altogether. It needs to be reformed rather than eliminated.

Government enterprise has also been an effective expansion and planning device. It has played an important role in Uruguay, Mexico, Chile, Brazil and many other countries. Where government enterprise fills a vacuum in economic development and is not unduly inefficient, it should be used. It is unlikely that private enterprise will be attracted into all fields and government enterprise is needed for balanced growth. This has been especially true in Mexico. Here again, Americans should not be overfearful of this "socialism" in Latin America.

Taxation in Latin America, another control device, is a subject about which there is much confusion. There is a tendency of Americans to recommend sweeping reforms which would increase the progressive part of the tax system, i.e., higher income tax rates. But here again, what is good for an advanced country may not be good for an unadvanced country. There is grave doubt whether highly progressive tax systems would benefit Latin America. If the problem there is one of increasing saving, regressive taxation is desirable and even a moderate amount of taxation of low incomes through inflation, if the result is to increase saving and investment. Where taxes are levied on the upper incomes, they should take the form of luxury taxes and favor saving and investment. Business taxes also should be geared to this purpose. Some of our insistence on tax reform in Latin America may not be defensible in terms of economic advancement, although it may be in terms of social justice.

In addition to taxation, wage rates also affect saving and investment. In underdeveloped countries, wages should be relatively low and profits high. This was true in the early stages of the development of the United States. Very high wages, featherbedding, and union restriction on productive efficiency could be far more injurious in Latin America than in advanced countries. As scarcity economies, Latin American nations need high productivity, low labor costs, and high profits as incentives to a large amount of investment.

To summarize, a valid economic theory for Latin America must include not only industrialization and foreign investment but (1) heavy investment—i.e., the "big push," (2) balanced and diversified investment, (3) taxes, wage levels, and profit levels that promote heavy saving and investment, (4) tariffs and exchange controls to divert the economy to domestic industrialism, (5) government enterprise to fill investment gaps and stimulate private enterprise, and (6) strong government planning. In this paragraph we have stated the *new economic development theory* urgently needed by Latin America. In effect, this is a theory that economic development requires *balanced growth* and a *big push* that can be provided only by a *take-off* induced by great domestic saving and investment and economic control through *nationalist, capitalist,* and *socialist* measures. It is the real theory behind the economic policy revolution.

2. THE SOCIAL AND POLITICAL FRAMEWORK

From a social and political standpoint, the elements needed for rapid Latin American development have already been discussed. It remains only to summarize them briefly here. The needs are (1) political stability, (2) removal of the threat of expropriation, (3) removal of the threat of communism, (4) more general and technical education, (5) education in the values and goals favorable to economic enterprise and to productive work in an industrial system, (6) the reduction of too rapid population growth, (7) the rapid development of social overhead capital, and (8) the replacement of the *hacendados* and military by the new middle-class liberal businessmen and politicians in the seats of political power.

Dangerous Pitfalls

In the development of society, the difficulty is sometimes not lack of knowledge but the persistence of older inapplicable beliefs, or the acceptance of panaceas. Latin America, however, is not so likely to succumb to the former as to the latter. The obsolete system of the *hacienda* has no strong ideology behind it, and the *laissez-faire* of the *cientificos* hardly got a foothold in Latin America before it was replaced by a new economic nationalism. Latin American economics, moreover, has been unorthodox. Thus, Latin America has no firm traditional ideology and is likely to succumb to the lure of easy or dramatic paths to progress.

Among these primrose paths are (1) land redistribution without land reform, (2) the expropriation of foreign property, (3) the belief that communism can induce more rapid development than planning under a state capitalist system, (4) social security programs that cannot be afforded, (5) the belief that an undeveloped nation can raise itself wholly by its own bootstraps and with virtually no capital, foreign or domestic, (6) belief in the promotional effect of excessive population, (7) belief in the expansionist effect of heavy inflation, and (8) belief in pump-priming or in the expansion induced by one or two "key" industries.

Various Latin American nations can be cited as examples of accepting one or more of these erroneous policies at different times in their history. For example, Mexico, Cuba, and Bolivia have overemphasized land redistribution. Mexico, Cuba, Bolivia, and Brazil have indulged in expropriation. All over Latin America, but especially in Venezuela, Brazil, Argentina, and Chile, the belief in communist planning is widespread. Argentina was notorious for its social security program under Perón. Argentina, Bolivia, Brazil, and Chile have attempted to speed up development through excessive inflation. Belief in pump-priming and key industries has characterized Brazil.

There is no defense against these various forms of economic quackery except education by moderates as to their unwisdom, and the proof of greater progress through the adoption of sound policies. The extreme version of the bootstrap concept is especially hard to cope with. It is assumed that, for economic development, little or no capital is required. Through the use of improved techniques or better seed, for example, a revolution in agriculture is expected. From agricultural advancement will come the income and savings needed for industrialism. No foreign aid is needed, no planning, and little capital. Even in the United States there is a tendency to expect too much from the Point Four program and the technical assistance programs of some of the foundations. These efforts are valuable, but they cannot be expected to solve all problems of economic development by themselves.

The Interest of the United States in
Latin American Development

At an earlier point in this book the advantages of Latin American economic development for the United States were mentioned. These advantages are very real. One of them is the outlet Latin America provides for our capital. Since Latin America desperately needs our capital, exports of our capital goods will be stimulated if our loans, investments, and aid to Latin America are great. There will be large purchases of capital goods by governments with funds loaned or granted to Latin America by the United States, or of equipment and materials in the United States by American or mixed corporations for direct investment in plants in Latin America.

In recent years the exports of the United States have not grown rapidly. Dollar shortages have become dollars in abundance. We have lost gold. The late President Kennedy, along with members of Congress and many businessmen, was concerned about the need for a greater volume of American exports. The Marshall Plan and the reconstruction of western Europe created a great demand for American goods after World War II. Now Europe is on its feet and progressing rapidly. There is far less need for our goods. An increase in trade with Latin America could become a substitute for American sales of goods and investment in Europe. As such, it could materially aid in preventing economic stagnation in the United States. We should be vitally interested in Latin American economic growth for our own sake. This interest was great and American direct investments were large until 1957. A combination of depression, anti-Americanism, communism, and expropriation reduced American investment in Latin America drastically. As investment revives, it will aid not only Latin America but the United States as well.

Ultimately a rising standard of living in Latin America may enable the countries to the south to buy not only capital goods, but more consumer goods from the United States. This will also help our economy. But there will be a period of adjustment because of greater production in Latin America of consumer goods which were formerly bought from us. However, the volume of consumer-goods imports can be expected to grow. Our export of capital goods will increase Latin American production and income and ultimately result in greater imports of consumer goods from the United States. Apart from the political advantages of strengthening a noncommunist Latin America, our own economic development and welfare will be promoted.

Planning Is Crucial

The development of Latin America desperately requires planning. If the Committee for Economic Development regards this as dangerous "Prebischism," it is nonetheless true. The Latin American nations have been planning, are now planning, and will continue planning. We are encouraging them to plan as a prerequisite for Alliance for Progress aid. What we need is a greater understanding of the nature of the planning in the different nations and their special problems. Although general theories of development may be stated, to accomplish anything they must be applied to the specific economic problems of Latin America. In the following pages we will discuss the problems of Latin America as a whole, and the application of our development theory to them. Later we will consider the problems as they are found in individual countries and the economic history and forms of planning developed in these countries.

But we must emphasize the point that there cannot be real and sustained economic progress in Latin America unless the Latin American nations and the United States formulate cooperatively a broad plan based on the economic theory we have outlined. Thus far (1964), both the United States and the Latin American nations have failed (1) to understand the meaning and significance of the economic policy revolution, (2) to accept a development theory which is based on it, (3) to assess realistically the seriousness of the obstacles standing in the way of a sound development plan, and (4) to accept the extreme importance of promoting Latin American middle class leadership. The programs have been piecemeal and diminutive. There has been little cooperation between Latin Americans and the administration of the Alliance for Progress in Washington. There has been little encouragement of Latin American business. Idealism has not been tempered with realism. Social development has been promoted by our aid program to the neglect of economic development.

In short, there are many critical obstacles to the achievement of the ideal plan for progress outlined in this chapter which are not being met by adequate leadership, cooperation, and sound economic theory. There are (1) obstacles arising from the current economic problems of Latin America as a whole which we outlined briefly in Chapter 4, (2) obstacles due to the past history and mishandling of economic problems in specific nations and (3) the failure of the Kennedy Administration and, as yet, the Johnson Administration to provide the kind of economic planning and leadership on the part of the United States needed to make the Alliance for Progress succeed.

We will deal with the first type of obstacle in the next chapters.

References

1. United Nations Economic Commission for Asia and the Far East, *The Economic Development of Latin America and Some of Its Problems,* United Nations, New York, 1949.

2. M. K. Atallah, *The Long-term Movement of the Terms of Trade Between Agricultural and Industrial Products,* Netherlands Economic Institute, Delft, 1958.

3. Dr. Prebisch and other Latin American economists have strongly emphasized the need for economic planning. They have been severely criticized for this position by American businessmen.

III

The Economic
Problems Analyzed

SEVEN

POOR RESOURCES, OVERPOPULATION, AND LOW INCOME

FROM THE OUTSET, WE HAVE CITED FIVE BROAD FACTORS AFFECTING the wealth of nations: resources, population, capital, technology, and institutions. The unadvanced nations of the world are usually deficient in all of these factors. Latin American countries are no exception to the rule. The majority of the people are poor farm workers. They live on and from the land. Nature provides only a meager living and even this pittance is often reduced by excessive population growth. The Latin American struggles year after year with the land to get more out of it, despite the frustrations caused by backward institutions, poor technology, and a severe shortage of capital. The first question then to ask in exploring Latin American economic problems is, How much are these land resources? How great is the Latin American's resource potential? Let us assume that he could get more capital, learn modern technology, curb population growth, and change his customs and attitudes to suit modern industrial life. What basically has he to work with? How much and of what quality are his land and raw materials? Also, how serious is the pressure of population and how low actually is his income? We will begin with the resource problem.

Minerals and Energy Are Lacking

Opinion differs widely as to the natural wealth of Latin America, some contending that potentially it is one of the richest areas in the world, others that it is one of the poorest. Insufficient geological exploration of Latin America makes it difficult to arrive at a sound estimate of the natural riches in this area. Three geological regions should contain much mineral wealth—the cordilleras, or southward extension of the mountain chain of western North and Central America; the sedimentary area which extends from Venezuela and Colombia down through the eastern parts of Ecuador, Peru, and Bolivia into Argentina and has a lateral tongue extending eastward to the Atlantic along the valley of the Amazon; and the two Cambrian shields in northern and southern Brazil. These regions resemble similar ones in North America. If they follow the same mineral history, the cordilleras should yield much copper, tin, lead, and precious metals; the sedimentary region, much oil and coal; and the Cambrian shields, iron, nickel, and ferro-alloys.

The balance of opinion in 1960 was, however, that Latin America lacks productive resources, and that its resource potential is uncertain. Latin America was producing only 2 percent of the world's total mechanical energy. Venezuela was producing a large quantity of oil, and Mexico a smaller amount, but oil production in Argentina, Brazil, Chile, and Colombia was trivial. Although potential oil reserves have been variously estimated in recent years as between 15 and 25 percent of the world total, they are largely confined to Mexico and Venezuela. Brazil, Colombia, and Bolivia are reputed to have large reserves, but there is as yet no proof of this. Coal is decidedly scarce in Latin America. Mexico, Chile, Cuba, and Brazil have small amounts of bituminous coal, and Colombia and Peru have a little anthracite suitable for coking purposes. Coking coal, little as it is, lies far away from the really large deposits of iron ore in Venezuela and Brazil. For this reason steel manufacturing must depend largely upon imports of coal from North America and Europe.

Latin America's major resource problem is the lack of fuel and energy resources. Unless more coal and oil can be discovered, Latin American countries will have to resort to water power or atomic energy. Fortunately, there are great possibilities for the development of hydroelectric power. But the exploitation of this power potential requires a great deal of capital. It requires also the use of foreign technicians. In the ABC countries, resource development has been set back by opposition to both American capital and technicians.

Latin America is much better endowed with iron ore than coal. Venezuela has two great deposits in the Cerro Bolivar and in El Pao. These deposits are easily accessible to water transportation and Venezuela has become an important exporter of ore. Mexico has at least one sizable deposit in the Cerro del

Mercado, and there are large deposits in Minas Gerais in Brazil and in the Oriente province of Cuba. Bolivia is also thought to have significant deposits, but Argentina, Chile, and Peru have very little.

In contrast to iron ore, Latin America is rich in other metals such as copper, tin, lead, nickel, zinc, and the ferro-alloys. Peru is now the largest exporter of vanadium. Considerable quantities of molybdenum are produced in Mexico and Chile. But the ferro-alloys are of little use locally unless industrialism grows and steel can be manufactured. Aluminum, another important industrial metal, is found in large concentration only in the Guianas, which are technically outside Latin America. Bauxite could easily be exported to Mexico, and the north and east coasts of South America, if aluminum plants were built in the more industrialized countries. However, Brazil and Mexico are the only nations which as yet are making any considerable progress in aluminum production.

In summary it can be said (1) that fuel-energy resources are limited except for oil, (2) that steel manufacturing, the basis of much modern industrialism, is hampered by lack of coal and the location of what little coking coal there is at a great distance from the iron deposits, and (3) that mineral resources generally are poorly located for the rapid industrialization of some of the more advanced countries such as Argentina and Chile.

Land As a Resource Is Poor

Latin America, although desperately in need of industrialization, is still largely agricultural. In 1960, 53 percent of the labor force worked on the land.[1] In many of the countries the percentage on the land was very high. In Brazil, Bolivia, the Dominican Republic, El Salvador, Guatemala, Haiti, Honduras, and Panama it ranged from 60 to 80 percent. In Argentina, Chile, and Uruguay, however, the percentage on the land was less than 30. Since Latin America is still largely agricultural, land remains its most important natural resource.

But there is little more cause for optimism in regard to the land as a resource than with minerals.. Only 5 percent of the huge land mass of 7.7 million square miles in Latin America was actually being cultivated in 1953, and probably only 8 percent was in any condition to be used for agriculture. In the United States, 18 percent of the land is cultivated. Thus a population in Latin America larger than that of the continental United States was attempting to feed itself and also grow large quantities of export products on less land than we used. The mountains make considerable amounts of land useless for agriculture in addition to causing serious transportation problems. Vast areas such as the coastal regions of Peru and Chile are deserts and in need of irrigation. Still other vast areas, such as the eastern slopes of the Andes in Ecuador, Peru, and Bolivia and the enormous rain forest valley of the Amazon, are jungles and in need of clearance. In Central America and the Caribbean area, the climate makes agricultural diversification difficult with the resulting reliance on monoculture and the necessity of meeting its problems. Thus Latin America lacks land and it needs to meet this lack through irrigation, clearance, reforestation, the damming of rivers, and the resettlement of some of its peasant population on better land. It needs new agricultural frontiers with "pioneers" to settle them. In an earlier chapter we have mentioned the peculiar extremes in the land-man ratios. In general, some areas have too great a population density. Other areas have too little density. To some extent, the population can and should be redistributed.

Population Grows Too Rapidly

The population of Latin America had reached 196,000,000 by 1958 and in 1960 was 210,000,000.[2] The rate of population growth in Latin America is one of the most rapid in the world. According to Paul S. Henshaw, population growth in the United States was only 1.70 percent a year in 1955, and the rate of growth for the world at large was only 1.20 percent.[3] Latin American growth rates had a median of about 2.90 percent, more than twice as large as that of the world as a whole and two-thirds larger than that of the United States. The rates of increase ranged from 1.94 percent in Peru, 2.28 in Argentina, and 2.34 in Brazil to 3.20 in Mexico, 3.50 in El Salvador, and 4.10 in Costa Rica. It is estimated that the total population of Latin America will be 303 million in 1975.[4] Most Latin American countries will double their populations in 25 to 30 years.

The rapid rate of growth is due to very high birth rates, and a decline in the death rate in the last twenty years. Despite the fact that life expectancy is much lower in most of the countries than in the United States, the birth rates are so high that the rate of population increase is more than double that of the world as a whole. Life expectancy ranges from a low of 36 years in Guatemala to 57 years in Argentina. The high birth rates and low expectancy rates cause the population of Latin America to consist of a high proportion of children and young people. In most of the countries 40 percent of the population is less than 15 years of age.[5] This fact has a number of important implications which will be discussed later.

There is nothing remarkable about the population "boom" in Latin America. In A.D. 1650 there began in the world at large an acceleration in the rate of population growth because of various factors which caused a decline in the death rates while the birth rates remained high. The change has been called the "population revolution." Industrialism in its early stages of development from 1750 to 1850 still further accelerated the growth. By 1920, however, the birth rates in most advanced countries began to decline to such an extent that some countries approached population stability. After World War II a new rise in the birth rate occurred, but it may only be a temporary consequence of the prosperity following the war. However, Latin America is in the stage of development in which the United States was during the early days of industrialization, and until industrialism becomes widespread, high birth rates are likely to continue.

As we pointed out in Chapter 4, the quantity of population may create serious economic problems. The most serious current population problem is the rapid rate of growth. With a population growth of 3 to 3½ percent a year, production must grow at this rate merely to prevent a fall in per capita income. For progress, the production rate must rise to at least 4 or 5 percent a year. For rapid progress, it must be even higher. Unfortunately, however, the growth rate of 5 percent reached after 1950 has not been sustained. Growth has fallen to 2 percent and less, which means that Latin American production is entirely offset by population increases. In some countries, where the rate of growth has dropped below 2 percent or is even negative as in Argentina, the standard of living is falling. Income per capita fell 10 percent in Argentina in 1962. Latin America must either curb the birth rate or reach rates of production growth greater than those in advanced industrial countries.

The birth rate tends to decline as as country becomes industrial and urbanized. Greater industrialization, therefore, can ultimately be counted on to reduce Latin American birth rates. But the present high rates retard industrial progress and in some countries even prevent it altogether. Population pressure is part of a vicious circle. The rates of increase should be reduced to promote industrialism, but unless industrialism grows, the rate of population increase will not decline. The circle needs to be broken. There are only two ways to do it: either increase production growth, or reduce the birth rate. Although the latter is possible, it is not the probable solution. Cultural patterns and indifference to poverty may be even more serious obstacles than widespread Catholicism. But a serious effort should be made. It will not be made, however, so long as Latin Americans are insufficiently aware of the retarding influence of excessively rapid population growth.

A second major population problem closely related to the rapid rate of growth is the youthful composition of the population. Peter Grace has pointed out that Americans do not realize the extreme youthfulness of Latin America, and that the political proposals we make for Latin American progress should be of a nature to appeal to young people. Although the political consequences of youthfulness are important, the economic results are equally important. Out of a total of 210 million people in Latin America in 1960, the estimated age composition was as follows:[6]

Age	Number in Millions
0–4	32
5–9	27
10–14	24
15–19	20
20–24	18
25–29	15
30–34	13
35–39	11
40–44	10
45–49	8.7
50–54	7.3
55–59	6.0
60 and over	13.23

Economically the most productive years are between 20 and 44. Out of 210 million people, only 67 million were in this age group, or about 32 percent of the entire population. This was a considerably smaller percentage in the most productive ages than in the United States and Europe. Also, a far larger percentage were under 15, and a much smaller percentage in the older working ages above 45. A decline in the birth rate and an increase in life expectancy are both needed to create a population composition which is not burdensome and is economically efficient. When one considers other qualitative problems such as illiteracy, ill health, lack of training in productive habits, and lack of technical training, the picture of the Latin American labor force is not bright. Reduction of birth rates and the rapid increase of literacy are imperative. Although birth rates probably cannot be reduced by means employed in more advanced countries, there are great possibilities in the newly discovered methods of reducing female fertility through simple medication. Puerto Rico is already having some success through medication, and a new vaccine is being perfected which in a few more years may be ready for use.

This is an area of controversy. Some contend that because population density is comparatively low in Latin America except in the Caribbean region, a reduction in the birth rate is only imperative there. They reason also that in other parts of Latin America population growth is needed not only for a more efficient land-man ratio, but to stimulate production by creating a rising demand for goods. To some extent both these points are valid, but the relation of population growth to production growth must be considered. Unless the latter exceeds the former, population growth will neither stimulate production nor improve the man-land ratio. All the advantage of production growth will be absorbed by additions to the population. It will not raise the standard of living.

Declining Income Growth

In the years after World War II there was an economic boom in Latin America. The gross product of Latin American countries increased rapidly. Using 1950 as the base year of 100, the total and per capita gross product increases by years were as follows:[7]

Year	Gross Product	Gross Product Per Capita
1950	100	100
1951	106	103
1952	108	102
1953	112	104
1954	119	108
1955	126	111
1956	129	111
1957	135	114
1958	138	114
1959	141	113
1960	143	112
1961	145.5	111
1962	147.5	110
1963	150	109.5

The table reveals several things. (1) The total gross product rose by about 5 percent annually from 1950 to 1957. (2) The most rapid growth occurred between 1950 and 1951, 1952 and 1954, and 1956 and 1957. (3) Between 1957 and 1959 the rate of growth fell to 3 percent, in 1960 to 20 percent, and in 1961 to 1½ percent. (4) The growth of population largely offset the effects of the 5 percent rate of growth in raising the standard of living between 1950 and and 1957. (5) With a 3 percent rate of growth in the gross product in 1958 and 1959 and a 2 percent rate in 1960, population growth more than offset production growth and per capita gross product declined. The importance of sustaining growth rates of more than 3 percent or else curbing population growth is here revealed statistically. *By 1959 Latin America was going backward economically.* This is at the bottom of the political and economic crisis. Democratic governments and the economic policy revolution have not promoted a rapid enough rate of growth. They have not even prevented a reversal of the upward trend in per capita gross product.[8]

There are wide differences between the Latin American nations both as to their rates of growth in gross product and in their per capita incomes. The estimation of over-all per capita incomes and growth rates is difficult. The estimation of comparative growth rates and per capita incomes approaches the impossible. To be comparable, both growth in the gross income or gross product must be deflated for price changes in the various countries. The price indexes are not always comparable. Per capita income figures must not only be deflated by dubious price indexes, but related to some common denominator such as the American dollar. At this point, problems arise as to the exchange rate to use in converting Latin American currency into dollars. There may be several exchange rates to choose from, such as the official rates or the open market rates. Which one is chosen may make a great deal of difference. In any case, exchange rates do not accurately reflect differences in the purchasing power of the dollar in various countries. The Mexican pesos one can get for a dollar will buy much more in Mexico than the bolivars one can get for a dollar in Venezuela. Thus in 1963, the 335 bolivars were worth much less in income than the 100 American dollars they represented, and the 1,250 Mexican pesos represented much more purchasing power than the 100 dollars into which they could be converted.

Estimates of growth and income for 1960 based on studies of gross domestic product by the Economic Commission for Latin America were submitted in 1963 by the Chase-Manhattan Bank.[9] Although these figures seem somewhat more reliable than earlier estimates, they are still subject to qualification and are derived from inadequate basic statistics, points readily admitted by the Chase-Manhattan Bank. A thorough general study of Latin American growth and income is yet to be made.

According to the Chase-Manhattan Bank, the growth of the GDP from 1950 to 1960 was as follows:

Country	Yearly GDP Increase, Percent
Argentina	0.2
Bolivia	0.3
Brazil	5.6
Chile	2.4
Colombia	4.6
Costa Rica	5.4
Dominican Republic	5.9
Ecuador	4.8
El Salvador	4.2
Guatemala	4.3
Honduras	3.9
Mexico	5.8
Panama	4.9
Paraguay	4.05
Peru	6.1
Venezuela	7.7

The per capita real income figures of the Chase-Manhattan Bank for 1960 based on GDP were as follows:

Country	Per Capita Income
Argentina	505
Bolivia	100
Brazil	250
Chile	375
Colombia	325
Costa Rica	350
Dominican Republic	330
Ecuador	180
El Salvador	260
Guatemala	195
Honduras	210
Mexico	320
Panama	503
Paraguay	110
Peru	240
Venezuela	1,120

The average per capita income in Latin America based on the sixteen nations studied was $325.

Conclusions

In regard to the resources, population, and income of Latin America, the following conclusions may be reached:

1. Latin America has a fuel-energy resource problem because of poor oil resources except in Mexico and Venezuela, and the scarcity of coal. It will have to rely heavily on hydroelectric power.
2. Latin America is land poor because of lack of land clearance, erosion control, and irrigation and the failure to cultivate all of the available agricultural land.
3. The rate of population growth is one of the most rapid in the world and it absorbs the increased income resulting from production growth.
4. Despite the rapid rate of income growth in some countries between 1950 and 1960, the average income of Latin Americans remained pitifully low.

Thus we can readily understand from a brief analysis of Latin American resources, population, and income that all three present serious obstacles to the adoption of a broad development plan which would within twenty or thirty years raise the level of living in Latin America much closer to that in the advanced nations. How are resources adequate for such a plan to be provided? How can population growth be prevented from absorbing all of the annual increase in production? How can Latin Americans save and accumulate capital for a development plan from such low per capita incomes? Unless satisfactory answers can be found for these questions, Latin America cannot plan successfully for economic progress.

References

1. Chase-Manhattan Bank, *Latin American Business Highlights*, vol. II, no. 3, p. 3. Data from ECLA.
2. United Nations, *Demographic Yearbook*, New York, 1960.
3. Paul S. Henshaw, *Adaptive Human Fertility*, McGraw-Hill, New York, 1955.
4. United Nations, *The Future Growth of World Population*, New York, 1957.
5. United Nations, *op. cit.*, p. 35.
6. United Nations, *op. cit.*, p. 36.
7. United Nations, *Statistical Yearbook* and ECLA. (Figures for 1960, 1961, 1962, and 1963 are the author's estimates.)
8. The probable fall in per capita income in 1961 and 1962 in Argentina and Uruguay was 10 percent, and in Chile 5 percent. Growth in some countries like Colombia and Ecuador stopped.
9. Chase-Manhattan Bank, *Latin American Business Highlights*, vol. 13, no. 1, 1963. GDP adds to GNP income earned in Latin America, but remitted abroad by Latin Americans as dividends, interest or wages.

EIGHT

AGRICULTURAL OBSTACLES
TO PROGRESS

THE HISTORY OF ECONOMIC DEVELOPMENT REVEALS THAT MOST advanced nations started from an agricultural base. In fact, those well-developed nations that now rely on foreign trade for a considerable part of their food first so improved farm productivity that they could release farm labor for manufacturing. England, for example, had an agricultural revolution before its industrial revolution. Thus, whether Latin America is to remain agriculturally self-sufficient or not, the improvement of agricultural productivity is essential for the development of industrialism and a high standard of living. The current failure to increase agricultural productivity rapidly is one of the main obstacles to the development of an effective economic plan for Latin America based on the economic theory we have outlined.

Most of Latin America is seeking greater industrialization and urbanization. If cities are to grow, however, a greater proportion of the labor force must devote itself to manufacturing, service, and trade. This means that a smaller number of workers on the farms must feed a growing number of workers in the cities. We have seen this happen in the United States. One farmer can now feed himself and his family and more than five families living in the city in addition. In fact, the productivity of farming has become so great that we have problems of surplus food. Latin America has not reached this degree of productivity, but it must reach it or the growth of industrialism will be seriously retarded. The current agricultural backwardness of Latin America is one of the greatest obstacles to economic development.

As was revealed in the previous chapter, Latin America is not well endowed agriculturally. Mountains and forests reduce the amount of land available for cultivation. Less than 5 percent of the land was cultivated in 1961. In the world as a whole, 7 percent was under cultivation and in the United States, 18 percent. The picture in Latin America seems brighter if land in pasturage is added to that in cultivation. Land in both uses amounted to 25 percent of the total land.[1] But there is no denying that the basic agricultural problem is the lack of good land. Not much more can be brought into use unless great forests and jungles are cleared in Brazil and on the slopes of southern Venezuela and eastern Colombia, Ecuador, Peru, and Bolivia. Some desert lands can also be reclaimed in Chile, Peru, and other countries. It would be very costly to create this new land, and at present the countries involved do not have the funds to do it.

Not only is there a scarcity of good land, but the best land is unequally distributed among the Latin American nations. A third of the cultivated land is in Argentina. Brazil, Mexico, and Chile have 47 percent of the total. Fifteen nations which have 37 percent of the population have only 20 percent of the farming land. In Paraguay and Bolivia, less than 3 percent of the land has been made suitable for cultivation.[2] The unequal distribution of good farming land is one reason for greater interregional trade. Some nations could become more industrialized, and others increase their agricultural productivity. They could then exchange their products. But such an exchange will be possible only if agricultural output expands much more rapidly in countries like Argentina, Brazil, and Uruguay than it has since World War II.

It may be necessary also for Latin American countries to stress production of food for local consumption at the expense of exportable commodities such as coffee and sugar. But this will create problems of foreign exchange. The great agricultural exports have supplied Latin America with much needed raw materials and machinery. How are these to be obtained, if less coffee and sugar are exported? The answer lies in speeding up both food production and industrialism so that Latin America can begin to become less dependent upon imports of raw materials and manufactured goods.

Despite the fact that Latin American nations have difficulty in feeding themselves or in developing an agricultural base for their industrialism, they provide, paradoxically, great farm surpluses for export. They supply 73 percent of the world's coffee, 57 percent of the sugar, 78 percent of the bananas and 8 percent of the cacao. Since World War II the paradox has been increasingly recognized. Latin Americans are endeavoring to divert agriculture from export to domestic production. Before the war, only half of the production was for food consumed at home. Since the war, two-thirds of the production has been devoted to home consumption.

"The Agricultural Problem"

Traditionally, Latin Americans have attributed most of their economic and social problems to agricultural difficulties, and have regarded the unequal distribution of land as their main agricultural problem. In more recent years interest has shifted from concern over the great estates, the *latifundia,* to other agrarian difficulties. "The agricultural problem" is not simply a problem of latifundism. Other problems, equally serious, are: monoculture; the lack of adequate transportation, refrigeration, irrigation, fertilizer, and machinery; and above all, the need for modern methods of farming which will save the soil from erosion, provide better seeds and herds, and generally increase the productivity per acre.

Although latifundism may not be the whole story, however, it is still important as one factor affecting productivity. It is also a great cause of social discontent and an important political issue. Equalization of land distribution was one of the twelve objectives of the nations signing the Charter of Punta del Este. It was also one of the main early objectives of the Castro Revolution in Cuba, and the illusion that all farm problems can be solved by dividing up the land will long be regarded by the poorer and less informed people of Latin America as of prime importance.

How important, therefore, is it—as the Charter of Punta del Este recommends—"to encourage, in accordance with the characteristics of each country, programs of integral agrarian reform . . . with a view to replacing latifundia and dwarf holdings by an equitable system of property . . ."? Certainly the facts of land distribution are cause for concern. Of farm land, 50 percent is owned by 1½ percent of farm owners, and 73 percent of the small owners have only 4 percent of the farm land.[3]

The unequal distribution of land varies from country to country, but it is present in all except Cuba, Haiti, and Mexico. The most extreme inequality is to be found in Ecuador, El Salvador, Guatemala, and the Dominican Republic. The situation of eleven nations is given in the adjoining table.

Country	Percent of Farm Units	Percent of Land Owned
Brazil	1.6	50.9
Colombia	0.4	26.7
Costa Rica	0.2	34.7
Ecuador	0.2	37.4
El Salvador	0.1	19.9
Guatemala	0.2	40.8
Honduras	0.1	20.6
Nicaragua	0.7	32.8
Panama	0.1	12.2
Dominican Republic	0.1	24.3
Uruguay	4.2	56.4

Source: Organization of American States.

Large estates have been the subject of bitter criticism for many years. A great many objections to land concentration have been raised. It is insisted that widespread tenancy prevents self-respect and a genuinely democratic social structure. Latifundism divides society into rich and poor, "haves" and "have-nots," with the former wielding great political power. Peons obtain only subsistence incomes, are often perpetually in debt to the landlords, lack educational and health services, and cannot better their economic condition. To many, it seems that all this could be changed merely by expropriating the landlords and dividing land equally among the landless. Redistribution was gradually effected in Mexico after 1917 and it has now also been accomplished in Cuba, but the results are questionable.

There are, however, many economic objections to the *latifundia*. (1) Large landlords are able to keep their taxes very low, with the result that funds are not available for schools, roads, and health services. (2) Landlords use the land for export crops to obtain large cash profits when food is badly needed for domestic consumption. (3) They also "mine" the soil by failing to use cover crops, and by allowing erosion to occur. (4) They invest their profits abroad or use them for lavish living instead of buying farm machinery and better herds. (5) They fail to adopt the best method of cultivation out of pure conservatism. (6) They allow large acreages to go uncultivated in periods when the prices of export crops are low, thus creating underemployment of agricultural labor and preventing the use of land for much-needed food. (7) They are responsible for unintegrated systems of transportation in which roads and railroads lead to seaports where crops can be exported rather than to domestic market areas. (8) Many of the large estates have absentee landlords with resulting mismanagement and lack of concern for the welfare of the tenants.[4]

In spite of these many criticisms, there has been a tendency in recent years to defend the large-estate system. An attack has been launched on what might be called *minifundism,* or the fragmentation of estates. Mexico's mistakes are cited. In Mexico, the large estates were broken up without providing enough aid to the poor farmers who got the land, and inefficient collective farming was encouraged. Castro is derided as attempting to repeat these mistakes. Large landlords are defended on the following grounds: (1) Many have spent heavily to import better agricultural machinery and cattle. (2) Many types of farming are not efficient or profitable unless conducted on large farms. (3) Some of the land left uncultivated should not be used, because it leads either to crop surpluses or to soil exhaustion. Much of it also is of such poor quality that it is not worth cultivating. There is no point in giving it to the poor farmers.

The balance of the argument against minifundism is perhaps greater than the arguments against latifundism. Where poor farmers are given a few acres of their own, they are usually unable to farm in an efficient manner because they cannot afford expensive machinery, or plough and plant on fields of efficient size. Economical and productive farming requires a reduction in the manpower employed per acre, and a shift from hand to machine methods. If land is divided into many small plots, hand labor is inevitable. The redistribution in Mexico, moreover, resulted in control of farming by poor farm workers who were not educated in the best methods of farming. As a result, crop yields per acre declined, erosion become worse, and soil was "mined" to a greater extent than had been the case with the larger estates. In countries where minifundism has existed, such as Haiti, Colombia, and Mexico, agricultural progress has been slower than in Argentina and Brazil.

Early in the land reform in Mexico the inefficiency of co-operative farming also was realized. Cooperative farming had existed in the *ejidos* or farm communities. Much of the ex-propriated land was turned over to the *ejidos,* and farmed under arrangements resembling collective farms in other parts of the world. A study made in 1958, however, reveals that yields of wheat and cotton per hectare are much higher on private land than on *ejidos.*[5] The yield of wheat on *ejidos* was 1.02 metric tons per hectare, and on private land, 1.39 tons; on cotton the yield for *ejidos* was 2.97 tons, on private land, 4.54 tons. Although the large *haciendas* had been inefficient, and the land was not intensively worked, there is little evidence that small private farms and the *ejidos* have been more efficient. In fact the reverse seems true, and wasteful and unscientific farming still prevails in Mexico. This is so despite the government's strong efforts in recent years to improve farming through education in modern techniques, disease control, loans for agricultural machinery, and irrigation and erosion-control projects.

In addition to other difficulties in Mexico it has been discovered that collectivization results in poor incentives. At one time it seemed that ultimately all the farm land would be turned over to the *ejidos.* But the advantages of private farming, as well as the persistence of economic individualism in Mexico, retarded the extension of the *ejidos.* From 1917 to 1932, 20 million acres of expropriated land were turned over to 783,000 *ejiditarios* who owned the land in common in *ejidos* of varying sizes. In 1934, the growth of *ejidos* was accelerated under the socialistic Cardenas. But more moderate presidents who succeeded him reversed the trend and private holdings grew. In 1950 the *ejidos* had only 44 percent of the crop land and 27 percent of the total farm land.[6]

The early years of the Revolution had seen a great decline in agricultural production as the land was expropriated and turned over to the *ejidos* and small private owners. Food in basic staples such as corn, beans and other products fell below the production levels of 1910. Mexicans have come to realize that neither minifundism nor collective farming will solve their agricultural problems, and that the solutions lie in greater mechanization and improved methods of farming. Socially and politically, however, minifundism has had great value. Farmers no longer feel they are mere tenants on large estates controlled by inhuman landlords who exploit them.

In addition to Cuba and Mexico, latifundism has been reduced recently in both Bolivia and Venezuela. In 1953 a socialist government was established in Bolivia which began drastic agrarian reforms. These were accompanied by violence and disruption of production. Farm output fell a third between 1954 and 1955, and corn and staples had to be imported in great quantities.[7] The Bolivian land reforms followed the early Mexican pattern in that land was distributed without providing credit, machinery, and technical assistance. The peasants were worse off than they had been before. The Bolivian measures resembled Mexican agrarian reform also in that after a stormy beginning, equalization proceeded slowly. By 1960 only 11 million acres had been distributed, leaving 85 percent of the land still in the hands of the landlords. But the *political* power of the large landowners had been destroyed.

Pressure for land reform in Venezuela resulted in the passage of an Agrarian Reform Law in 1960. Both the Venezuelan law and laws in Colombia and Peru follow a new and reasonable approach to the land problem. The Venezuelan law has been drawn up by agricultural experts, and the landowners expropriated are to receive fair payment. Only land not cultivated or tenanted is subject to appropriation. The general purposes of the law are to bring unused land into cultivation and to force the full cultivation of land by taxes which are graduated upward in proportion to the amount of uncultivated land. In addition, a broad program of technical and financial assistance to new landowners has been provided, and plans are being made for roads, schools, and power facilities.[8]

What Is the Basic Agricultural Problem?

If unequal distribution of land is not the main cause of agricultural difficulties, what is the cause? *There is no one cause.* The difficulties result in part from poor land, lack of machinery, and unscientific methods. There is also a scarcity of good land, and too many people remain on the land. Without machinery, better methods, and higher productivity, the present rural population can obtain only a very poor living from the small amount of good arable land available. Some land is unused and it should be made available. Where irrigation and clearance can create arable land, these measures should be used. But even in the few places where all available land is in use, and modern machinery and good methods are employed, too many people remain on the land for even a moderate standard of living. Industrialism must be accelerated and, as in the United States, excess farm population drained off into the cities to engage in manufacturing, service, trade, and the professions. Even in our country the exodus from the farm has not gone far enough. *The basic agricultural problem of Latin America is industrialization.*

The need for industrialization and large-scale scientific farming can be granted, but even when land is held in plots too small to permit profitable use of machinery much can be done through extending credit to farmers to enable them to buy seed, fertilizer, and better implements. When credit is accompanied by an educational program, the yield per acre can be increased considerably. Credit and educational programs have been conducted by ICA and American foundations in Peru, Brazil, and Mexico with good results. Point Four programs have also greatly improved the situation. But these efforts, although valuable in the short run, are not the basic answer to Latin American agricultural difficulties. They can raise the productivity of the poorest farmers in Chile, Brazil, Mexico, Peru, Colombia, Bolivia, and other countries where much of the farming is still on a very primitive, small-scale, abject level. But this does not solve the basic land problem. It is merely a form of agricultural relief reminiscent of some of our farm programs in the depression of 1929.

Price Problems and Crop Control

The agricultural problems of Latin America have international as well as domestic aspects. On the domestic level, there are issues related to efficiency and land distribution. On the international level, there are difficulties due to monoculture, wide price fluctuations, and the oversupply of basic products such as sugar, coffee, cacao, bananas, wheat, wool, cotton, and meat. The oversupply of these products in some years and shortages in others lead to wide and sometimes disastrous price fluctuations. In bad years, foreign exchange earnings are cut sharply, trade balance deficits appear and become large, and much-needed machinery, raw materials, and consumers goods cannot be imported in sufficient quantities. In short, a sharp fall in the price of such products as sugar or coffee may lead to serious depressions in the whole economies of countries dependent on these commodities for foreign exchange earnings.

Periodic wide fluctuations in the export prices of farm products are serious. But much more serious is the long-run downward trend in recent years in the prices of two of the most important commodities, coffee and sugar. Countries heavily dependent on these commodities may become stagnated unless their decreased earnings in these fields are somehow offset by other forms of enterprise. The rise in the export prices of coffee and sugar in 1963 is likely to be only temporary.

In addition to wide price fluctuations and the long-run downward trend of some prices, Latin America suffers from declining terms of trade. We have made this point earlier but it largely is an agricultural problem, and should be mentioned again here. The prices of raw materials and food products have tended to fall in contrast to the prices of manufactured goods. Countries are becoming increasingly self-sufficient in food and raw materials. They import less, and the exporting countries suffer from declining demand at the same time that their export commodities increase in supply. Falling prices sometimes cause this increase because of an effort to recoup losses by larger volume. A more common reason, however, is that food and raw-material outputs are usually uncontrolled, whereas manufacturing outputs are controlled. At any rate, the falling or widely fluctuating prices of primary goods cause great hardships in Latin American countries, and one of the objectives of the Charter of Punta del Este is their regulation. Latin American countries believe that the United States should cooperate in this objective. Public opinion in our country, however, is not favorable to any extensive effort on our part to help them in price stabilization.

Summary

The following broad conclusions may be reached concerning agricultural problems in Latin America. Although it has been thought in the past that the latifundias or large estates were the root of all evil in Latin American agriculture, this belief is becoming less common. Minifundism is regarded as another serious problem. Some redistribution of land to equalize ownership is needed. But the plans used in Venezuela, Colombia, and Peru are preferable to those of Mexico, Bolivia, and Cuba because they do not cause social upheaval through expropriation. Greater agricultural productivity is the major need of Latin America. It can be improved by more education, better seed, more fertilizer, better roads, new equipment and machinery, and better housing and health services. Farm-credit plans which exist in some countries such as Mexico need to be expanded.

Price-control plans are of doubtful value when their object is to maintain unnatural world prices, as in the case of coffee. Only short-run price stabilization is defensible. It is also evident that the United States should not enter price-control plans which merely perpetuate the overproduction of coffee, sugar, and other Latin American products.

In general, the basic problem of Latin America—a better use of the resources supplied by nature—can be solved only by industrialization. Land equalization is not the answer. Mexico and Uruguay early came to this conclusion, and it is the foundation of the economic policy revolution. But industrialization has been viewed too narrowly. It does not consist merely of the growth of factories and large cities. What Latin America has not learned is that *agriculture must be industrialized simultaneously with manufacturing*. Without a productive, industrialized agriculture, total industrialization will be impossible. Latin America cannot at this stage repeat the history of England in the nineteenth century. It cannot become the workshop for the world and buy its food with exports of manufactured goods.

References

1. Chase-Manhattan Bank, *Latin American Business Highlights*, 1961, vol. II, no. 3, p. 3.
2. Chase-Manhattan Bank, *op. cit.*, p. 3.

3. Chase-Manhattan Bank, *Latin American Business Highlights,* 1961, vol. II, no. 3, p. 3.

4. Harry Stark, *Latin America,* W. C. Brown, Dubuque, Iowa, 1961, pp. 136–137.

5. Clarence Senior, *Democracy and Land Reform,* University of Florida Press, Gainesville, 1958.

6. Chase-Manhattan Bank, *op. cit.,* p. 7.

7. Chase-Manhattan Bank, *op. cit.,* p. 7.

8. Chase-Manhattan Bank, *op. cit.,* p. 8.

NINE

PROBLEMS OF INDUSTRIALISM
IN LATIN AMERICA

INDUSTRIALISM AND THE INDUSTRIALIZATION OF AGRICULTURE will bring a better economic life to Latin America. Beginning with the Presidency of Batlle y Ordonez in Uruguay and the regime of Obregon in Mexico, Latin American nations turned increasingly to industry as the means of removing poverty. But in most of the countries there are great obstacles to rapid industrialization.

To change from a handicraft and primitive agrarian economy into an advanced industrial nation requires a number of steps, although they may not be taken in the exact order in which we shall list them: 1) Agricultural technology must be improved and machinery and other capital applied to farming so that farmers can produce enough to feed not only themselves but also two to five additional families in the cities. (2) Excess population on the land, resulting from greater agricultural productivity, must be transferred to the cities and given employment there. (3) City employment requires the growth of manufacturing, services, and trade—but it requires mainly the growth of manufacturing. (4) The needed industrialism depends in its turn on the growth of capital. Capital can be obtained either from domestic saving or foreign investment. (5) Since people in poor underdeveloped countries cannot save very much, foreign aid and investment are needed. Without them, growth will be retarded. Somehow foreign investment and aid must be accepted despite strong nationalism. If foreign investment and nationalism prove incompatible, the consequences are unfortunate. There will be a slow rate of growth, and even impoverishment of the people, as in Cuba, by the premature adoption of extreme forms of economic planning. Either there will be economic isolation, or dependence on the dubious advantages of trade agreements with China and the Soviet Union.

In addition to economic progress, there must be simultaneous social development. It is needed not only for the welfare of the people, but for the growth of industrialism. A country which does not remove illiteracy and bad health, promote sanitation and good housing, and greatly increase technical and professional training cannot go far in the direction of industrialism. Transportation, marketing, and communication must also be increased. Industrialization is a simultaneous advance on many social and economic fronts.

The Latin American economies are all underdeveloped, and serious obstacles prevent the achievement of the various prerequisites for industrialism outlined above. Even nations like Argentina, Uruguay, and Chile have a long way to go to overcome these obstacles. But to understand the problems of industrialism in Latin America we must first be sure that we know what Latin American economic life is really like.

Economic Divisions and Leadership

What then is the nature of Latin American economy? It may be described by dividing it into basic sectors. (1) Primitive Indian culture consisting of subsistence agriculture. (2) Large estates producing basic crops such as coffee, sugar, bananas, cacao, wheat, wool, and meat. (3) Small land holdings or cooperatives producing basic or diversified crops. (4) Small handicraft manufacturing of products such as Panama hats in Ecuador, or leather goods in Argentina and Mexico. (5) Small-scale manufacturing using machinery. (6) Large industrial plants under government or private auspices. (Much direct foreign investment is of this nature.) (7) Retail and wholesale establishments, mostly on a small scale. (8) Service enterprises, for the most part also on a small scale. (9) The professions (doctors, lawyers, teachers, engineers). (10) Government employees. (11) Railways and other transportation services. (12) Telephones, telegraph, radio and television. (13) Building construction. (14) Public utilities providing gas and electricity. (15) Mining. (16) Banking, finance, and insurance. Perhaps a third of the whole economy consists of the first sector, more than another third of the second and third sectors. The remainder is made up of sectors four to sixteen.

Out of this organization of the economy is derived a number of economic groups. They consist of (1) the primitive rural Indian peasants who are often squatters, (2) the poor agricultural workers, tenants, and sharecroppers on estates, (3) the poor independent farmers, (4) the members of the cooperatives such as the *ejiditarios* in Mexico, (5) the wealthy landowners, (6) the handicraft workers, (7) the industrial workers, (8) the lower middle class, consisting of small businessmen, teachers, clergy, government employees and office workers, (9) the small upper middle class, consisting of well-to-do businessmen, bankers, doctors, lawyers, government officials and wealthy people living on their investments, (10) a considerable number of urban unemployed, and (11) the army and navy and their officers.

The first four groups and the sixth, which include the vast majority of the population, have little power or influence. Most of these people are illiterate. Industrial workers, however, are becoming organized, and where they are joined politically with the lower middle class they have achieved considerable power.

At the top of the socioeconomic scale, a shift of power is occurring. At one time, wealthy landowners combined with top military men to control political and economic life in virtually all Latin American countries. A dictator or *caudillo* assumed concentrated power, and represented the interests of these two groups. In more recent years, wealthy businessmen and leading politicians have combined with the military to assume power. In some cases they have represented the lower middle classes and organized labor. Economic and political leadership is now in a state of transition. Democratically elected presidents have succeeded dictators although, once in office, they often assume dictatorial power.

It is evident that a new type of political and economic leader is appearing in Latin America. In large business enterprises, men of lowly origin are rising to top managerial positions. A new wealthy class is also arising, a group of men who acquired wealth through business enterprise rather than land, and through the tactics of the so-called self-made man. Workers and small farmers, through savings, are getting into the lower middle class by starting small enterprises. Political leaders are beginning to come from these various new groups and are known as "the new men." They "got there" the hard way. They know the sufferings of the peon and the urban unemployed. They seek a fusion of economic development with social justice, and they are impatient to obtain it. Their goals are rapid economic reform and social progress with emphasis on better education, housing, and health services. These goals are similar to those of the welfare state. From the Andes to the Caribbean, a new generation of able and angry young leaders is battling against stupid and corrupt governments as well as poverty.[1]

The Nature of Manufacturing in Latin America

Although virtually all kinds of manufactured goods are produced in Latin America, there is a much greater proportion of manufacturing in light industries than in the United States. Textiles and food processing are the most important manufacturing fields. Heavy industry is largely undeveloped and most countries are severely handicapped because of lack of coal, iron, or both. Trade and service employ a smaller proportion of the labor force than in the United States, and railroads, electrical power, and telephone service are much less extensive than in our country. But these differences characterize most underdeveloped nations.

In general, the growth of manufacturing and industry depends upon the presence of technical know-how; skilled, semi-skilled, and unskilled industrial labor; much capital, saving and investment; adequate transportation facilities; supplies of fuel, energy and raw materials; and a domestic market with sufficient purchasing power to buy the manufactured goods produced. Latin America has lacked most of these prerequisites of industrialism. It has only begun to progress rapidly in these respects since World War II.

In the Latin American economic boom after World War II, manufacturing grew more rapidly than any other field. From 1945 to 1955 the increase in total production was 62 percent. But manufacturing grew 77 percent, and agriculture only 51 percent.[2] The growth was accompanied by greater diversification of manufacturing. There appeared new steel plants, the assembly of automobiles, the expansion of nonferrous metal production, greater shipbuilding, the new chemical and petro-chemical industries, and the development of paper and pulp, cement, bicycle, refrigerator, radio, diesel engine, TV, and plastics manufacturing. However, in spite of these new enterprises in the hard goods and heavy industries, the majority of the manufacturing in Latin America is in the consumers goods fields of food processing, textiles, shoes, and clothing.[3]

Iron and Steel

The basis of modern industrialism is still the production of iron and steel. Thus the leading industrial problem of Latin America is the development of steel production as the core of an expanding industrial system. Latin America has been producing about 1½ percent of the world's total steel. It produces only 2 percent of the world's iron ore. Steel production as yet consists largely of processing imported semifinished steel. The lack of coal is the chief obstacle to the development of the steel industry. There is a sufficient supply of iron ore in three countries—Brazil, Cuba, and Venezuela. The great deposits in the Cerro Bolivar in Venezuela and in the state of Minas Gerais in Brazil are among the largest in the world. Chile and Mexico also have a sufficient amount for steel production.

Coal could be imported from the United States by Venezuela and Brazil in return for exports of iron ore. In this way, or through the development of electrical steel based on water power, a sizable steel industry could be created in at least two nations.

Basic steel production on a relatively large scale began in Brazil with the construction of the mills at Volta Redonda. President Vargas, who came to power in 1930, proposed an *Estado Novo* which would bring Brazil out of the depression and start it on the road toward rapid economic development through the creation of a steel industry. With Vargas, the industry began to grow in Brazil, but there was insufficient capital. Eleven countries are now producing pig iron, steel ingots, or finished steel. Second in importance to Brazil is Mexico, but Venezuela will probably soon become the second largest producer. Production figures for 1956, 1957, and 1958 are given in the adjoining table.

Latin America, in spite of manufacturing 2.4 million tons of pig iron, 3.5 million tons of steel ingots, and 3.6 million tons of finished steels in 1958, was far from self-sufficient in steel. As production increased after 1950, the gap between production

Latin America: Production of Pig Iron, Steel Ingots and Finished Steel 1956, 1957 and 1958
(thousands of tons)

Country	Pig Iron			Steel Ingots			Finished Steel		
	1956	1957	1958	1956	1957	1958	1956	1957	1958
Argentina	35	34	29	203	221	224	631	703	878
Brazil	1,152	1,252	1,340	1,375	1,475	1,590	1,142	1,246	1,360
Colombia	116	126	149	100	125	135	83	105	101
Cuba	—	—	—	(12)	(14)	(17)	(15)	(15)	(15)
Chile	367	382	304	401	412	373	285	270	234
El Salvador	—	—	—	—	—	1*	—	—	0
Mexico	408	429	496	888	1,050	1,115	710	880	916
Panama	—	—	—	—	—	1*	—	—	0
Peru	—	—	—	—	—	21	—	4	25
Uruguay	—	—	60*	13	(13)	(13)	30	(36)	40*
Venezuela	—	—	—	38	59	56*	35	54	51*
TOTAL	2,078	2,223	2,378	3,030	3,369	3,567	2,931	3,312	3,621
Rate of increase in relation to that recorded in the preceding year	16.3	7.0	7.0	19.2	11.2	5.9	13.1	13.0	9.3

Source: United Nations, Economic Survey of Latin America, New York, 1958, p. 81. Figures in parentheses are estimates based on data for other years.

*Provisional estimates.

and consumption widened. From 1950 to 1957 steel imports increased from 2.8 million to 5.5 million tons. Steel consumption in Latin America in 1958 was nearly 15 million tons. If industrialism grows rapidly in the next ten years, 20 or 30 million tons will be needed, and local steelmaking capacity is not growing rapidly enough to supply even half of this. As the need for steel increases, larger imports will cause additional balance-of-payment problems. Obviously, the growth of steel capacity must be rapidly stepped up to sustain the rate of production growth Latin America experienced in the years from 1950 to 1958. It should be one of the main objectives of Alliance for Progress aid. In 1958 the rate of steel production growth fell off, mainly because little further expansion was possible, granted existing plant capacity. In 1959 crude steel production even declined in Argentina, Colombia, and Mexico.

As we have indicated, the main sites of additional plant capacity will be in Brazil and Venezuela. In some ways Venezuela has advantages over Brazil. Iron ore reserves are large and surpluses can be shipped to the United States in return for coal at a distance that is much shorter than the journey from the United States to Brazil.[4] Cuba, Chile, Colombia, Peru, and Mexico could also increase their capacity if capital were available. Despite limited resources, the cost of production is low in some of these countries. Steel has been produced in Colombia at costs that are the lowest in the world. Chile has been producing steel cheaply in the Valdivia area since 1924.

Metals and Machinery

Progress in the smelting and refining of nonferrous metals has been much slower than in steel. Latin America has large deposits of these metals, and it could retain some of the profits derived from them by smelting and refining them locally. They have been mined and shipped mainly to the United States for processing. But not much progress has been made in developing local smelting except in Peru where zinc smelting is increasing.[5]

Considerable advance has been made in the production of machine tools and machinery, especially in Argentina, Brazil, and Mexico. Among the types produced are machines for textile factories, construction, and paper and pulp mills. Large diesel engines are being manufactured in Argentina and Brazil.

In the field of metal fabricating, the most significant development in recent years has been the mass production of motor vehicles and tractors. There is still a great shortage of motorized equipment and spare parts in Latin America. These industries are among the newest and only Argentina, Brazil and Mexico have made any considerable progress.

Latin America: Manufacture and Assembly of Motor Vehicles 1955 to 1958
(Units)

A. DOMESTIC MANUFACTURE				
Country	1955	1956	1957	1958
Argentina	6,653	5,164	15,274	26,586*
Brazil	4,595	6,619	29,129	61,129
Mexico	—	—	—	203
Latin America	11,248	11,783	44,953	87,918

B. ASSEMBLY OF IMPORTED PARTS AND SEMIASSEMBLED VEHICLES				
Country	1955	1956	1957	1958
Argentina	—	—	7,089	1,495
Brazil	—	—	1,021	183
Mexico	31,740	41,500	40,733	41,163*
Venezuela	18,097	13,830	14,812	13,443
Latin America	—	—	63,650	56,283

Source: United Nations, *Economic Survey of Latin America*, New York, 1958, p. 84.

* Provisional estimates.

Three other fields of metal fabricating which show promise, although still largely undeveloped, are railway rolling stock, shipbuilding, and aircraft. Argentina, Brazil, Chile, and Mexico have had two decades of experience in the manufacture and repair of railway rolling stock, principally freight cars and spare parts. Modern plants for these purposes have been established recently in Brazil and Mexico, and production is expanding in these countries. In Argentina and Chile, however, excess productive capacity exists in proportion to the rate at which rolling stock is being replaced or increased. The aircraft industry exists on paper in most countries except Argentina and Brazil, where planes are being assembled mainly for military purposes. In most of the countries the aircraft industry could be developed to local advantage if capital, technical staff, and skilled labor were available.

Argentina, Brazil, and Colombia have been the countries most interested in developing merchant marines and ship-building and repairing facilities. But at present there are only small and poorly equipped shipyards. As in some other fields, there has been a great deal of planning but it has not resulted in concrete achievements. In Brazil there are plans for the expansion of shipbuilding from small to medium tonnage of 5,000 to 10,000 or even 20,000 tons. Brazil, however, has not been able to obtain the necessary capital, and it lacks the technical staff, skilled labor, and ancillary industries needed for growth in this field.

Shipbuilding is a corollary to the development of national merchant marines. Perón in Argentina created a national Merchant Marine between the end of World War II and 1952. A variety of objectives were sought. Because of the large foreign trade of Argentina, much-needed foreign exchange was being spent to pay for the services of foreign merchant ships transporting Argentine meat, grain, and other products. Brazil has rivaled Argentina in the development of a merchant marine. In both countries there is state planning and control, and the underlying purposes are about the same.

Chemical Industries

Another promising field for economic development in Latin America is the chemical industry. There is a rapidly increasing demand for chemical products such as sodium bicarbonate, fertilizers, and pharmaceuticals. Latin America has a growing market for these and other products, but two factors have thus far retarded growth in this field: (1) import restrictions on chemical raw materials imposed to save foreign exchange for products regarded as of greater economic importance, and (2) inability to develop a wide enough market demand to justify large plants in the field of heavy chemicals where low costs of production depend upon large-scale operations.

Because of agricultural needs, the most important chemical product at this stage in the economic development of these nations is fertilizer. Mexico has entered the field to a greater extent than any other Latin American country. However, it was estimated that in 1956 only 5 percent of tilled land in Mexico was fertilized.[6] Other fields that are growing rapidly are the manufacture of plastics, explosives, paint, insecticides, and detergents. Pharmaceutical companies are producing a wide range of products in many countries and the petrochemical industries are becoming important in Mexico. The soda alkalis are not being produced in sufficient quantities to meet demand except in Mexico, and, except in that country also, there has been little development of synthetic yarns and textiles.

Tires, Pulp and Paper, Cement

Most of the rubber manufactured in Latin America is used to manufacture tires. Tire plants have existed in Latin America for many years. They consist mainly of branches of American tire companies. Firestone and Goodyear have plants in Brazil; Goodrich, Goodyear, General Tire and U.S. Rubber in Mexico; and Goodyear and Goodrich in Peru. Goodrich and Firestone also have plants in Argentina and there is an important domestic tire company in Brazil,[7] and a government monopoly on tire manufacture in Uruguay.[8] The industry has not made much progress despite the fact that a shortage of tires created a need for local production during World War II, and the growth in the production and use of automobiles since the war has caused an upsurge in demand.

Several reasons explain the failure of the industry to grow rapidly. The first of these is a shortage of foreign exchange with which to purchase rubber. Exchange has not been allotted in large amounts for this purpose. An insufficient foreign supply of rubber has led to efforts to expand the growth of plantation rubber in Brazil, Peru, and Bolivia. But in 1958 only 23,000 tons were produced in Brazil, 2,400 tons in Peru, and 1,100 tons in Bolivia.[9] Although more plantation rubber is being grown, especially in Brazil and Bolivia, it is not expected that it will meet domestic rubber needs. As a result, Argentina, Brazil,

Mexico, and Venezuela are entering the field of synthetic rubber manufacturing.

The production of pulp for paper and paper itself are rapidly expanding in Latin America. In 1957 and 1958 the production of paper and board grew by 17 and 10 percent respectively. The production of pulp is growing at a more rapid rate than paper. But even the rapid growth in these fields has not closed the wide gap between supply and demand. Only Chile seems to produce more than it needs for self-sufficiency and is exporting newsprint. Mexico and Venezuela, however, are rapidly expanding plant capacity. The production of pulp and paper would seem to be an area in which Latin America has natural advantages due to the large supply of wood available for this purpose.

Cement is another industry which has been growing rapidly in Latin America. Two reasons are involved—government encouragement and the building boom in large cities since World War II. For a number of years the average rate of increase of production was 10 percent. But with the recession, and deteriorating economic conditions after 1958, the rate of increase fell to only 3½ percent. This decline may be temporary, and the governments of various countries were planning further expansion of capacity even in 1958.

The Limited Industrial Development

The picture of Latin American industry is one of limited advancement. The industrial core—the production of steel—is undeveloped. About 30 million tons would be needed for real progress. In 1958, only 3½ million tons of crude steel were produced locally, and about the same amount of finished steel. Even at the present low rate of use, Latin America can only produce half of the amount it uses. Only Argentina, Brazil, Chile, and Mexico have been actually producing steel in sizable amounts. In 1962 Venezuela, however, constructed a new plant. The production of other metals is virtually nonexistent except for small amounts of copper and lead produced in Chile and Mexico. Only a few countries assemble or manufacture automobiles, and the total production is less than one percent of the production of the United States. There is little shipbuilding. Aircraft production is still in the planning stage. The chemical industries are undeveloped except for pharmaceuticals, fertilizer, and a little rayon. Only nine countries produce automobile tires. In spite of vast quantities of wood, paper and pulp production is not great enough for self-sufficiency. Except for the production of cotton textiles, clothing, shoes, processed foods and beer, Latin America has made little progress industrially.

If the world were buying a steadily and rapidly increasing quantity of sugar, coffee, bananas, cotton, and other export commodities at steady or rising prices, industrialization would not be so necessary. But the demand for Latin American products is not rising rapidly, and the terms of trade are becoming unfavorable. Unable to rely increasingly on foreign trade, domestic industrialism has now become of crucial importance. Without it, Latin America will not progress. It will go backward. By 1959, Argentina, Bolivia, Brazil, Cuba, and Chile were declining and some of the other countries were at a standstill.

The Requisites of Industrial Progress

The primary need for rapid industrial progress is capital. Latin America has neither been attracting enough foreign capital nor creating enough of its own. Capital formation, which is discussed in the next chapter, should be occurring at the rate of $6 to $12 billion a year, or from 10 to 20 percent of the gross national product. Capital accumulation had become so low that production increased only 2.6 percent in 1959—an amount barely offsetting the rise of population. Production per capita was at a standstill.

The older classical economists were fully aware of the need for capital as the basis of economic progress. Latter-day economists have stressed other factors. We have discussed them in Chapter 5. Balance in growth was one of these. Our brief survey of Latin American industry clearly reveals a great lack of balance in growth. Although steel production has begun to grow, ferro-alloy production, which must accompany steel production in advanced industrialism, has scarcely grown at all. Moreover, except for building construction, the industries that use steel such as machinery, automobile production, and shipbuilding are not growing fast enough. Also, granted the lack of energy resources, new sources of power should be growing at a rate at least equal to the growth of industries using power. Electrical power, one major power source that Latin America must use, is seriously lagging behind industrial needs. Venezuelan oil is not supplying Latin America with power to any great extent. It is being shipped to other parts of the world. Although Latin America, as we have just seen, has a great supply of wood, paper production is far behind paper needs. Although the demand for clothing is growing, the rayon and nylon industries are almost nonexistent. The textile industry, one of the most advanced in Latin America, has to rely on imports of cotton because cotton farming has not grown enough to meet the local demand. Rubber must still be imported in large quantities, because of the failure to expand rapidly the production of plantation rubber. Throughout the whole of Latin American industry, trained managers, engineers, technicians, and skilled workers are scarce. The supply of trained labor lags behind the demand for it. One could go on and on giving examples of unbalance.

Lack of balance is partly due to the lack of "a big push" or "take-off." These in their turn are due to a lack of capital. But both unbalance and lack of capital are caused by lack of planning. The "free market" which under capitalism is supposed to lead to balance, is not maintaining it in Latin America. To a large extent there is no free market. It is doubtful whether any unadvanced region can achieve growth balance through a free-market price system, assuming that there is one. Unadvanced areas, however, are riddled with monopoly and government control. *The only way out is planning.* Our survey of Latin American industry reveals not only the need for capital, but careful growth planning as well.

Virtually no one, however, is providing the necessary planning, because most of the nations operate on a purely national basis. The planning should embrace Latin America as a whole, and include its over-all economic relations with the United States. Although a promising beginning has been made by the economic organizations of the two common markets, they have not thus far provided the kind of comprehensive planning that is required. But perhaps more serious is the fact that the United States under the early administration of the Alliance for Progress has not provided it. One of the major contentions of this book is just that. The policy pursued by the Alliance for Progress thus far has led only to piecemeal unilateral action. Under

President Kennedy, at any rate, we were failing to lead in the over-all economic planning needed in Latin America.

References

1. Peter Drucker, "A Plan for Revolution in Latin America," *Harper's Magazine*, July 1961, p. 31.
2. Chase-Manhattan Bank, *Latin American Business Highlights*, Sept. 1956, p. 4.
3. Foods, including beverages, were 32 percent of the total in 1957, and textiles, shoes, and clothing, 23 percent.
4. At present, however, the Venezuelan government is planning to use electricity instead of coal in a new government-financed plant.
5. United Nations, *Economic Survey of Latin America*, New York, 1958, p. 82.
6. United Nations, *Economic Survey of Latin America*, New York, 1958, p. 86.
7. *Companhia Brasilera de Artefactos do Borracha.*
8. *Fabrico Uraguaya de Neumaticos.*
9. United Nations, *op. cit.*, p. 86.

CAPITAL FORMATION, FOREIGN INVESTMENT, AND FOREIGN AID

THE INDUSTRIALISM SO GREATLY NEEDED IN LATIN AMERICA CAN only be achieved if there is a rapid accumulation of capital. Advanced countries usually have no trouble in amassing capital. In fact, they sometimes "oversave." But low incomes make it hard for people in poor countries to save. As a result, capital accumulation in underdeveloped countries is too little and too slow for the rate of industrial growth they need. Either loans or aid should be obtained from rich countries like the United States.

But vigorous nationalism is often an obstacle. Underdeveloped nations resist the foreigner's loans or aid for fear of "imperialist domination." Their desire for independence and their fear of the imperialist powers make them try "to raise themselves by their own bootstraps." Some nations, such as Mexico, have been relatively successful in this endeavor. But her rate of growth has been retarded by it. Even the United States had to rely heavily on Great Britain and France for capital in its economic infancy. Fortunately, the nationalism generated by the two wars with England did not prevent us from accepting British capital. Until the take-off point is reached, a poor country needs outside assistance. But, in most Latin American countries the take-off point has not been reached. These countries need our capital even to prevent a decline in per capita production.

Post World War II Foreign Investments

The inflow of capital from foreign sources in the thirties and forties was not large. It was confined to the relatively small loans of the Export-Import Bank, and to some small loans obtained from Great Britain, France, and Germany. The inflow of capital has been described as a "mere trickle."[1] Moreover, the total amount of investments outstanding at the beginning of the war in 1939 was $9 billion, only half a billion higher than in 1914. The actual value in 1914 purchasing power of these investments was only $6.3 billion, representing an actual shrinkage.

The significant growth of foreign funds began after World War II when the total annual gross inflow increased from $588 million in 1947 to $2,240 million by 1957.[2] Except for short-term private credits, most of these funds were either official loans made by government agencies, or direct private investments. Between 1941 and 1950 there were no long-term private portfolio loans. From 1950 to 1959 the total accumulated *net* inflow of long-term capital from the United States and the World Bank for the ten-year period was $8.3 billion.[3] Of this total $5.8 billion, or 70 percent, came from private United States sources, and was largely direct investment. Additional direct investment from other nations, mainly those in Western Europe, amounted to $1.6 billion. The inflow of capital exhibited radical fluctuations from year to year, but there was a general upward trend until 1957. Since that year, private direct investment has declined sharply, more than offsetting the recent increase in government loans and aid.

The number of public agencies making loans increased after World War II. Before the war, there were only the loans of the Export-Import Bank. Among the additional agencies or funds participating after the war were the United States Development Loan Fund, the Inter-American Development Bank, the International Finance Corporation, the International Development Association and the International Bank for Reconstruction and Development (World Bank). The Inter-American Bank, the latest and most important of these, was organized in the spring of 1961 under Felipe Herrera of Chile. In 1961 it made loans amounting to $294 million. Capital from the United States Government and other public sources has not been limited because of too few public lending agencies. The trouble was that insufficient loan funds were allocated to these agencies. Until the Alliance for Progress program, inaugurated in 1961 in the administration of President Kennedy, not enough capital had been made available from public sources. The decline in the inflow of private capital after 1957 made a compensating increase in public capital im-

Loans Granted By The International Bank for Reconstruction and Development. 1952–1959
(millions of dollars)

Year	New Authorizations	Disbursements	Amortization Payments	Net Contributions
1950	53	39	—	39
1951	85	57	—	57
1952	54	66	—1	65
1953	30	60	—2	58
1954	100	69	—7	62
1955	123	73	—13	65
1956	73	100	—20	80
1957	80	162	—30	132
1958	174.27	72	—32.3	39.7
1959	80.65	68.6	—35.5	33.1

Source: Based on official reports of the International Bank.

Latin American Net Inflow of Capital (Public and Private)[4]
(1955–1962 in millions of dollars)

1955	760	1959	(600)
1956	1,080	1960	(100)
1957	1,730	1961	(250)
1958	715	1962	(—100)
		1963	(—200)

Source: ECLA based on International Monetary Fund, *Balance of Payments Yearbook*, and U.S. Department of Commerce, *Survey of Current Business*, and official statistics of Latin American countries.

perative if the high rate of economic development in Latin America after 1950 was to be sustained.

American Aid Programs

In the years after World War II, the United States granted over $70 billion in aid to various parts of the world for military and economic purposes. Of this amount, Latin America had received scarcely a billion dollars by 1960. Half of this consisted of surplus and outmoded war material. Latin Americans have complained vigorously of our neglect. Aid has been given to forestall communism in other parts of the world. But until recently we have not regarded the communist threat in Latin America as serious. Certain forms of aid, although not financially large, have had significance, however. These consist of technical aid from the Departments of Agriculture, Commerce, Interior and Health, Education and Welfare, and from ICA and the Point Four program. By 1953 the United States was granting $45 million a year for technical assistance. But Latin Americans were far from satisfied with this type of American aid, and believed that we had greatly neglected them.

The mounting discontent was one of the reasons prompting the visits of Vice President Nixon and Dr. Milton Eisenhower to South America. Dr. Eisenhower returned recommending loans rather than aid, and only loans for "sound" projects to countries that were "good credit risks." Nothing came of these recommendations. But a sizable aid program of $500 million was proposed at Bogota in 1960. Acceptance of the principle at the Bogota meeting that we should make large grants for social and economic development was a direct result of the communist threat posed by Castro.

At an earlier point[5] we have described the beginning of this program known as the Alliance for Progress. Aid was made conditional upon the drawing up of plans for social and economic development, and the adoption of basic tax and land reforms. The meeting in Punta del Este in August, 1961, established the framework by which the funds were to be administered, and set up the twelve program objectives. The United States committed itself to grant $1,029,576,000 between March, 1961 and February, 1962. In March, 1962, President Kennedy asked Congress to approve $3 billion for 1963.[6] The total program calls for the spending of $20 billion in ten years. Although $1,029,576,000 had been committed for 1961, the program was slow in getting under way and only about $250 million had been spent by March, 1962.

During the first year the Alliance for Progress was severely criticized both in the United States and in Latin America. The communists and Perónists called it a form of American imperialism. Conservatives opposed it on the ground that it compelled the Latin American nations to make social reforms that they considered premature. In the United States it was insisted that the funds would merely get into the pockets of wealthy Latin Americans, and that the Latin American nations were not living up to their agreements to introduce tax and land reforms. In

Brazil, Colombia, and Peru both types of reform were postponed because of impending elections. In Argentina, the ardent supporter of the program, Frondizi, was forced out of office by a military coup on the eve of Perónist victories. In Chile, extensive land reform could not be introduced without upsetting the political balance of power and bringing about communism. Under these circumstances, President Kennedy could only urge Congress to have patience.

The future of the Alliance for Progress was bleak on its first anniversary. More serious than congressional opposition was the drying up of American private investment in Latin America in 1962, and the renewed flight of American and other capital. Despite the Alliance for Progress, there was probably a net outflow of $100 million in 1962 and $200 million in 1963. Thus the inflow caused by the Alliance for Progress was more than offset by private capital outflow. The Alliance for Progress did not promote much progress. But it did prevent utter economic collapse in Latin America.

The Alliance for Progress Commitments
(March 3, 1961 to February 28, 1962—thousands of dollars)

Argentina	$ 9,128	Honduras	$ 5,076
Bolivia	22,420	Mexico	106,321
Brazil	357,190	Nicaragua	10,729
Chile	135,489	Panama	11,926
Colombia	69,162	Paraguay	16,282
Costa Rica	20,024	Peru	65,969
Dominican Republic	25,024	Uruguay	4,925
Ecuador	39,505	Venezuela	99,358
El Salvador	23,514	Central American Bank	2,000
Guatemala	3,669	Undistributed	1,550
Haiti	2,840		
	Total	$1,029,576	

Source: *New York Times*, March 12, 1962.

Direct Private Investment

As we have said, private capital inflows into Latin America, which had become net outflows by 1962, were heavy between 1950 and 1957. Almost all of this capital took the form of direct investment. Portfolio investments had virtually disappeared as a result of the bond defaults after 1930. Direct investments, which consist of the building of foreign-owned plants and equipment in Latin American countries, became the substitute for the purchase by Americans of Latin American securities. Direct investments were regarded as safer. The American investor could determine the uses to which funds were put, and control the efficiency with which they were used. Moreover, the high tariffs of Latin American countries made it difficult for American industries to produce goods at home and sell them in Latin America. To sell, they had to build plants in the countries involved. Between 1946 and 1958, direct investments of the United States rose by about $5½ billion. By 1958, however, the inflow of direct investments declined sharply. In 1957 it had been $1,350 million. In 1958 it fell to only $475 million. In 1959, the total over-all value of direct investments of the United States in Latin America amounted to $9 billion, and the goods and services produced annually from these industries amounted to about $7½ billion a year. Of this amount, about $4½ billion of products were sold and consumed in the Latin American countries and about $3 billion were products made in Latin America, but exported to other countries.[6]

American direct investments have gone mostly into petroleum, and most of these funds have been invested in Venezuela. Not only were the main petroleum resources in Venezuela, but the climate for foreign investment was favorable there. These factors, coupled with the rising demand for petroleum in the United States, explain not only the great increase in direct investment but account in no small measure for the rapid increase in the gross national product of Venezuela. After 1952, however, direct investment in petroleum became less important, and the flow of American capital shifted to some extent to manufacturing and the production of metals.

Direct investments in petroleum declined, partly because of the recession of 1953 but also because petroleum productive capacity had reached a peak in relation to demand. Further investment in petroleum could be made from the reinvestment of profits rather than from the inflow of new capital. In 1955 direct investment in petroleum again turned upward, due to the Suez Canal crisis. Simultaneously new concessions favorable to investment were made by the Venezuelan government. New capital flowed into Venezuela despite the curb placed on American imports of Venezuelan oil, and was based on the confidence investors had in the long-run prospects of the petroleum industry. In these years also, the United Kingdom and the Netherlands made considerable investments in Venezuelan oil. But after 1957 investment in oil again declined. The Suez crisis was over and investors again became dubious about the long-run prospects of oil.

Although oil resources exist and need to be developed in Argentina, Brazil, Chile, and Mexico, their development by foreigners is opposed. There is also opposition to the use of private capital even if domestic. Despite these handicaps, oil production has increased in these countries.

Of long-run significance is the expansion of direct investment in manufacturing. Immediately after World War II purchasing power in Latin America grew, partly because of the favorable balance of trade during and immediately after the war, and the boom in Latin American industry. The increased purchasing power created a potential market for many new types of manufactured goods. The demand for manufactured products increased rapidly. Tariffs and trade controls blocked imports, and domestic capital was insufficient to supply the rising demand. As a result, direct foreign investment began to fill the gap. Argentina, Brazil, and Chile also provided tax and other incentives to encourage the investment of foreign capital in local factories. At the same time, direct investment in manufacturing in Europe was becoming less attractive for a variety of reasons. Even Japan began to make direct investments in Latin America. Brazil has attracted the most manufacturing capital, but Mexico, Peru, Chile, and, until the days of Castro, Cuba also received a great deal of these foreign manufacturing funds. Argentina and Venezuela have not attracted much of this capital, but by 1960 some of it began to flow to these nations also. Automobile assembly, chemicals, textiles, machinery, consumer durables and a variety of products for consumers have been developed, especially in Brazil, Chile, and Mexico. Foreign investment in utilities has greatly declined except in Central America and the Caribbean countries.

A number of factors encouraged direct private investments between 1945 and 1960. The United States Economic Cooperation Act of 1948 provided arrangements by which investments could be insured against loss from expropriation, and inconvertibility of principal or profits into American currency. Although this law required mutual agreements in regard to specific investments and few of these have yet been made, the prospects of the development of this form of insurance were encouraging to American capital. Much more important was the insurance against unfair treatment or expropriation derived from the formation of mixed companies in which both Latin Americans and United States citizens jointly invested. Also, various Latin American countries began to relax their restrictions on the remittance of profits, and some guaranteed the conversion of profits into foreign exchange. On the negative side, however, was the unfavorable tax position of American direct investors, who were taxed on business earnings both in the countries where they were earned and in the United States. However, some progress was being made even in this area in the direction of mutual agreements by which deductions were allowed for taxes paid in the United States and in the United States for taxes paid in Latin America.

The Investment Climate

Psychological factors affect the willingness of people to invest whether at home or abroad. During certain periods of Latin American history the climate or psychological atmosphere for investment has changed from excellent to very poor. The chief factors affecting these changes have been governmental. When dictators such as Porfirio Diaz established governmental stability and encouraged the inflow of foreign funds, large sums were invested in Mexican railways. But subsequently during the revolutions extending from 1910 to 1917, and in the period of governmental uncertainty that followed, foreign investment was discouraged. Expropriation of foreign property which occurred later brought investment to a standstill. Widespread defaults in the thirties discouraged investment in any form in the other Latin American nations, and destroyed portfolio investment. Since World War II, the tendencies toward socialism, the anti-Americanism, and the threat of communism have all played a part. Insistence on domestic exploitation of oil and other resources has inhibited the flow of capital into these fields in

Argentina and Brazil. Castroism has been the most recent deterrent.

Unless Latin American nations can maintain an atmosphere of friendliness toward the major investing nations, and a degree of governmental stability which gives some hope that communism will not engulf South and Central America, they cannot hope for the continuation of even direct private foreign investment on a large scale. Castroism, economic and political crises after 1957, and restrictions on the taking out of profits were largely responsible for the sharp drop in direct private investment. By 1960, only governmental aid from the United States in the Alliance for Progress program could prevent the collapse of Latin American economic growth. But as we have seen, after an upturn in private investment in 1961, a large flight of capital occurred in 1962. The departure of American private capital due to the bad investment climate offset all of the advantage gained from the Alliance for Progress. The jibes of communists had some truth. They referred to the new aid program as the *alianza para* (against) *progreso.*

But the climate favorable to investment is reciprocal. Latin Americans may deter North Americans, but the opposite can be true. We can invest in ways that arouse antagonism and cause fear of imperialism. The Committee for Economic Development has pointed out that American subsidiaries in Latin America should (1) employ a very large percentage of Latin American labor and attempt to advance native employees to top managerial and technical positions,[7] (2) attempt to develop local sources of supply of manufactured goods not formerly produced in these countries and meet the needs of local communities, (3) offer capital stock to local buyers, and (4) attempt to increase joint ownership or enter into joint enterprises with local businessmen. As a result, the local attitude toward foreign investment will become more favorable and governmental cooperation greater.

From the standpoint of many Latin Americans, direct investment by foreigners, especially Americans, is an imperialistic menace. At times, the opposition to foreign capital has been so great that leading politicians, although strongly favoring these investments themselves, have not dared to solicit foreign capital openly. The reasons for opposition are (1) general anti-Yankeeism, (2) belief that foreign companies steal and exploit the resources of the nation, (3) belief that excessive profits are made, and that these profits, which really should belong to domestic citizens, are taken out of the country to enrich foreigners, (4) belief that foreign companies exploit domestic labor and deny natives the really good positions in the companies, and (5) belief that foreign companies exercise sinister influences over the government of the country.

In recent years these charges against foreign companies have proved unfounded. Although oil, iron ore, and other minerals are taken out of the ground by foreign companies, the nations involved have been paid handsomely in rents, royalties, taxes, and shares of the profits. In Venezuela, for example, the government takes 60 percent of the profits of the oil companies. Moreover, the wages paid by the companies are well above those of domestic concerns. At least 98 percent of all employees are domestic, and as natives are trained, they are advanced to the highest positions in the foreign companies. The profits may in some instances be too high, but profits are generally high in Latin American business. Far from exercising undue influence upon the governments, foreign corporations have frequently been victims of unjust tax treatment and governmental frustrations of various kinds.

In the United States also there is a form of imaginary superficial liberalism that assumes the existence of a great American imperialism in Latin America. This is the communist line, although many who follow it are not communists. Some of the "viewers with alarm" come from the academic world, and "lean over backward" to make sure that we see the case for the Cuban or Bolivian Revolutions, or the Argentinian and Brazilian anti-Americanism.

Grants-in-aid are also under attack. In Latin America, the Perónist line is typical. It consists of two parts. American aid is destructive of national independence. American aid merely enriches a few people who are already wealthy. It is true, of course, that aid and loans given indiscriminately may not only enrich the few but help to impoverish the many. Loans and aid can be given for unproductive or ill-considered projects such as unneeded roads, public buildings, water power projects, etc. As a result, labor and resources are misdirected and wasted through the encouragement provided by foreign loans for unwise projects. Often the funds are entirely used up for construction, and nothing is provided for depreciation and maintenance.

Domestic Private Investment

The economic development of Latin America must ultimately be based on domestic investment, and it must also be private, if these nations are to remain substantially capitalist. In the development of any nation, production and income must reach a level which can allow a sufficiently large volume of domestic saving and investment for independent, self-sufficient capital formation. The nation then "takes off" on its own. There is much dispute as to when and how this point is reached, but it must be reached. No nation can continue forever to rely on foreign investment or aid. However, the point where "capital independence" begins can come much earlier in some countries than in others. For example, it may be that Mexico, although on a lower level of per capita income than Venezuela or Argentina, has reached this point.

It is difficult to measure the amount of domestic investment and even more difficult to make valid comparisons between nations. Apart from special studies of economic development in a number of the countries, we must rely on the United Nations' national accounts statistics. From these data it would seem that except for Costa Rica, Mexico, and Venezuela, the total level of saving and investment was too low for rapid economic advancement.

Other studies of investment lead one to conclude that the rates of domestic investment and saving are especially high in Mexico. Since Mexico received little foreign capital in the postwar years, it would seem that it may provide a clue to the stimulation of domestic investment. Mexico has achieved a high rate of economic growth without much foreign capital. The possible causes of the growth of saving in Mexico will be discussed at a later point.[8]

Conclusions

Latin America is still an area that lacks capital for development. Before World War I, it sought and received about $8.5 billion of foreign capital. At the time of World War II, foreign investment was still around $9 billion, but its actual value had shrunk to $6.5 billion because of inflation. After 1945, a large influx of foreign capital began and continued until 1957. Foreign direct investments in Latin America grew to $13 billion, of which American capital was $8.5 billion. Portfolio lending had disappeared, and most of the new capital consisted of direct investment in petroleum and manufacturing. But a great loss of confidence occurred after 1957. The net inflow of capital fell to $715 million a year in 1958, $250 million in 1961, and became minus $100 million in 1962 and minus $200 million in 1963. Although domestic capital formation has been growing in some countries like Mexico, it is not great enough to sustain the rapid rate of growth in production that existed from 1945 to 1957. Without sufficient domestic investment, no foreign portfolio investment, the tendency of direct foreign investment to fall, and the flight of American capital, Latin America desperately needs foreign government loans and grants. Although considerable funds have been obtained from the Export-Import Bank and the new Inter-American Development Bank, the real hope lies in speeding up the Alliance for Progress program, and in restoring the confidence of American direct business investors. It is possible also that some Latin American nations can accelerate domestic saving and actually begin to rise by their bootstraps. This is "doing it the hard way." But in the end, the *hard way* may be the *only way* to achieve real progress. As we have pointed out, capital accumulation must come mainly from domestic saving. Foreign loans and aid can only accelerate the process.

Foreign Trade and Capital Formation

The problems of capital formation in Latin America are closely related to problems of trade, both between Latin America and other parts of the world, and between the Latin American nations themselves. The ability of Latin America to purchase machinery and capital equipment in the past has depended considerably upon foreign trade earnings. Part of the progress made between 1945 and 1957 can be attributed to this source of funds which could be used for industrial investment after World War II. The decline of these earnings was an important causal factor in the Latin American downturn after 1957. A second trade factor concerns inter-American trade. Many of the Latin American nations are too small or poorly endowed with resources to develop industrialism successfully in economic isolation. A common market is essential. Industrial expansion depends on broad markets. If only the internal market can be supplied, expansion may be slow. The foreign trade problem of Latin America is therefore logically the next topic for discussion.

References

1. Cf. United Nations, *Economic Survey of Latin America*, New York, 1957, p. 51.
2. United Nations, *op. cit.*, p. 51.
3. Cf. Committee for Economic Development, *Cooperation for Progress in Latin America*, April 1961, p. 35.
4. United Nations, *Economic Survey of Latin America*, New York, 1958, p. 44. Also N.Y. *Times* and author's estimates (in parentheses).
5. Cf. Chap. 3.
6. Congress subsequently cut the appropriation by 20 percent.
7. Committee for Economic Development, *op. cit.*, pp. 38–40.
8. Only about 2 percent of the employees of American subsidiaries were Americans in 1957, but they held most of the top posts. Cf. Committee for Economic Development, *Cooperation for Progress in Latin America*, p. 43.
9. See Chap. 16.

FOREIGN TRADE PROBLEMS

FOREIGN TRADE IS AN IMPORTANT ELEMENT IN THE ECONOMIC LIFE of Latin America. Failure to solve some of the persistent and critical problems of foreign trade is another important obstacle to the achievement of an effective plan for rapid economic development in Latin American countries. For many years they have exported large quantities of food products and raw materials. In earlier times, these exports were largely exchanged for consumer goods, but, after 1930, capital goods and industrial raw materials became increasingly important. Because of the scarcity of domestic and foreign capital, the capacity to import, based on the volume of exports, is an important source of capital funds. The downturn in the Latin American economy after 1957 was a joint result of declines in the inflow of foreign capital and import capacity. Unless the capacity to import can be increased, Latin America will need to save even more drastically than we indicated in the preceding chapter and foreign aid will have to be greater.

The Latin American Trade Picture

Foreign trade is about a quarter of the gross national product of Latin America. Since a large sector of Latin American economic life functions without money, the gross national product, which was about $60 billion in 1960, does not measure the entire economy.[1] Thus foreign trade may account for as little as one fifth of *all* economic activity. But even this amount is three times the proportion of the economy devoted to foreign trade in the United States. Latin America is much more dependent on trade than we are, and trade fluctuations often make the difference between prosperity and depression. In 1959 exports and imports

138

combined amounted to about $16 billion. Imports were $7,790 million and exports $8,270 million.[2]

The strong emphasis on capital goods and raw materials is illustrated by the fact that in the first half of 1958 only $764 million of consumer goods were imported by Latin American nations, while $420 million of fuel, $1,265 million of raw materials and intermediate goods and $1,568 million of capital goods were imported.[3] Latin America imports textiles, chemicals, drugs, transportation equipment, machinery, iron and steel products, fuel, lubricants, metals, paper, wood, rubber, coal, coke, cotton, electrical equipment, and many other goods which are not in a form for immediate consumption. In the field of consumer's goods, it imports automobiles, airplanes, and various consumer durables. Cotton goods and food products such as wheat and rice are also imported. Some of the countries, such as Bolivia and Mexico, are not self-sufficient in food.

The Caribbean, Central American, and northern South American countries have had trade relations primarily with the United States. The other South American countries before World War II exported more to the United Kingdom than to the United States. These Latin American nations also have had a considerable amount of trade with Germany, France, and Japan. By 1959, however, the United States was the leader in Latin American trade, in both South and Central America. Latin America exported 45 percent of its goods to the United States, 37 percent to Western Europe and the United Kingdom, 3 percent to Japan, 8 percent to other Latin American countries, 1.8 percent to the Soviet bloc and 5.2 percent to other parts of the world. It imported 46.3 percent from the United States, 33 percent from Western Europe and the United Kingdom, 3 percent from Japan, 9.1 percent from other Latin American nations, 2 percent from the Soviet bloc and 7 percent from other nations.[4] Over the years, the trend in Latin America has been both to export and import a larger percentage of the total to and from the United States. Trade relations with the United Kingdom and Germany have declined proportionately.

Although inter-American trade has grown and is the major trade relationship of Latin Amercia, *inter-Latin American* trade is not large. It has amounted to about 10 percent of the total. Moreover, during the boom of the fifties when Latin American production was advancing, inter-Latin American trade declined. In 1956 a Latin American trade commission was appointed by

Latin American Trade With the United States (1959)
(thousands of dollars)

Country	Exports To U.S.	Percentage of Total L.A. Exports	Imports From U.S.	Percentage of Total L.A. Imports
Argentina	124,489	12	229,802	23
Bolivia	6,905	11	23,313	36
Brazil	611,172	47	401,388	29
Chile	156,133	31	136,432	32
Colombia	339,794	72	204,161	52
Costa Rica	32,709	41	40,762	39
Cuba	467,219	74	434,747	71
Dominican Republic	75,151	58	59,482	50
Ecuador	60,181	43	48,503	52
El Salvador	37,377	32	36,843	37
Guatemala	64,906	55	64,084	49
Haiti	16,075	57	23,410	76
Honduras	24,588	36	32,335	51
Mexico	428,649	57	726,434	72
Nicaragua	15,396	23	27,585	42
Panama	24,938	74	90,066	93
Paraguay	8,457	26	7,814	31
Peru	105,340	33	121,590	42
Uruguay	19,006	19	33,338	20
Venezuela	881,066	37	734,735	52

Source: United Nations, *Yearbook of International Trade Statistics* and *Department of Commerce.*

ECLA to study the situation. Ultimately, the common markets were established which will be discussed later. The decline in inter-Latin American trade is revealed by the following data:

	PERCENT OF WORLD TRADE			
	1953	1954	1955	1956
From Latin America	9.5	9.1	9.5	7.8
To Latin America	12.0	10.5	11.0	9.0

Source: W. S. Woytinsky, *The United States and Latin America's Economy, The New Leader,* Nov. 24, 1958, p. 28.

The Decline in Total Latin American Trade After 1957

The decline in Latin America's capacity to import had become acute by 1958. It created serious balance-of-payment problems, and was one of the major factors causing a slowdown in the growth of production to 2 percent a year. Latin America had enjoyed certain advantages in trade during and after World War II. The United States was anxious to buy from Latin Americans to prevent them from selling to the Nazis. We had greater need for minerals and oil. African, Indian, and Philippine supplies of coffee and sugar were cut off. Coffee supplies dropped in Brazil because of lack of replanting and a year of bad weather. Moreover, during World War II, because of the inability to import many commodities, Latin American nations had built up great foreign exchange reserves which greatly increased their capacity to import after the war.

Latin American exports reached a peak in 1957 of $8.6 billion. In 1958 they fell to $8.2 billion and in 1959 they recovered slightly, but were almost $400 million less than they had been in 1957. Exports to the United States declined from $3.5 billion in 1959 to $2.5 billion in 1961. In some countries the export decline began before 1957. This was true in Argentina, Bolivia, Brazil, Chile, Colombia, Guatemala, Haiti, and Uruguay. For some nations the decline from the high point in the 1950s amounted to more than 25 percent. Examples of extreme decline are Argentina, Bolivia, Brazil, Haiti, and Uruguay. Although some improvements in trade have occurred since 1960, the situation is still critical. Export trade continued to decline in 1963 in Argentina, Bolivia, Guatemala, Haiti, Panama, Paraguay, and Peru.

In world markets, prices for basic commodities like coffee, sugar, meat, and petroleum fell. The falling value of exports reduced the trade balance of many Latin American nations. Some of the countries, such as Argentina, Bolivia, Brazil, Cuba, Guatemala, and Uruguay had even developed unfavorable balances by 1958.

The price problems faced after 1957 and lasting into 1962 were due to (1) overproduction and the accumulation of surpluses of basic commodities, (2) the failure of the world market demand for sugar, coffee and other exports to rise at a rapid rate. (3) the declining terms of trade under which Latin American products were sold, and (4) certain special difficulties affecting some of the countries and their products. The principal products affected were coffee, sugar and petroleum. These three commodities account for over 50 percent of the value of all Latin American exports. Petroleum trade alone is 26 percent of the exports. Serious overproduction had begun even before the Suez crisis.

Problems Of The Balance Of Payments

A nation's trade balance is the difference between its exports and imports. It can balance its total international payments, however, by other items which become credits or income payable. These are insurance, shipping, banking and tourist services; income from investments; foreign private direct investments; grants or loans by foreign governments; exports of gold; reductions in credits or cash balances held by its citizens in other countries; and reductions in international fund balances. Most of these items are not of much assistance to Latin Americans. They must balance their trade either by more exports or by private foreign investments or government grants or loans. When they faced a 2 percent decline in their trade balances in 1959, Latin Americans could not rely on private loans and direct investments. These sources of capital and payment balances had sharply declined. Consequently, Latin Americans sought grants under the Alliance for Progress program and resorted to other measures to gain a balance in their total international payments. With their sources of foreign capital dwindling, with their capacity to import reduced, and with funds from grants and loans from the United States largely needed to balance payments, they could not rely on foreign trade for the extra capital needed to continue the high rate of economic development prevailing before 1957. Although by 1961 international payments had been balanced through various expedients, the problem is of a long-run nature. It is not likely, despite the sharp rises in 1963, that the prices of petroleum, coffee, sugar, cacao, bananas, the non-ferrous metals, wool, cotton, and meat will rise enough or the volume of sales increase at a rapid enough rate to supply the amount of capital goods imports needed for rapid industrial expansion. Grants-in-aid from the United States are the solution at this stage in Latin American economic history.

Some light may be thrown on these difficulties by outlining the ways in which some of the Latin American nations met their payment balances in 1958 and 1959. Latin America began to have a negative balance of payments in 1957. This means that the value of exports, services, income from investments, direct investments, loans and grants did not add up to an amount equal to the value of imports, amounts owed on foreign debts, and other withdrawals. There was consequently a balance-of-payments deficit. It amounted to $115 million. In 1958, however, the payments deficit reached the large figure of $1,107 million or about 8 percent of the total foreign trade. In 1959, the situation was less critical. The payment deficit had been reduced to $509 million.[5] But in 1960 it rose again. In 1961 a trade-balance surplus of about $100 million was achieved, but only because of the large surplus balance of Venezuela. The rest of Latin America had a trade deficit of $1,110 million.

The reduction in the payment deficit in 1959 was achieved through the development of a trade surplus of $228 million. Subsequently the reduction in the payment deficit in 1961 was due to this cause, since another trade surplus of $100 million was achieved in that year. A trade surplus can be created either by a rise in the value of exports or by a decline in imports. Except for a few countries, one of which was Brazil, Latin Americans could not offset the falling prices of their exports by an increased volume of sales or by new exports. Also, loans and aid were not forthcoming in 1958 and 1959. The only way out was to restrict imports. Some countries have adopted strong restrictive measures since 1958. Balance was thus achieved, first by drawing heavily on international fund balances in 1958,[6] and second by restricting imports through exchange controls in 1959 and subsequent years. In 1961 only $250 million had been disbursed through the Alliance for Progress program. American private investments in terms of capital inflow were only $400 million, and the actual disbursements of the government lending agencies were less than $200 million. There was a large flight of capital from Latin America which partly offset inflows. To achieve balance, imports had to be restricted. Imports from the United States alone fell from $4.7 billion in 1957 to $3.5 billion in 1961.

Latin American Trade Recovery Efforts

The decline in trade in 1958 and 1959 gave rise to a number of policies intended to correct the situation or solve the problems created by it. One of these was an attempt to find new markets for coffee and other products in Europe and behind the Iron Curtain. Another was a change in Latin American foreign exchange policy. In general, this consisted of a drastic rationing of foreign exchange available to importers, and a shift from multiple fixed to uniform fluctuating exchange rates. Selective restriction of certain types of imports was accomplished in a majority of the countries through foreign exchange deposit permits and licenses rather than through different exchange rates. But to fully grasp the nature of the change, one must be familiar with the development of the foreign exchange systems which preceded the changes in 1958. It would get us too far afield to discuss it here.

The chronic scarcity of many capital and consumer goods in Latin America and the inability to build enough import capacity to meet all these needs through the expansion of exports have caused an excess in the demand for dollars, pounds, francs, and other foreign currencies. Just as Latin America is land poor and capital poor, it is also exchange poor. Only rigid exchange control prevented the collapse of its currencies through an excess of imports over exports too great to be covered by foreign loans and grants or the expansion of Latin American services. Imports have been classified according to essentiality, usually in this order: (1) service on the foreign debt, (2) capital goods, (3) raw materials, (4) essential consumer goods, (5) unessential consumer goods and luxuries, (6) the withdrawal of profits by foreigners, and (7) the transfer of wealth abroad by nationals. Permits are granted or multiple exchange rates charged to give preference to the more important items.

The Declining Terms of Trade and Price Support

Another way out of the trade dilemma in Latin America is to find some means of reversing the unfavorable terms of trade through price supports. Latin American economists have been concerned for years over the deteriorating terms of trade under which Latin American exports are sold. The prices of the goods imported by Latin America have fallen since 1957, but the prices of Latin American exports have fallen at a much more rapid rate. In times past the prices of imports have even risen while

the prices of Latin American exports fell. As an example of
the deterioration in the years 1956–58, the money value of exports increased 26 percent but the purchasing power of the
exports increased less than 20 percent. Thus about a fifth of the
result of the increased trade was nullified by the declining purchasing power of the exports.[7] A direct comparison of the relative fall in import and export prices for more recent years states
the case more dramatically. Between 1957 and 1961 the index
of import prices paid by Latin America based on 1953 prices as
100 fell from 104 to 98. The export prices received by Latin
America, however, fell from 95 to 83.

Dr. Raoul Prebisch, as we have pointed out earlier, is one of
those who stresses the declining terms of trade and the serious
disadvantage resulting from it for the Latin American nations.
He has calculated that the tendency of raw material and food
prices to fall more than the prices of manufactured goods resulted in the 1930s in the same manufactured goods costing 58.6
percent more primary products in exchange than in the 1860s.[8]
He has maintained that there exists a long-term trend toward
worsening terms of trade for agricultural and primary products.
His belief seemed to be refuted by an improvement in the terms
of trade in the 1940s, but by the 1950s the downward trend had
begun again. Just as agricultural prices fail to keep up with industrial prices within a country, the export prices of agricultural
nations deteriorate in purchasing power in terms of industrial
goods imports.

The effect of this disadvantage is to cause a demand for price
supports on the part of farmers within a nation or of farmers
in primarily agricultural nations. Latin Americans have taken
a position about the role of the United States in this respect
whch, although logical, is extremely difficult for us to accept. The
Latin American knows that he sells a major part of his coffee,
sugar, and other basic commodities to the United States. In this
respect, he feels that he is in the same economic position as
American farmers who grow wheat, corn, cotton, and other farm
products sold in the United States. The American government
supports the prices of these commodities. Why should it not also
support the prices of the agricultural and primary products
grown or produced in Latin America and sold in the United
States? If we are willing to support the price of wheat, why not
the price of coffee? An example of this attitude was the in-

sistence of the delegates at a conference held by the Inter-American Development Bank in Buenos Aires in April, 1962 that the funds of the Alliance for Progress be used to support and raise the prices of Latin American exports. The finance minister of Colombia, Jorge Mejia Palacio, made a fiery speech threatening that if this were not done, the Alliance for Progress would fail.

Americans, of course, believe that it is enough to subsidize their own farmers. There is also much sentiment in the United States against farm subsidies of any sort on the ground that they keep in operation marginal farms which should be allowed to go out of business. At any rate, extension of our subsidy system to farmers of other nations is unthinkable. We would rather aid them in a more general way. And yet our unwillingness to accept any obligation to support the prices of Latin American exports is an important cause of Latin American anti-Yankeeism.

Monoculture and Duoculture

In addition to declining terms of trade the export and foreign exchange problems of Latin America are due to lack of diversification in foreign trade. Most of the countries have "put their eggs all in one basket," or, at the most, in two. When the price of their one main export drops, their over-all trade receipts are seriously diminished. If they were exporting several commodities in large quantites, a fall in the price of one would have less effect on the total receipts, and it might be offset by a rise in the prices of other exports. The extent of the dependence on one or two exports is revealed in the accompanying table.

In recent years, some countries—notably Mexico, Brazil, Chile, Colombia, Peru, and Venezuela—have attempted to diversify their agriculture to reduce the emphasis on mono- and duoculture. Cotton, rice, cacao, and fish meal have been promoted, but the diversification has also taken the form of greater food production for home consumption. In an indirect way, home production of food will assist the foreign trade problem by reducing the importation of food products. Assuming that the production of exports does not diminish as home food production increases, a greater import capacity for capital goods will result from these policies.

Percent of Export Earnings From One or Two Commodities In Latin America (1959)

Country	Percent from One Commodity	Percent from Two Commodities
Argentina	26 (meat)	39 (meat, wheat)
Bolivia	62 (tin)	71 (tin, lead)
Brazil	58 (coffee)	64 (coffee, cacao)
Chile	66 (copper)	76 (copper, nitrates)
Colombia	77 (coffee)	92 (coffee, petroleum)
Costa Rica	51 (coffee)	86 (coffee, bananas)
Cuba	77 (sugar)	83 (sugar, tobacco)
Dominican Republic	48 (sugar)	65 (sugar, cacao)
Ecuador	57 (bananas)	75 (bananas, coffee)
El Salvador	72 (coffee)	88 (coffee, cotton)
Guatemala	72 (coffee)	85 (coffee, bananas)
Haiti	63 (coffee)	80 (coffee, sisal)
Honduras	51 (bananas)	70 (bananas, coffee)
Mexico	25 (cotton)	36 (cotton, coffee)
Nicaragua	39 (coffee)	73 (coffee, cotton)
Panama	69 (bananas)	72 (bananas, cacao)
Paraguay	24 (timber)	46 (timber, meat)
Peru	23 (cotton)	38 (cotton, sugar)
Uruguay	54 (wool)	68 (wool, meat)
Venezuela	92 (petroleum)	—

Source: Benton, William, *Voice of Latin America*, 1961, p. 35.

The Latin American Common Markets

In general, the great dependence on one or two export products and the other trade problems of Latin Americans are a reflection of their limited industrialization, and their failure to trade among themselves, exporting and importing a variety of products. There is a great need for common markets.

While the export problems of Latin America were growing, news came of the establishment of the European common market. The first reaction was to propose a Latin American common market as a means of protection. Presumably, the European market would exclude Latin American coffee in favor of African coffee. Deals might be made with European and Asian exporters of other Latin American products such as sugar and cotton. But these fears were not warranted, and the interest in a Latin American common market shifted to its possible effects on economic development. Instead of fearing damage to the coffee market, they feared damage to infant industries that would lose protection if one were adopted.

As a result of the various uncertainties, the Economic Commission for Latin America made an exhaustive study of the possible effects of a common market. The resulting report is one of the most significant documents on Latin American economic problems to appear in recent years, and was prepared under the supervision of Dr. Prebisch.[9] It went far beyond an analysis of the common market, and set up goals for Latin American economic development with trends projected to 1975. A thorough description of this report cannot be given here, but its major conclusions can be stated:

1. The Latin American boom and growth of national production at rates of 5 to 6 percent a year and of 2.7 percent per capita could not be sustained. They were based on the large exchange reserves and favorable terms of trade prevailing after World War II.

2. The collapse of the boom was inevitable because of the fall in the prices of the primary products exported and the declining terms of trade.

3. To continue the high rate of growth, machinery and equipment imports would have to grow at a higher rate than could be financed by the falling export earnings. Latin American nations would not have a sufficient import capacity for rapid growth.

4. As a result, "import substitutes" would be needed. By this was meant that the production of machinery and equipment *within* Latin America would have to increase from a mere $240 million in 1958 to $6.5 billion by 1975.

5. Apart from foreign capital and aid, this great growth would require the stimulation of a wider market than could be provided within the boundaries of the separate Latin American nations. Large steel and machinery industries could not grow, with the resulting higher specialization that makes for efficiency, unless a large market were provided. Hence the crucial need for a common market *to promote rapid economic development*.

6. The fear that a common market would expose the existing industries to too much competition and destroy Latin American development was unfounded provided free trade was allowed only for the steel, machinery, automobile, and "more complex" industries which had hardly begun to develop by 1958. As the report puts it, "the more complex industries in question have not yet been established, or are still in the early stages of development, and it is in their case

that the reduction or abolition of customs duties implied by the common market can be effected with relative ease."[10]

The recommendations of the report, however, were not followed in the actual development of extensive common markets. The subsequent agreements were, in fact, largely gestures in favor of the common market principle rather than vigorous free-trade agreements although they may become much more effective in the future. The two "common markets" were established in 1960 by the Treaty of Montevideo, and the Treaty of Managua. The Treaty of Montevideo includes Argentina, Brazil, Chile, Colombia, Ecuador, Mexico, Paraguay, Peru, and Uruguay—or about 70 percent of the population of Latin America. It provides for the removal of all tariffs between the nine participating nations within twelve years in four stages of reduction. No tariffs were reduced in the first stage for agricultural products. Ths means that virtually no tariffs of consequence have been reduced since the trade between the nations is largely agricultural. As trade in manufactured products grows, the treaty may have some significance, but there are three stages yet to be introduced. Will the steps leading to free trade actually be taken? Moreover, can trade develop to any large extent between the nations, in view of the great lack of marketing and transportation facilities? Transportation has been adapted to trade outside Latin America. It would seem that the development of inter-Latin American transportation is as important, if not more important for interregional trade than the reduction of tariffs.

It is possible, however, to become too pessimistic about the future of the Latin American common markets. It is possible also to misunderstand the significance of the effort which has recently been made to establish them. By 1964, the Montevideo treaty organization, known as the Latin American Free Trade Association (LAFTA), had been in existence for over three years, and had at least served as an effective forum for the exploration of economic problems by Latin American businessmen and government officials. It had succeeded in lowering some trade barriers and trade between its member nations had grown 37 percent during the first two years of its operation.[11] Total intra-Latin American trade, however, still remained less than 10 percent of total trade since the increase was from a base of only 8 percent. Intra-Latin American trade was still only of real importance for Paraguay, where it constituted 32 percent of total trade. But Chile had reduced her tariff on Argentine meat to 30 percent. Argentine razor blades entered Brazil with only an 8 percent tariff and Mexico, the chief beneficiary from the agreements, had increased her exports of manufactured goods to Latin America by 150 percent.[12] In addition, the new Inter-American Development Bank had made arrangements to underwrite loans of the banks of the member nations granted for intra-American trade.

Hopeful also was the rapid organization of The Central American Common Market (CACM). The visit of President Kennedy in April, 1963, and his talks with the six central American presidents stimulated action in this area. An elaborate organization was set up including a Central American Economic Council, an Executive Council, a Permanent Secretariat, a Central American Bank for Economic Integration and a Central American Clearing House. But Panama refused to enter the agreement, and Costa Rica continued to delay her entry. All tariff barriers were to be removed by 1965, and by 1963 interregional trade had grown 300 percent above the level of 1957. Most of this growth, however, cannot be attributed to the Common Market but to the growing trade between Panama and Costa Rica.

The real significance of these common markets thus far lies in the economic planning and cooperation they represent, and in the growing awareness of Latin Americans of the need for a common solution of common economic problems. To be sure, a great deal of insularity and nationalism still persists which might in the end frustrate any serious efforts to arrive at a common plan for Latin America. But the basis for the planning exists and reveals vitality. Moreover, it is planning for Latin America by *Latin Americans*. It is one of the most hopeful signs that Latin Americans will attempt seriously to solve their own problems, in part at least, *by their own efforts*. This indigenous planning is a far more significant sign of this than the few tax reforms or anti-inflation efforts that Latin American nations have made since the beginning of the Alliance for Progress. It also represents a regional approach which is far sounder than the unfortunate bilateralism which the United States introduced under the administration of our end of the Alliance by Martin and Moscoso.

Conclusions

The Latin American nations, we can conclude, had flourishing exports and a high capacity to import until 1957. This favorable situation was due to high prices and high demand for their exports of coffee, sugar, bananas, cotton, and minerals. It was also due to their ability to draw on large foreign exchange reserves built up during World War II when the demand for their products was high and their ability to import was restricted for war reasons. The great capacity to import (1) enabled them to obtain the raw materials and capital needed for industrial expansion, and (2) to raise the standard of living through greater imports of consumer goods. But the great period of growth between 1945 and 1957 came to an end partly because of the declining prices and demand for their exports and the worsening terms of trade. The great foreign exchange reserves also were gradually used up. Inability to revive import capacity is another great obstacle to the development of an effective plan for Latin American economic progress.

But economists who fix their attention on trade factors are likely to underemphasize and even overlook the fact that during the great boom between 1945 and 1957, Latin American nations were receiving a great inflow of foreign capital mainly in the form of direct investments and government loans. In addition to great import capacity, foreign capital was also an important cause of the boom. In some countries, moreover, there was a great increase in saving and domestic investment. After 1957, not only did import capacity decline, but foreign and domestic capital declined also. Import capacity was by no means the only source of investment capital during the boom, and its decline is not the only serious obstacle to further economic development and needed planning for it.

As a means of obtaining capital, import capacity does not have a bright future. Prices of Latin American exports have risen again, and new markets have been found for coffee, sugar, bananas and minerals, especially in the centrally planned economies. Sugar prices in 1963 reached an all-time high as a result of the rising demand for sugar in the Western nations. But the conclusion of Dr. Prebisch that Latin America may have to trade increasingly with itself through common markets seems well founded. The alternative is the development of totally new products for export and, at present, this seems unlikely.

Latin America's economic crisis, therefore, cannot be met solely by reviving foreign trade. The solution for Latin America's economic problems is industrialization. Because foreign trade is still important and has been so important in the past, it may serve as a mirage. Overemphasis on it is yet another obstacle to planning in Latin America. There must be less dependence on foreign trade and more industrial independence. This was the lesson of the economic policy revolution which began in Uruguay and was pursued in Mexico. The lesson was not entirely learned. Instead of making basic structural economic changes between 1945 and 1957, Latin America was contented with the marked improvement resulting from a temporary boom in export earnings and the use of past export earnings held in reserve.

References

1. In 1950 dollars. It was $80 billion in current dollars.
2. United Nations, *Statistical Yearbook,* New York, 1960.
3. United Nations, *Economic Survey of Latin America,* New York, 1958.
4. United Nations, *Monthly Bulletin of Statistics,* June, 1960.
5. United Nations, *Economic Bulletin for Latin America,* October 1960, vol. V, no. 2, p. 23.
6. Fund balances or gold and foreign exchange reserves were reduced by $737.5 million in 1958. Some countries also had to resort to compensatory loans from the International Monetary Fund and Eximbank.
7. United Nations, *Economic Survey of Latin America,* New York, 1958, p. 49.
8. United Nations, Economic Commission for Asia and the Far East, *The Economic Development of Latin America and Some of Its Problems,* New York, 1949, pp. 1–3.
9. United Nations, Economic Commission for Latin America, *The Latin American Common Market,* 1959. Dr. Prebisch is sometimes referred to as the Jean Monnet of Latin America, or the father of the common market.
10. ECLA, *op. cit.,* p. 6.
11. Chase-Manhattan Bank, *Latin American Business Highlights,* vol. 13, no. 2, p. 5.
12. *Ibid.,* pp. 5–7.

INFLATION AND PUBLIC FINANCE

UNCONTROLLED INFLATION IS A PERSISTENT PROBLEM IN LATIN America. It has seriously disrupted business activity, halted the inflow of foreign capital, discouraged thrift and domestic investment, and subjected thousands of people to injury from price and income inequities. Along with inadequate resources, excessive population growth, lack of domestic and foreign capital and the decline of import capacity, it is another great obstacle to the development of an effective economic plan for Latin America.

The monetary problems of Latin America began when the nations achieved their independence in 1824. The royalist Spaniards, the *gachupines,* departed, taking with them all the fluid capital consisting of gold and silver. Lacking monetary reserves, Mexico and other nations experimented with fiat paper currency in their early history. The results were disastrous, even when currency was issued by banks with fractional reserves.[1] After a long period of attempts to operate on fiat paper money, beginning with Mexico in 1900, Latin American nations adopted the gold standard. None of the nations was able to establish completely free gold standards. But the period 1900–29, when gold standards operated in some form, was one of relatively stable prices and exchange rates.

The Evil Effects of Inflation

From time to time Latin Americans have thought that inflation produces prosperity and economic growth. There is no question that a moderate degree of inflation may have stimulating effects. For a while prices rise faster than wages and other costs, causing higher profit margins. Goods are stockpiled because higher prices are anticipated. This leads to a boom in orders. Buying in general becomes active because prices are expected to go higher. But wages and other costs eventually catch up with the rise in prices, and may cause prices to spiral in their upward movement. If inflation becomes extreme, it disrupts production. Why? There are many reasons.

1. There is little money offered for investment, or business loans. The value of the money paid back may be far less in purchasing power than the value of the original loans.
2. Interest rates for these reasons become exorbitant.
3. Money-making shifts to speculation in land and in other physical goods such as consumer durables, and turns away from productive processes.
4. Saving declines, or becomes nonexistent because one loses purchasing power by accumulating assets in the form of money.
5. Foreign exchange earnings from exports are held abroad in the expectation that their value will be much higher later in domestic currency.
6. There is a flight of domestic capital abroad. With the inevitable depreciation of the currency, the capital can be repatriated later at a much higher value in domestic currency.
7. Uncertainty pervades the entire economy, with the result that those with money assets convert them into a physical form and "sit tight."

In addition to these economic evils which have to do mainly with production, investment, and saving, there are moral evils as well. In any extreme inflation, prices, wages, and incomes do not all go up simultaneously and in the same degree. Those with fixed incomes, or savings which cannot readily be converted into physical goods, suffer grave injustice. In terms of purchasing power, their savings and incomes may be virtually wiped out. Pensions and social security payments become meaningless. Thousands become unemployed because of cuts in production. A general economic and social demoralization sets in. Argentina, Brazil, Uruguay, Paraguay, Bolivia, and Chile have experienced all these evil social effects since World War II. They have affected Colombia and Mexico also, but to a lesser degree.

One conclusion can be stated emphatically: the higher the rate of inflation, the lower the rate of economic growth. The Chase-Manhattan Bank made a careful study of this question based on data of the International Monetary Fund for the period 1950–58.[2] With average annual price increases of 20 to 70 percent, Bolivia and Paraguay grew at less than 2 percent of gross national product per year, and Argentina at less than 3 percent. With annual rates of inflation of 4 to 10 percent, Colombia, Mexico, and Peru grew at rates of 4 to 6 percent. With inflation rates of 1 to 2 percent a year, Costa Rica, the Dominican Republic and Venezuela grew at rates of 6 to 9 percent. Chile and Brazil seem exceptions to the rule. With a 20 percent inflation rate, Brazil had a 3½ percent growth rate, and Chile, with a 40 percent inflation rate, grew at a rate of 4 percent. A later study of the Chase-Manhattan Bank for the period 1950–60 confirms these conclusions and shows Chile with a growth rate for this period of only 2.3 percent.[3]

Another inflation evil is the unwise price, wage and exchange controls it causes. Although such controls may be reasonably fair and effective if they are planned intelligently and put into effect slowly, this is only possible when inflation is occurring at 10 percent or less a year. When inflation gets to the level of 20, 40, or 80 percent a year, extreme inequities and restrictive effects occur. An example is the control of beef exports in Argentina in the 1940s and 1950s. The costs of producing beef rose rapidly due to the inflation, but the export prices were kept low through exchange control. The margin of profit was squeezed between rising costs and a stable foreign price to the point where it did not pay Argentine growers even to renew their herds. The exports of beef fell off sharply and the foreign exchange position of Argentina was seriously deteriorated. If Argentine pesos had been allowed to depreciate, foreigners could still have bought Argentine beef at low prices in terms of their own currency. They would have been able to get more pesos for the pound, dollar or franc. At the same time, Argentine growers could have received enough more pesos to make beef growing profitable.

The Causes of the Inflation

But what has caused the great inflation in Bolivia, Paraguay, Chile, Argentina, and Brazil, and the less extreme inflation in Mexico, Peru, Colombia? Among the reasons for the inflation are (1) a decline in the value of exports; (2) inadequate tax systems, (3) unwillingness to exercise central banking controls which restrict inflation, (4) deficit financing, (5) deficits of government enterprises, (6) politically inspired spending, (7) overambitious social security programs, and (8) the desire to eliminate debts.

A decline in the value of exports leads to inflation for at least two reasons. The decline usually must be offset by a decline in imports, if the balance of payments is to be maintained. A decline in imports means a decline in tariff revenues. It may be substantial enough to cause a large budget deficit and the deficit usually leads to further inflation. Latin American governments finance deficits through the sale of bonds to the central banks, and the banks are seldom able to sell the bonds to the public, thus absorbing the deficit through saving. Instead, additional amounts of money are issued based on the government bonds, and additional money means higher prices.

As we have already stated, export or foreign exchange earnings are sources of capital for domestic investment. If this supply of capital is reduced, unemployment may grow. Pressure on the government develops to provide public works as substitutes for private investment employment derived from foreign exchange earnings.[4] An ambitious public works program could be financed through raising taxes. But this is unpopular if the higher taxes are imposed on the masses. Also it is usually impossible to impose them on the wealthy privileged groups if they control the government. The only acceptable solution is borrowing, which increases deficits and results in inflation. Latin American economic history is replete with examples of large deficits caused by public works programs undertaken for the promotion of prosperity.

Inflation in Latin America is partly due to the backwardness of the tax systems. Many countries have not learned that the increasing economic role of government requires a progressively higher tax yield. Both the absolute amount of the taxes collected and the percentage of personal income taxed must increase. A greater level of government activity can be financed temporarily through deficits in wealthy countries, or countries where there is underproduction and unused economic capacity. But poor countries cannot indulge in deficit financing without disastrous inflation. The temptation is naturally greater than in the case of rich countries, but the results are much worse. In Latin America, Bolivia and Argentina may be contrasted. Both resorted to deficit financing, but inflation and the general economic consequences were worse in Bolivia than Argentina.

Until recent years the central banks in Latin America have not made much effort to curb inflation. This is not surprising, since the banks are government bodies, and government policies have been inflationary. Because the banks made little effort to arrest inflation through high interest rates and restrictions on rediscounting, inflation due to public borrowing was further enhanced by unrestricted private borrowing. Some of the inflation also may be attributed to the Keynesianism in Latin America. Latin America economists are not orthodox. They believe in multiplying-income effects of public works, and are not overly concerned about deficit spending. But Keynesianism, instead of promoting production, has caused inflation because it is applied in countries which are essentially scarcity economies.

Argentina under Perón's regime provides a good example of two other causes of inflation, the deficits of government enterprises, and overambitious social security programs. The Argentine railways were heavily featherbedded with unnecessary employees. Their costs became much greater after nationalization than they had been when operated by the British. But the fares were kept low. As a consequence, in some years a third of the government deficit was due to the railway deficit. In addition, the social security program of Argentina has been greater than the nation could afford.

Finally, it is commonly believed that some of the groups influencing the Latin American governments have favored inflation as a means of reducing their debts. Where large debts have been incurred, it is desirable to have prices double or triple. Higher money incomes are received by those who are in debt, making it easier to make repayments, since the debts are in fixed amounts which do not change with inflation. Some of the inflation in Chile, for example, has been attributed to the control of the government by debtors. Inflation is sometimes wanted also to pay public as well as private debts.

The Degree of Inflation

The degree of inflation in Latin America ranges from virtual price stability to the runaway variety. The worst inflation took place in Argentina, Bolivia, Brazil, and Chile. Between 1850 and 1950, prices in these countries rose over twenty times above the

1850 level. In addition to these four countries, two others, Paraguay and Uruguay, had extreme inflation.

A general picture of the changes in prices which occurred after World War II can be obtained from the consumer price

UNITED NATIONS: WHOLESALE PRICES (1953 = 100)

Country	1948	1951	1952	1953	1954	1955	1956	1957	1958	1959
Brazil	53	79	87	100	130	147	176	197	221	305
Chile	37	66	81	100	157	277	454	646	811	1053
Colombia	73	96	95	100	107	108	117	145	170	187
Costa Rica	101	116	105	100	104	107	108	108	108	107
Cuba	–	–	–	100	97	96	97	100	100	–
Dominican Republic	106	98	100	100	94	95	94	103	103	97
Ecuador	–	–	97	100	99	98	97	99	100	99
Guatemala	89	101	100	100	105	101	101	100	101	102
Mexico	66	98	102	100	109	124	130	136	142	143
Paraguay	–	28	61	100	122	144	193	233	252	297
Peru	46	90	97	100	112	121	138	141	147	181
Venezuela	102	102	103	100	103	103	100*	100	102	104

Source: United Nations, *Statistical Yearbook*, New York, 1960, pp. 445–450.

* Venezuela begins 1956 base here.

CONSUMER PRICE INDEXES (1953 = 100)

Country	1948	1951	1952	1953	1954	1955	1956	1957	1958	1959
Argentina	31	69	96	100	104	117	132	165	217	464
Bolivia	23	40	50	100	224	404	1126	2428	2498	3005
Brazil	59	67	82	100	118	142	173	206	237	326
Chile	39	65	80	100	172	302	471	627	752	1043
Colombia	68	95	93	100	109	109	116	133	153	164
Costa Rica	80	102	100	100	103	106	107	110	113	113
Dominican Republic	97	100	101	100	98	98	99	104	102	102
Ecuador	—	97	100	100	103	105	100	101	102	102
El Salvador	67	95	94	100	100*	105	107	102	108	107
Guatemala	83	99	97	100	103	105	106	104	106	105
Haiti	99	—	108	100	104	106	113	112	112	107
Honduras	83	100	98	100	112	117	107	102	104	104
Mexico	71	89	102	100	105	122	128	135	150	154
Nicaragua	65	88	89	100	108	—	100*	94	101	96
Panama	—	—	101	100	99	99	99	99	99	99
Paraguay	8	26	59	100	120	148	180	209	222	240
Peru	60	86	92	100	105	110	116	125	135	152
Uruguay	71	82	94	100	112	122	130	149	175	244
Venezuela	85	100	101	100	100	100	101	98	103	108

Source: International Labor Office, quoted from UN, *Statistical Yearbook*, 1960, pp.451–456.

* In the cases of El Salvador and Nicaragua the bases of the indexes change to 1954 and 1956 respectively.

indexes of the International Labor Office and the United Nations indexes of wholesale prices. The Latin American nations are divided about equally between those with little inflation (some even less than in the United States such as Ecuador, Panama, and Guatemala) and those with extreme inflation, Argentina, Chile, Brazil, and Bolivia.

In Argentina, Bolivia, Brazil, Chile, Colombia, Mexico, Paraguay, Peru, and Uruguay, inflation continued steadily upward at large annual rates of increase with few periods when there was much control or reduction in the rate of increase. Argentina seemed to control its price rise between 1952 and 1955, but prices rose rapidly again between 1956 and 1958, and doubled between 1958 and 1959. Colombia showed restraint between 1951 and 1956, but considerable inflation occurred between 1957 and 1959. Mexico curbed inflation between 1952 and 1955, but prices rose 54 percent between 1953 and 1959. Peru also had a period of price stability in the early 1950s, but resumed rapid inflation in 1956.

Recent Efforts to Curb Inflation

In 1960 and 1961 Latin America seemed to be returning to economic orthodoxy. Various countries attempted to balance their budgets, commercial credit was tightened, rediscounting at the central banks was reduced, and even proposals for tax increases were made. Argentina, Chile, and Bolivia took the lead in the new drive to check inflation. Quadros in Brazil promised austerity, but he did not remain in office long enough to put it into operation. His successors made only feeble efforts to curb the price rise. In 1960 the cost of living rose only 13 percent in Bolivia, 8 percent in Argentina, and 4 percent in Chile.[5] These three countries had had price increases of 20 to 70 percent a year. In addition, Peru balanced its budget in 1959, and by 1960 the annual rate of inflation had been reduced to only 2 percent. In Colombia, inflation fell to less than 7 percent in 1960. Colombia not only balanced its budget but developed a surplus. Mexico also made progress in reducing inflation. In addition, an austerity program was introduced in Ecuador. This country had had a good record on inflation, but was faced with a deficit. The austerity programs of both Argentina and Ecuador played a part

in the overthrow of presidents Frondizi and Ibarra. Some wonder
how long orthodox budget and price policies can be maintained.
They are unpopular not only because austerity is unpopular, but
because many consider the United States responsible. Alliance for
Progress aid commits the recipients to budget and tax reform.
Not only must belts be tightened, but hated Uncle Sam says so,
and makes it a condition of foreign aid.

The Tax Systems of Latin America

Although promising headway was being made in 1960 and
1961 in budget restraint and central bank credit control, Brazil
and some of the other countries began a new inflation in 1962.
Little progress was also made in the direction of tax reform. In
some countries the tax systems are antiquated and inadequate.
They have suited the interests of the ruling groups for years, and
there is little likelihood of immediate and drastic changes. Low
and regressive taxes have favored the wealthy. They are justified
on the same grounds in Latin America as in the United States.
Saving and business enterprise is supposedly promoted. But
unlike the wealthy in the United States, those of Latin America
have not assiduously invested their growing wealth in domestic
enterprise. Much of the wealth has been sent abroad to promote
foreign business, or accumulated for safety in Swiss bank accounts. The argument seems to have some validity in Mexico,
however. Low wages and low taxes there have resulted in greater
domestic investment. Even Mexican inflation has had the same
result. It has forced savings by the poor which have been invested by the profit makers in new enterprises. These investments can ultimately raise the standard of living of all groups.

Whatever else may be said in criticism of Latin American tax
systems, Latin American nations, unlike some American states,
have not neglected the use of certain forms of taxation. Almost
every Latin American government has almost every form of tax
used in the United States, and some not used. The tax difficulties
arise from the relative emphasis placed on different tax sources,
and the rate structures. Unlike the United States also, there is
little periodic re-examination of the tax systems, and changes
are far less frequent. Because of the tendency toward deficit
financing, less attention has been given to the adequacy of rev-

enue. In contrast, there is more concern over the political consequences of tax changes.

In 1961, over-all studies of Latin American tax systems were being made by a tax research project at Harvard University, and by the research staff of the Organization of American States. We shall know much more about the Latin American fiscal systems in a few years. At present, however, the following generalizations can be made:

1. All forms of direct and indirect taxes are in use in most of the countries.
2. Most taxation is administered by the national governments, including land and property taxes.
3. Latin American governments obtain funds from national lotteries, gambling, government monopolies, taxes and royalties on the severance of petroleum and minerals, and revenue stamps for legal and business transactions to a much greater extent than the United States.
4. The tax systems are inadequate in yield in view of the deficits, and the great need for expenditures on education, health, housing and welfare.
5. The tax structure is regressive in most countries. Heavy reliance is placed on customs and excises. In a few nations, taxes may be mildly progressive because of the incidence of consumption taxes rather than because of progressive income tax rates. Income tax rates are low and not very progressive. They are also widely evaded.

From the data of five countries—Chile, Colombia, Costa Rica, Ecuador, and Peru—one gets an idea of the typical Latin Amer-

Forms of Revenue (1959)	Chile	Colombia	Costa Rica	Ecuador	Peru (1958)
			Millions of		
	escudos	pesos	colones	sucres	soles
Income from property and entrepreneurship	17.0	234	19.8	565	103
Indirect taxes	390.0	1,545	272.6	1,410	1,937
Direct taxes on corporations	153.0	435	4.3	195	1,413
Direct taxes on individuals and households	262.5	616	89.4	370	1,115
Other revenues	22.7	16	80.4	127	—
Total Revenues	845.2	2,844.0	466.5	2,667	4,568

Source: Adapted from United Nations, *Yearbook of National Accounts Statistics,* New York, 1960.

ican revenue picture. In three countries—Colombia, Ecuador, and Peru—sizable amounts of revenue were obtained from government property and enterprises. In all the countries, by far the largest source of revenue was indirect taxation. Taxes on corporations were large revenue items in four out of the five nations and in one, Peru, exceeded the receipts from direct taxes on individuals. The latter were an important revenue source in only three out of the five nations.

It is often charged that the tax systems of Latin America discourage foreign investment. On balance, this does not seem to be the case. The tax systems of Latin America generally do not discriminate between foreign and domestic investors. A number of countries have offered liberal tax concessions for the initiation of certain types of business enterprise. These usually consist of the exemption of part or all business income or other taxes on the new enterprises for a specified period. Such concessions were introduced in Argentina, Chile, Costa Rica, Cuba, the Dominican Republic, El Salvador, Guatemala, Mexico, Nicaragua, Panama, and Uruguay. The enterprises most favored have been those which process local raw materials.[6] Foreign investors have benefited from these tax exemptions.

In general, the taxation of business is much lower in Latin America than in the United States, with the exception of severance or production taxes on the extraction of oil or other raw materials. Various types of special tax relief are provided, such as tax reductions on profits used for reinvestment, or exemption from import duties on machinery imported for new enterprises. But these tax advantages are sometimes more apparent than real so far as United States and United Kingdom investors are concerned. They apply mainly to manufacturing, and much of the investment of these countries has been in mining and utilities. Moreover, both our country and the British tax income earned abroad at higher rates than the Latin Americans tax this same income. Tax credits for taxes paid in Latin America are allowed, but since the Latin American taxes are not higher than ours, no tax benefit results.

In the case of mining taxes, which are usually levied on gross product, no compensating tax credits are allowed in the United States and mining by American companies is much more heavily taxed than similar operations would be at home. The recent tendency of Latin American countries to shift to the income basis of taxation has at least one advantage. It makes it more profitable to mine the lower grades of ore, and thus promotes conservation. Where taxes are on a production basis—or, in other words, on quantity of output—it pays to mine only the better grades of ore. If the United States would lower its taxes on foreign income, there would be another advantage. American investors could credit the taxes against American income taxes and thus reduce their tax burden. In view of the need to stimulate American investment in Latin America, the United States should reduce its income taxes on foreign earnings. In 1954 President Eisenhower recommended a reduction of 14 percent. This was a step in the right direction. In 1963 President Kennedy recommended a reduction of 33 percent, but Congress has not accepted either proposal.

Conclusions

Serious inflation has retarded economic growth in Latin America and is one of the main obstacles to effective planning for economic growth. But inflation and public finance are interrelated. Unwise spending for public works and social security programs contributes to inflation by causing large and chronic deficits. Government enterprises used as make-work agencies and run at a loss also cause deficits. Even the normal growth of government causes inflation if it is not financed by taxes. The tax systems of Latin America are too antiquated to yield enough even for normal growth.

Thus tax reform in Latin America seems urgent. It is needed (1) to balance ordinary budgets and prevent inflation, (2) to provide for growth in social expenditure, and (3) to provide greater justice in taxation. The prime need seems to be heavier and more progressive personal income taxes. Certain consumption taxes such as those on liquor and gasoline might be raised also, and heavier taxes should be imposed on the owners of large estates. But we must not agree too readily that these tax reforms are desirable. Other factors are involved, such as the widespread failure of Latin American countries to collect more than a small percentage of the taxes due under the present laws. Perhaps the major tax reform needed in Latin America is fairer and more complete tax collection. But this matter will be discussed more fully in a later chapter.

More serious, however, is the question as to whether higher taxes on the upper incomes may not reduce the already inadequate domestic saving and investment in Latin America. Higher tax yields are desirable, but higher taxes on the wealthy at this stage in Latin American economic history are questionable. They could easily retard much-needed capital accumulation. It is true, of course, that in the long run, unless taxes are made to fall more heavily on the rich, the benefits of economic progress will not go far toward aiding the improverished masses.

Summary of the Obstacles to Economic Planning for Progress in Latin America

At the beginning of this book we attempted to dramatize the crisis in Latin America. It is genuine and acute and arises from a worldwide social revolution of the underprivileged who will no longer be denied a higher standard of living. A great boom occurred in Latin America after World War II under the dictatorships which temporarily gave the people hope. It was fostered by the great import credit balances left over from World War II, and the heavy direct investment in industry by the United States and other countries. The dictatorships followed to a limited degree the program of the economic policy revolution which had developed earlier in Uruguay and Mexico and which was a mixed system consisting of economic nationalism, socialism, and the promotion of domestic private enterprise. But despite some efforts in the right direction and a promising beginning, the boom collapsed after 1957. The exchange balances were exhausted. The rise of communism and especially the revolution in Cuba frightened both domestic and foreign capital. A great flight of capital began.

Unemployment, excessive inflation, and the decline of export earnings brought Latin America to a stage of acute crisis between 1958 and 1960. As a result, the dictatorships were overthrown and new liberal democratic governments undertook to cope with the multitude of problems. But the situation was out of hand. The new middle-class men who had taken over from the dictators from 1957 on were faced with almost insuperable difficulties.

They had inherited the basically sound theory of the economic policy revolution, but needed to implement it fully. They lacked a basic and suitable theory of economic development, and a common economic plan for Latin America based on it. Perhaps these are and still remain the chief obstacles to further economic progress.

But there are other obstacles to planning and progress. They consist of two kinds: (1) those that are common to Latin America as a whole, and (2) those that arise from the recent history of political and economic policy in individual nations. In the preceding six chapters we have discussed the first category of obstacles. They include inadequate and inadequately located resources, a rate of population growth which tends to absorb the results of economic growth and cause a stable or falling per capita income, the low per capita income generally which makes it almost impossible to save enough domestically to promote rapid economic growth, and the failure to promote economic productivity and efficiency in agriculture so that agriculture can support a growing population and release workers to the cities for the rapid expansion of industrialism. In addition, industrialism has not gotten under way on a large scale through the development of the steel, automobile, cement, paper, and chemical industries. Even in countries like Argentina, Brazil, Chile, and Venezuela industrialism is unbalanced and retarded. Also, domestic capital formation is not taking place rapidly except in a few countries. Both the lack of domestic capital accumulation and a large inflow of foreign capital stand as serious obstacles to planning for progress. Even the Alliance for Progress has failed to meet these capital needs because of poor leadership and planning in Washington and lack of cooperation between Latin America and the United States. Moreover, the foreign trade situation is an obstacle due to the decline of export earnings, the declining terms of trade, and the failure to develop effective common markets rapidly. Finally, as though the foregoing were not sufficiently frustrating, there has been severe inflation and a lack of tax reform. Although inflation may have contributed to the economic boom before 1957, it got out of hand and became a very serious obstacle to further progress or reasonable economic planning in about half of the nations.

In the chapters that follow, we will discuss obstacles to planning and progress arising from the recent history of the Latin

American nations. These obstacles are specialized versions of those already discussed, but an analysis of what happened in some of the nations will make the planning needs of Latin America much clearer. Finally, we will attempt to prescribe for the economic and political ills of Latin America, and make predictions concerning its future.

References

1. Cf. W. C. Gordon, *The Economy of Latin America,* Columbia University Press, 1950, New York, p. 217.
2. International Monetary Fund data, cited in Chase-Manhattan Bank, *Latin American Business Highlights,* vol. II, no. 2, 1961, p. 17.
3. Cf. *Latin American Business Highlights,* vol. 13, no. 1, 1963.
4. Cf. Harry Stark, *Latin America,* W. C. Brown, 1961, Dubuque, Iowa, p. 126.
5. Chase-Manhattan Bank, *Latin American Business Highlights,* vol. II, no. 2, p. 14.
6. United Nations, *Foreign Capital in Latin America,* New York, 1955, p. 24.

IV

The Nations
of Latin America

THIRTEEN

ARGENTINA

THE ECONOMIC DEVELOPMENT OF LATIN AMERICA IS OCCURRING under a variety of conditions. The twenty-two countries have special problems determined partly by their resources, climate, and racial composition, and partly by their economic, political, and social history. Some nations are well advanced, such as Argentina, and have a relatively high standard of living. Others, like Bolivia and Haiti, are extremely poor and have a long way to go. Some are highly literate and their general education is good. Others are highly illiterate and educational facilities are meager. There are many possible classifications. The point to emphasize is that an economic program appropriate in one country may be inappropriate in another.

Of great importance also in understanding the problems faced by each country is their recent economic and political history. The way the different countries have attempted to solve their problems, the cultural pattern of each country, and the mistakes they have made may throw more light on their inability to make rapid economic progress than broad economic facts concerning economic organization and resources. In fact, as we pointed out in the preceding chapter, the history of these countries since World War II reveals many obstacles to progress. The second type of obstacle to sound planning for rapid economic development consists of the "wrong turns" made by many of these countries since 1945, their frustrating beliefs and social patterns, their old-guard reactionary social groups, and their insularity and perverted nationalism.

The General Character of Argentina

It is appropriate to begin with Argentina because in some ways it is the most advanced Latin American nation. Some

question whether it should still be considered an underdeveloped nation. Until 1950 it had the highest per capita income
in Latin America. Venezuela then went ahead of it due to the
huge Venezuelan oil earnings. Also, the economic collapse due
to the Perón regime greatly decreased its per capita income. In
1959, according to one income estimate, it was even worse off
than Chile and Costa Rica. In real terms, however, the majority
of the population has had a fairly high income because the
national income is more evenly distributed than in some of the
other countries. As a result, the Argentine worker has had more
meat and cereals in his diet, more cotton goods and shoes, and
better housing.[1] Although a very serious housing problem exists
in Argentina, the slums are not as degraded as those of Rio de
Janeiro, Lima, or Colon.

Moreover, Argentina is well advanced culturally. Literacy is
the highest in Latin America (90.3 percent) and the country is
highly urbanized. More than two-thirds of the population are
living in cities or towns of 2,000 or more. It is probably the most
nationalistic and vain of the Latin American nations. Argentinians consider themselves superior to other nationals and, in
their opinion, they have a "manifest destiny" to lead the "underdeveloped" nations of South America. Buenos Aires, the
second largest city in Latin America, is regarded by Argentinians
as the Paris of the Western Hemisphere. Their German-trained
army is the largest and most formidable military force in South
America. The "Colon" is South America's most famous opera
house, and Mar del Plata, its greatest seaside resort. Nahuel
Huapi is its finest mountain lake.

In addition, Argentina is proud that it has virtually no race
problem. The twenty and a half million people are largely of
European origin, and racial intermixture has created the most
homogeneous population in South America. The Indians were
exterminated under the dictatorship of Rosas in the middle of
the nineteenth century. The Negro population was never very
large, and many of the Negroes died in the revolutionary army of
San Martin. Most of the population has come from immigration
and almost half the immigrants were Italian and a third Spanish.
The remainder in order of importance were Poles, Russians,
French, and Germans. The immigrants built up the population
of the large cities, Buenos Aires, Rosario, Sante Fe, Cordoba,

Mendoza, and Tucaman. They also became *vaqueros,*[2] or settled
on the land as grain farmers.

Although there is no racial conflict in Argentina, social, cultural and economic conflicts have at times been severe. The
portenos, or city dwellers, believed in Europeanizing the nation.
The great landowners, who were often descendants of the most
vigorous *gauchos,* the half-breed cowboys who had fought the
Indians for possession of the *Pampa,* believed in "Americanism."
A rural-urban struggle existed for many years which was finally
resolved by Perón through uniting the rural and urban working
classes. The peons became "workers," identifying themselves
with the workers in the cities. The landlords could no longer rely
upon them for loyalty and political support. But until Perón,
there was a struggle for power between the farm landlords and
the *portenos.* At times, as in the case of Rosas, the landlords won,
and dominated the cities. At other times the urban middle classes
seized power, as in the case of Irigoyen.

The struggle between the "Europeanized" cities and the
"Americanized" *estancias* constituted a serious cultural and technical dualism which retarded the growth of industry. It was not
until World War I, when imported manufactured goods were
scarce, that domestic industry began to grow. The rule of Argentina over long periods by the rural landlords had confined
economic life to export trade in meat, wool, and grain. The only
industry that grew on a large scale was meat packing. Foreign
investment was devoted largely to building an extensive railway
system designed almost entirely to bring agricultural products to
Buenos Aires and Rosario for shipment. Although a sizable
middle class developed in the cities, it was confined to the professions, civil service, trade, and the handicrafts. Argentinians
invested their surplus capital abroad or in urban housing. The
typical middle-class investment still consists of urban real estate
mortgages.

The rural landowners, however, were progressive. Fields
were fenced with barbed wire, new strains of cattle imported,
and the herds improved. Farming was efficiently conducted over
wide areas with the use of machinery. But progressive farming
on what is probably the best soil in the world made agriculture
too profitable to encourage investment in other forms of enterprise. Also, the need to export farm products created the need
to import manufactured products in return, and this precluded

much development of domestic industry. Because of the importance of agriculture, Argentina remained a free-trade country, and at no time prior to the dictatorship of Perón accepted the economic policy revolution of its neighbor, Uruguay. When exchange control and tariffs were introduced, it was largely to cope with trade deficits resulting from a decline in the prices of meat, wool, and wheat.

The Economic Dilemma of Argentina

Two basic changes caused the prosperous agricultural era of Argentina to come to an end. First, during the great depression the demand for Argentine farm exports and their value in terms of trade declined. Also, the free-trade world collapsed, and Argentina was confronted with hostile foreign tariffs. Other countries were producing more of their own meat and grain. The second development was the rise of the economic and political power of the Argentine urban working class. It became self-conscious. It organized, and demanded higher wages. Labor productivity declined. Eventually, it brought Perón to power, and Perón introduced destructive antiagrarian measures.

With the decline of agriculture, Argentina was seriously in need of greater industrialization. Industrialism was urgently wanted by the majority of the population. There was a great unused labor force waiting for employment in the cities. Thousands had migrated there since they could no longer earn a decent living on the land. Argentina was ready for industry because of this large unused literate labor force, but it did not have the resource base for a great industrial development. It lacked coal and iron ore. Such coal as there was had to be brought more than a thousand miles to Buenos Aires, Rosario, Cordoba, and Sante Fe where the bulk of labor was located. Other energy resources were inadequate. There was not enough oil and water power.

Capital was also lacking. Local capital continued to flow abroad, or find investment in real estate. Although the Argentine middle class saved, there was little investment in industrial corporations. Purchase of securities in the stock market is a new phenomenon in Argentina. The Economic Commission for Latin America, however, has maintained that saving in Argentina is "satisfactory." But this is not true. To be sure, gross national product figures in recent years indicate a relatively high rate of saving and domestic investment. But this high rate is only apparent and is the result of inflation. In real terms, there has been dissaving since 1957. It is revealed by the decline in real per capita income, and the failure even to cover depreciation on such important capital assets as the railways and the merchant marine. It is doubtful whether real saving has ever been as great in Argentina as in some of the other Latin American countries such as Colombia, Chile, and Mexico. Argentina also did not direct surplus export earnings into industrial investment through exchange control until Perón. This form of forced saving and investment did not exist until 1946 after he had become dictator.

To sum up, Argentina frantically wanted to industrialize, but it was not prepared for industrialism because of lack of raw materials, saving, and capital. A large top-heavy working class with great political power crowded the cities, but there was not enough industry to utilize it effectively. Argentina was a great urban factory filled with workers who were trying to work without materials, machinery, or power.

Juan Domingo Perón

At this critical juncture dictatorial power was seized by Colonel Perón and his wife, Eva Duarte. In 1943 a military revolution occurred because the pro-German Argentine army feared the election of a pro-Ally president. Unable to secure civilian support for the revolution from landowners, industrialists, or the middle class, the military regime turned to the working class through Perón who was appointed Minister of Labor. Between 1943 and 1945 Perón rapidly organized labor in unions through government fiat. Collective bargaining was made compulsory. The period resembled that which immediately followed the passage of the Wagner Labor Relations Act in the United States. But there was a vast difference, Perón dominated the unions he organized, and made them not only tools of the government but a political force loyal to him personally. As a result, his power grew enormously. In 1945 the leaders of the military regime became fearful and tried to remove Perón. They imprisoned him for a short time, but huge mobs of workers, incited by Eva Perón, marched on the capital. Perón was not only released from prison, but from that time until his fall, became the absolute dictator of Argentina.

The economic policies pursued by Perón go far toward explaining the special developmental problems of Argentina today. Perón created a privilege-seeking working class. He organized city labor into unions. He allied the farm peons with the urban workers. In fascist style, unions were integrated with the government so that the real direction of organized labor was in the hands of the Ministry of Labor. Having organized labor behind him, Perón attempted to force industrialization rapidly on the country and exploit agriculture for this purpose. Among the main features of the Perón program were the following:[3]

1. *National Economic Planning.* Under Perón there were two five-year plans, those of 1947–51 and 1953–57. The first included projects for public health, housing, sanitation, a merchant marine, roads, tourism, and the development of oil, gas, coal, and hydroelectric resources. The plan was to cost 18 billion pesos. The second five-year plan used the target principle. Goals were set for agriculture, mining, transportation and the various industries. Among the principal objectives were the development of the steel and chemical industries, the mechanization of agriculture, and the expansion of oil production. Neither plan was fully completed.

2. *The Sacrifice of Agriculture to Promote Industry.* Since Perón was nationalistic and attained his popular support in no small measure through appeals to the vanity of Argentine nationalists, he favored a "bootstrap" policy. The bootstrap was agriculture. Agricultural export earnings were to be used as the means of obtaining capital for industrialization. To do this, he introduced a new system of exchange control by establishing the *Institut por Produccion e Intercamio* (IAPI) in 1946. This government agency was given a monopoly of the purchase of grain and meat. These products were bought at prices lower than world prices and sold abroad at a large profit. The profit was used to buy machinery and industrial equipment, and to repatriate the foreign investments of Argentina. It was also used to create a merchant marine. Although IAPI was instrumental in promoting industry, it caused the deterioration of agriculture. Agricultural exports, the main source of capital, began to decline

rapidly. Perón was "killing the goose that laid the golden egg." The prices given to Argentine farmers cut farm profits. In addition, the higher wages of farm workers resulting from Perónist unionization further squeezed profits. In the end, farm profits declined so much that land was abandoned, farm owners moved into the cities, herds were not replenished, and the migration of farm workers into the already overcrowded cities increased.

3. *Deficit Financing.* Under Perón, Argentine economists followed a specious interpretation of Keynesian doctrine. It was thought that at least half of the first five-year plan could be financed by borrowing. Deficits grew great under Perón. But deficit spending was supposed to cause a Keynesian increase in employment and production, and a multiplication of income. To some extent it did, but Argentina was a scarcity economy, and the chief result was more and more inflation. Real savings declined, ordinary business profits were uncertain, and speculation increased.

4. *Raising the Incomes of the Workers at the Expense of Other Income Groups.* Although Perón and his wife dominated the labor movement, they did not control it in the interest of capitalists and the middle class. Wage demands of unions were not only accepted by the government, but made larger. In this situation, however, employers were temporarily saved by the inflation of prices. Otherwise, the end of the regime would have come sooner. Usually, industrialization has been accompanied by higher profits which lead to even more rapid investment. This was not the case under Perón, and both investment and saving were eventually curtailed.

5. *The Expansion of Social Security.* As in the case of the American New Deal, the Perón regime introduced widespread social security. Systems of retirement pensions were established for various types of workers under government offices, or *Cajas,* and the whole was coordinated by the *Instituto Nacional de Prevision Social.* Early retirement and liberal pensions were provided, but no health insurance. On the whole, the payments exceeded the financial ability of the Argentine government, and added to the deficit spending already induced by the five year plans.

6. *Government Enterprise.* Under Perón the railways were bought from their British and French owners, and run by the government. As a result, the number of employees became ex-

cessive and the lines lost money. This was another cause of government deficits. The government also organized and operated a merchant marine. A government agency was established to develop Argentine oil resources, *Yacimientos Petroliferos Fiscales* (YPF). Under Perón it was unable to produce more than 40 percent of the oil needed in Argentina. Finally, military expenditures were increased until they constituted almost 30 percent of all government spending.

7. *Government Loans to Private Business for Industrialization.* Perón sought also to promote industry by government loans to business. Through an Industrial Bank, easy credit was extended to new enterprises and for the expansion of old enterprises. In addition, some new foreign enterprise appeared. Kaiser established an automobile plant outside Cordoba. An agricultural machinery plant was constructed by FIAT.

8. *Tariffs and Agreements.* Finally, the Perón regime undertook to promote industrialism by protective tariffs and bilateral trade agreements. Free trade was completely abandoned.

One must not conclude that the results of Perónism were completely negative. On the contrary, industrialism was accelerated. The cotton textiles, metallurgical, chemical, automobile, tractor, and shoe industries grew. Argentina began to solve its fuel problems through the construction of gas pipe lines from the oil fields. Collective bargaining and social security became established parts of the economic system. But the measures Perón employed were essentially short-run devices. Perón had accepted Keynesian economics and his policies certainly reflected Keynes' emphasis on the short run. In the long run they were doomed to failure because, in a scarcity economy, spending cannot create capital. It can only provide the temporary economic stimulation of inflation. Perón adopted primrose paths and apparently neither cared about the future nor understood what headaches it would bring. He created a false hope also that Argentina could produce every variety of goods and could build up its productive capacity to a level approaching that of the United States within ten to fifteen years. As Herring says, "industrialization became a magic word for the Perónistas."[4]

The worsening economic conditions and the death of Eva Perón finally shook the dictatorship. To save his regime, Perón turned to attacks on liberals and radicals, introduced an austerity program, and tried to make peace with agriculture. The army and the labor movement remained loyal to him, but in June, 1955 a revolt occurred in the navy. Finally, the army also revolted, and Perón's rule was at an end.

After the revolt, the country was governed for two years by the army and navy under the provisional presidency of General Aramburu. Even the labor unions were controlled by the military. General Aramburu restored civil liberties and returned property expropriated by Perón. The Perónist party, however, was outlawed. Despite the dominance of the armed forces, and widespread anti-Perónism, support from the Perónistas was sought by other parties in the elections of 1958. The *Union Civica Radical Intransigente,* headed by Dr. Arturo Frondizi, adopted a social development and nationalist economic program not very different from that of Perón. It not only pledged itself to support organized labor, but also to secure the reinstatement of the Perónists politically through legalizing the party, or allowing its leaders to run for office as candidates in other parties. As a result, Perón advised his followers to support Frondizi. In the ensuing election, Frondizi won by a plurality of two million.

The Policies of Frondizi

Once in office, Frondizi, despite Perónist support, turned to policies which were completely anti-Perónist. He believed (and rightly) that the country should be stabilized financially, that industrialization should be promoted by more private and less public enterprise, that the peso had to be allowed to depreciate, that free-exchange rates should be established, and that Argentina should seek foreign financial and technical aid and new world markets. In pursuit of these policies, a new austerity program was begun. Wage rates were not allowed to rise, government spending was reduced, 75,000 unneeded workers were fired from their jobs on the railways, credit control was tightened, vigorous efforts were made to collect more taxes and eliminate the widespread tax evasion that existed, American loans were sought, contracts were signed with foreign corporations to exploit Argentine oil resources, and laws were passed to provide tax exemptions for foreign companies and to guarantee the withdrawal of their profits. Prices had risen rapidly in a heavy inflation in 1958 and 1959, but in 1960 and 1961 under the

Frondizi austerity program inflation was greatly diminished. Argentina's government budget deficit declined, and its foreign exchange position improved. Foreign capital began to flow in. In consequence of his austerity program and internationalism, Dr. Frondizi became increasingly unpopular with organized labor and the Perónists. He would not allow a rise in wages or the liberalization of social security. Real wages fell 26 percent between 1958 and 1959 and continued low in 1960.[5] The removal of workers from the railways caused a protest strike. The Perónists did not gain the political reinstatement they desired. They were antagonized by his acceptance of foreign capital and technicians. They attacked his support of the Alliance for Progress. By 1961 Frondizi had to rely on the military for the maintenance of his regime. A series of violent strikes occurred between 1958 and 1961. Communists joined with Perónists in attempts to cause disorder and embarrass the government. The Communist Party, as well as the Partida Perón, had to be outlawed. Frondizi appointed the arch anti-Perónist, General Montero, to command the army and restore order.

However, Frondizi had lost so much popular support that in 1962 he removed General Montero and again attempted to gain the backing of the Perónists. Perónists were allowed to run as provincial candidates in the spring elections. This tactical move was opposed by the military forces. But Frondizi gambled heavily on the possibility that the voters would remain loyal to the UCRI, his party, and would not elect Perónist candidates. The Perónists, however, won sweeping victories in twenty provinces, including Buenos Aires, where Frigerio, the leading Perónist, gained the governorship. The military then forced Frondizi to use his presidential powers to prevent victorious Perónists from taking office. But despite this concession, Frondizi, popular with only a small part of his own defeated party, was forsaken by the army, and arrested.

The military coup which forced Frondizi out of office was led by a group of competing army and naval officers. They were supported by the moderate General Aramburu who was brought in at the last moment to persuade Frondizi to resign. But Frondizi refused and was forcibly removed. The military turned over the presidency to José Maria Guido, the head of the Senate. Guido nullified the congressional elections which had been won by the Perónists and established a dictatorship. Assured that

President Guido would follow the economic policies of Frondizi and eventually restore democratic government, the United States supported the new regime.

In 1962 President Guido was confronted with an armed conflict between the forces of the competing generals. The differences between the military men were resolved only after extremely difficult negotiations. The regime also faced widespread criticism, and obstructionism by organized labor because of the continuation of austerity. Dr. Alsogarry, appointed to head the economic program, made a valiant attempt by radio propaganda to win support for austerity. He failed and was finally removed. Argentina made little economic progress in 1962, but it did succeed in holding the line against inflation. In 1963 the army generals attempted to dominate President Guido's government completely to insure success at the polls in the July elections. But in these elections Illia, an ardent nationalist and antiarmy candidate, won.

Current Economic Problems of Argentina

The economic problems of Argentina are largely evident from our historical survey of the policies of Perón, Frondizi, and Guido. They consist of the following:

1. The need for stability of (a) prices, (b) the balance of trade, and (c) the relations between prices, wages and profits.
2. Economic stagnation. The need somehow to get the economy to grow and grow rapidly.
3. The need to develop resources, especially those of power, and to concentrate on light rather than heavy industry.
4. The need to improve the railways, shipping and other transportation facilities.
5. The need to curb runaway inflation.
6. The need for greater saving and domestic investment.
7. The need to encourage heavy foreign investment and assistance both financial and technological.
8. The need for a larger and more vigorous entrepreneurial class.
9. The need for a degree of political stability that will allow continuous economic growth.

We cannot, of course, fully discuss these many problems here, but certain key points may be dealt with. Perhaps the prime difficulty in Argentina is instability. No nation can develop continuously and rapidly with an inflation that in some years is over 50 percent. Also, a nation as dependent on foreign trade as Argentina cannot survive if it continues to have large trade deficits. Either its trade position must be improved by finding new markets and obtaining better terms of trade, or it must drastically cut its imports.

Furthermore, no country can progress under capitalist institutions unless wages are low enough to allow reasonably high profits. Under Perón, wages in Argentina got out of line with both profits and productivity. If labor productivity is low, wages will have to be low. Under these circumstances, wages may be much lower than workers want them to be. But no advantage is gained by artificially raising wages. To do this makes acute inflation inevitable. Runaway prices badly disrupt the economy, and, in the end, real wages fall below their level prior to the dictatorial wage increases.

The real difficulty is that Argentina will not face facts about itself. The economy was stagnant before Perón. Under him it spent twelve years in a dream world of promises that could not be fulfilled. Perón boosted the economy to some extent in his early years, but then it bogged down. Frondizi attempted to set Argentina's house in order in a rational fashion, but the Argentine people could not accept the austerity program or the internationalism needed as the basis for future development. Argentina, to be sure, requires a "big push," and Perón attempted to supply it, but in the wrong way. The only realistic big push is one which will come from heavy foreign investment, and heavy real domestic investment and saving. The latter cannot be provided without relatively low wages, high profits, and high labor productivity.

Another basic unrealism of Argentinians is found in the way they picture themselves as an economy. Without adequate industrial resources, Argentina can never become (as they think) the industrial center or leader of Latin America. Argentina will have to concede this role to Brazil or Venezuela. But few Argentinians want to concede it.

Argentina is not the United States of Latin America. The most it will be able to do is to develop light domestic industry, and become the chief food-producing area for Latin America. It resembles Canada and Australia. It also resembles in some respects such Midwestern American states as Iowa, Nebraska, and Montana. It would be ridiculous indeed for these states to cut themselves off from the United States and attempt to become leading industrial centers like Illinois, Pennsylvania, and New York. Argentina needs unity with Brazil and Chile, which have a much higher industrial potential. It can even be argued that some of its labor force should emigrate to Brazil and Chile where it can be used more effectively.

Illustrative of Argentina's dreams of heavy industry are the attempts to build a steel industry. After World War II, General Savio had a vision of a steel plant on the Paraná River large enough to meet all of the country's steel requirements. But he was unable to obtain the needed capital, and the project was taken over by the government, which began a plant at San Nicolas. By 1962, one 1500-ton blast furnace and two 225-ton open hearth furnaces were about completed. This would give Argentina a steel capacity of only 630,000 tons of ingot steel, whereas the annual needs, if the economy actually began to grow rapidly, would be more than four million tons. With all the ore and most of the coal imported, the costs of production would be high. It would seem that Argentina should rely on Brazil or the United States for steel, and center its efforts on the development of other industries such as textiles, chemicals, paper, lumber, clothing, and shoes. In these fields it has the needed raw materials and natural advantages.

Another Argentine "will-o'-the-wisp" is oil. Argentina is proud of its "victory in the three-year battle for oil." To quote government propaganda under Frondizi, it was asserted in December of 1961 that "self-sufficiency in oil production, a dream for forty years, is realized; but [the] nation must gird for a new battle in 1966."[6] Despite this claim, Argentina, even in a stagnant state of general development, was still importing over 20 percent of its oil in 1961 although three foreign companies had invested $132 million through YPF to exploit Argentine oil in the remote region of Comodoro Rivadavia. There is some oil in Argentina, and it should be exploited, but the volume of production is not likely to increase enough to provide self-sufficiency if the economy begins to grow rapidly. Yet another dream is the development of coal in Rio Turbio. In this area, there are supposed reserves of 450 million tons, but they lie 1,575 miles away from Buenos Aires!

There is no doubt that the further industrialization of Argentina requires an ample supply of power. But there is perhaps more to be gained in Argentina from the development of water power than from oil, gas, or coal. The development of water power can also be combined with plans for regional improvement through irrigation and flood control. In 1961 plans were being made for an Argentine TVA in El Chocon-Cerros Colorados. This area, which is partly in Patagonia, contains the Limay and Negro rivers, and it was proposed to build a dam on each. The dams would supply considerable water power and provide irrigation for some of the arid regions of northern Patagonia.

Yet another urgent need is the improvement of the transportation system. The railways require new equipment, the elimination of excess personnel, the elimination of at least 3,000 miles of unused or little used track, and general improvement in the efficiency of management. Some argue that the railroads should be returned to private operation. Shipping is also in need of replacements and should be expanded. Under Frondizi, it was planned to purchase twenty new ships by 1970, and to enlarge the shipbuilding industry. Argentina also lacks roads. There are only 12,000 miles of paved roads.

Housing is so scarce in Argentina that in 1962, to catch up with the shortage, 1,500,000 units were needed. It was estimated that the cost of this much building would come to three times the entire annual budget of Argentina. Obviously, Argentina cannot make much headway with a problem of this size unless it receives foreign aid. Some of the funds of the Alliance for Progress program will have to be used for this purpose.[7]

Some final points may be made relating Argentina's economic problems to economic theory. Argentina cannot afford to follow Keynesian economics. Its progress obviously depends on a combination of greater capital and greater capital efficiency. Greater capital means more saving, and more foreign loans and aid. More capital efficiency means less inefficient government operation of industry and greater labor productivity. Despite serious handicaps, Argentina could progress rapidly if it would give up some of its dreams of political and economic leadership, face the hard facts about its economic development, capitalize on its head start in culture by doing things better technically than other countries, and move closer economically to its neighbors

Chile and Brazil. But even in 1963, after the election of Illia, Argentina remained stagnant with a declining per capita income, and gave signs of returning to militant isolationist nationalism and anti-Yankeeism. The foreign oil contracts were abrogated and there was little cooperation with the Alliance for Progress. The bootstrap policy returned in the attempt to rely more on foreign-export earnings for capital. The rising price of wheat gave encouragement to this point of view. Thus Argentine nationalism and unrealism constitute the main obstacles to this country's growth.

References

1. Cf. Robert Alexander, *Labor Relations in Argentina, Brazil and Chile,* McGraw-Hill, New York, 1962, p. 155.

2. Cowboys.

3. Cf. Alexander, *op. cit.,* pp. 141–144.

4. Hubert Herring, *A History of Latin America,* A. Knopf, New York, 1960, p. 650.

5. Cf. R. A. Potash, "Argentina's Quest for Stability," *Current History,* February 1962, p. 74.

6. *New York Times,* Dec. 17, 1961, special supplement, p. 59.

7. Under Frondizi, a valiant effort was made to direct private savings into housing. A Federal Housing Administration was established which tried to increase the flow of savings into housing and a Federal Savings and Loan Department which encouraged the establishment of reliable savings and loan associations by private interests.

BRAZIL

[handwritten annotation: slightly more than 100 million]

BRAZIL IS THE LARGEST COUNTRY IN LATIN AMERICA. IT HAS A population of over 70 million, and its area is greater than that of the continental United States. It is rich in resources. There is a great amount of iron ore and manganese. Other minerals and metals are found in substantial quantities such as chromite, mica, molybdenum, lead, vanadium, and bauxite. There is some oil and more extensive geological surveys may discover greater reserves. Brazil, with the possible exception of Venezuela, has the best endowment of the resources needed for rapid industrialization in Latin America. Its only serious limitation is the scarcity of coal.

Brazil has a large labor force located mainly in the southern cities of Rio de Janeiro and São Paulo. Brazilian workers, a large part consisting of immigrants from Italy, are alert, energetic, and resourceful. There is no shortage of manpower. Population has grown in recent years at the rate of 2 percent or more. Over a half million new workers enter the labor force annually.

Brazil, unlike Argentina, is heterogeneous racially. There is a great mixture of whites of European origin with Negroes. In 1950 Brazil was 61.7 percent white, 11.0 percent Negro, 26.5 percent mulatto, and about 0.8 percent Asiatic or of unknown origin. But despite the wide interracial mixture there is a race problem.

Brazil in many ways is a nation set apart from the rest of Latin America. Its language and cultural traditions are Portuguese, and there is a strong feeling of superiority. Like Argentinians, the people of Brazil believe that they can lead Latin America, and play the same role in the Southern Hemisphere as the United States has in the North. Unlike Argentina, however, Brazil has been friendly to the United States. In the minds of some, there is a father-son relationship. With American aid,

Brazil hoped to grow to economic maturity, and assume an equivalent role of leadership. In more recent years, however, friction has developed. Brazilians charge us with neglect. Senator Benton quotes one leading Brazilian as saying, "You rebuilt the roads of Italy for nothing. You gave her money under the Marshall Plan to rebuild her railroads. Yet you won't lend us— we who supported you loyally during World War II and in Korea—you won't lend us the money to build our power plants and dredge our harbors and put in our highways."[1]

The economic life of Brazil has been characterized by Professor Alexander as "a series of spurts of development."[2] Brazil began as a great source of wood. There followed a period when sugar cane was the chief product, and in the eighteenth century gold dominated the economy. In 1830 the era of coffee production began, and in 1860 the production of rubber. Finally, after 1930, the economy of Brazil became increasingly industrial.[3]

One outstanding fact about Brazil is its very rapid rate of growth in recent years. The International Monetary Fund has estimated that the real gross national product of Brazil grew 6 percent between 1948 and 1959. Brazil's rate of growth may have been even higher for part of this period. Professor Alexander states that it was 7.5 percent between 1948 and 1952. Even when the rapid growth of population is taken into account, the growth per capita was 5 percent. Industrial production increased 9.7 percent a year, and even agricultural production rose 3.8 percent.[4] More remarkable is the apparent continuation of a 6 percent annual rise in production between 1959 and 1961, a period when Brazil, along with other Latin American countries, was undergoing severe economic strain.

Brazil's development is uneven. The states of São Paulo, Minas Gerais, Rio Grande do Sul, and Paraná have become rapidly industrialized, and in these states there is much wealth. To the north, however, in the Amazon Valley and in the great arid northeast there is extreme poverty and economic stagnation. The poverty of the northeast has created a situation favorable to the organization of pro-communist peasant leagues. The failure of the Brazilian government to move rapidly enough in its efforts to alleviate the poverty may result in local communist revolutions. A great deal of Alliance for Progress money should be spent in this part of Brazil.

Brazil and Argentina

In understanding Brazil, it is useful to contrast it with Argentina. There are both similarities and differences. To begin with the similarities, the regimes of Perón and Vargas were alike and their heritage of economic disorder explains in part the current difficulties of both nations. In addition, both nations have suffered in recent years from serious trade deficits and extreme inflation. In both there has been a flight of domestic capital. Domestic saving is not great. Deficit-spending policies are common to both countries. In both countries, there is too great a tendency to invest in real estate, and yet there is a serious housing problem. Also in both, rural workers have migrated to the cities, creating an excess labor supply and much unemployment. Finally, in both, two ex-presidents recently attempted to establish economic order through austerity measures. Each failed, and both countries are at this writing drifting without effective leadership. Brazil, under Goulart, drifted toward a Castro-like communism. The Brazilian army seemed unreliable because it was infiltrated by communists.

But despite great similarities, Brazil differs in many fundamental respects from Argentina. The major difference consists of the greater industrial progress of Brazil. Moreover, if Brazil could solve its main problems, its future would be much brighter than that of Argentina. It has a far greater industrial potential and from 1950 to 1961 was growing at a rate of 6 percent or more a year.

But at the present time, average income is much lower in Brazil than in Argentina. The working class is exceedingly poor. In the northeast it is so poor that thousands are slowly starving to death from malnutrition. Furthermore, the country is infested with almost every horrible disease known to man. Illiteracy is over 50 percent. Two-thirds of Brazilian students never go beyond the second grade in grammar school. The male expectancy of life at birth is only 38 years. Infant mortality rates are among the highest in the world. In fact, it has been said that no matter what sort of economic, social, or health problem you think of, Brazil has it.

Other important differences are the greater inflow of foreign capital and American aid, and the greater size, resourcefulness, initiative, and ability of the entrepreneurial class. This group is largely composed of Italian, German, Polish, and other European immigrants. They began in many cases as skilled workers, established shops, then factories, and then large enterprises. Examples are the economic empires of the Lafers, the Matarazzos and the Renners. Brazil went through a stage of "robber barons" not unlike that of the United States.[5] Although, as in other parts of Latin America, the great planters and agrarian landlords were not much interested in industry, in southern Brazil some landlords actually shifted to industry. Perhaps more than any other country in Latin America except Mexico, Brazil exemplifies the value of an entrepreneurial class as the spearhead of economic growth under capitalism. The Brazilian entrepreneurs have overcome inflation and dictatorship, and seem to continue pushing the economy rapidly forward notwithstanding adverse conditions.

Yet other differences are the greater degree of laissez-faire in Brazil, and the relative weakness of the labor movement. During the many years of the Vargas dictatorship (1930–45), the government aided business in a number of ways, but did not regulate it to any great extent. The one exception is the introduction of exchange control which was manipulated to the economic advantage of some of Vargas' followers. Although it was unfairly administered, it did, however, result in increasing industrial enterprise.

Under Vargas, the government of Brazil assumed a paternalistic role toward labor. Workers looked to the government and to Vargas personally for aid. He was called "the father of the poor." As a result, there were few strikes and little violence until the cost of living began to rise rapidly due to inflation in the fifties. On the whole, Brazilian wages have been too low and labor has been exploited. The reverse is true in Argentina. There is little doubt that wage levels in Brazil stimulated industry, whereas they retarded it in Argentina. Brazil unconsciously followed the Marxian doctrine that capitalism thrives on low wages.

There has been some speculation as to the reasons for the docility of labor in Brazil. Perhaps it can be explained partly by the large proportion of Negroes in the labor force. The Negroes, whose ancestors were slaves, are an unusually docile group. The plantation system has also played its part. As in Argentina, the peon looked to the patron for aid. There was a strong personal tie. The Brazilian worker, as though he were still looking for a friendly landlord, casts about for a sympathetic employer or foreman, and establishes a close personal relationship with him. Vargas for many years was *the great national patron* or "father figure." Labor looked to him for help in a feudalistic way as if Brazil were his large *fazenda*. As a result, unions were not very militant, and communists made little headway for many years.[6] A somewhat similar relationship was established by Trujillo in the Dominican Republic.

Getulio Vargas

The ghost of Getulio Vargas is as influential in Brazil as that of Perón in Argentina. Both men had a powerful influence on their countries, and the current problems cannot be understood without some reference to their beliefs and policies. On the whole, Vargas' policies were more constructive than those of Perón, and his influence was exerted almost fifteen years earlier. A revolution occurred in 1930 which made Getulio Vargas the provisional president. He had been governor of the state of Rio Grande do Sul. The revolution was the work of young military men, but it did not result in a government dominated by the military because Vargas was a rancher rather than a soldier, and he favored civilian government. He was able to divide the military men and base his government largely on the support of the working class and the growing middle class. He was also skillful in defeating communist influences.

From an economic standpoint, Vargas' triumph was extremely significant. Before 1930, Brazil had been ruled by the coffee planters in São Paulo, and the ranchers in Minas Gerais.[7] Other states had little political influence. The working class and the middle class had little power. Industry was frustrated. There were even tariffs between the Brazilian states.

Before his actual dictatorship in 1937, Vargas began a series of useful reforms. He removed internal tariffs, threw out of office the reactionary state governors, raised new taxes, and curbed the overproduction of coffee. Like Perón, he believed strongly in industrialization. He encouraged new industry, introduced exchange controls to stimulate the importation of machinery and raw materials for industrialization, and in a broad sort of way accepted what we have called the economic policy revolution.

In the early 1930s, while Vargas was functioning as a constitutional president, having been elected by a constituent assembly called after the 1930 revolution, threats of both communism and fascism appeared in Brazil. The communists, who have always dangerously infiltrated the Brazilian army, staged a revolt in Rio de Janeiro and Pernambuco. Luis Carlos Prestes, the romantic leader of the communists, was arrested and jailed. In the meantime a group of green-shirted sun worshipers, following Plinio Salgado, and calling themselves *Integralistas*, threatened a fascist revolution. Whether justified or not by the circumstances, Vargas, who was ineligible for re-election in 1938, declared a state of emergency, proclaimed himself president for another term, and announced the formulation of a new constitution for a *Novo Estado*.

The *Novo Estado* was to be a "disciplined democracy." On paper, something like the fascist corporate state was established. Labor and business were both to be organized in associations and made subservient to the state. Actually, as we have pointed out, Vargas interfered little with the conduct of business. Labor was held in line by improvements in housing and medical care, and by slight wage increases. They were appealed to on a paternalistic basis, and, through the Labor Party (*Partido Trabalhista Brasileiro*), they obtained numerous civil service positions. Labor unions were incorporated in *sindicatos* which were combined associations of workers and employers. These, in turn, were controlled by the Ministry of Labor which also controlled the Labor Party. Collective bargaining was conducted and wage agreements were reached not through union-management negotiations, but through special labor courts. One effect of this procedure seems to have been the same as the labor control in Argentina. Through the Ministry of Labor the government dominated the labor unions, and labor supported the government politically on the basis of personal allegiance to Vargas. The effects differed in another important respect. Employers seem to have benefited at the expense of labor.

The *Novo Estado* had broader aspects. It was an outright acceptance of the need for social reform and industrialism. It promised to develop heavy industry, and to bring Brazil in a short time into the ranks of the advanced industrial countries.

In this, it was similar to Perón's five-year plans for Argentina, but it was more realistic. Brazil had at least part of the resource basis for advanced industrialism. Also the Brazilian *Novo Estado* was not militantly antiforeign or anti-Yankee and thus did not choke off the inflow of foreign capital needed to speed economic progress.

In the main, however, Brazil's industrial development under Vargas was the work of private businessmen and investors. Much of the enterprise grew through the process of ploughing back profits. What Vargas contributed was the shift of political power to the urban centers, and the removal of the stultifying effect of landowner control. The defeat of landowner influence came much earlier than in Argentina and most of the other Latin American countries, and Brazil's industrial progress can be attributed in no small measure to this change. In addition, Vargas gave much informal business aid, and the Banco do Brasil promoted industry through exchange control. Low wages and lack of union interference played their part, as we have pointed out. Vargas also made headway in linking the parts of the country together by roads and railroads.

In 1940, however, Vargas began to promote public industry and to work vigorously for an increase in the rate of development. The leading projects were the National Steel Factory at Volta Rodonda and the National Motors Factory outside Rio de Janeiro designed to produce motors and trucks.

Vargas also understook to aid industry through a Brazilian RFC.[8] He established the Banco Nacional de Desenvolvimento Economico, the Brazilian counterpart of development corporations which have been established in Chile and Puerto Rico. This body made loans to industry on a large scale, and was financed by a 15 percent income tax on corporations and individuals. It concentrated on critical industrial needs such as the improvement of transportation. In addition, it aided other industries which the government regarded as basic. The government also entered the field of hydroelectric power. In 1939, a National Council of Hydraulic and Electrical Energy was established. This organization made plans for the use of the vast water power of Brazil's rivers. Another field of government activity was the drainage of swamplands. Vargas also negotiated a barter agreement with Germany by which Brazil received locomotives, iron, coal, dyes, and chemicals in return for coffee, cotton, and tobacco.

The End of the Dictatorship

By 1945 much opposition had developed to Vargas. Although elections had been announced, it became apparent that Vargas did not intend to hold them. The appointment of his notorious brother as chief of police in Rio de Janeiro aroused great opposition, and the army acted to force Vargas out of office. He retired to his ranch in Rio Grande do Sul, and asked that his followers support General Eurico Dutro, his minister of war, who was the candidate of the conservative Social Democratic Party. Dutro subsequently won the election, and Brazil returned to free democratic constitutional government. The army pledged itself to defend the constitution.

Much of what Vargas did while in office from 1930 to 1945 was good for Brazil. But by the time he was forced out, inflation had begun, and there was much corruption in the government bureaucracy. Vargas, however, profited little personally. But he was either unwilling or unable to prevent the venality of his family and followers. General Dutro, who sought to clean house, found the problem too much for him. During his five years in the presidency, however, he succeeded in providing completely democratic government and in protecting civil liberties. He was plagued not only with corruption but with serious communist agitation, inflation, and unwise spending. Disgruntled at being thrown out of the presidency, Vargas planned to return, and courted the communists in Brazil. He incited them against Dutro. Prestes, the communist leader, who was out of jail and in the Senate, made untiring efforts to win the support of the masses both for Vargas and communism. In 1948 Dutro hit back by declaring the communist party illegal and expelling Prestes from the Senate.

Dutro's chief difficulty, however, was inflation. Business enterprises went on an investment spree with borrowed money. All sorts of projects were started: textile mills, cement works, automobile assembly plants, farm machinery plants, and chemical and fertilizer enterprises. There was also a boom in housing. Many new hotels, apartment houses, and homes were built.

The government also expanded its activities. Volta Redonda
was enlarged. A Rio Sao Francisco TVA project was planned.
Dutro himself came forward with a five-year plan in which 20
billion cruzeiros were allotted to projects for sanitation, food
production, transportation, and power development.[9] Professor
Herring says that "by the time this plan was announced in 1950,
the Brazilian economy had become so demoralized by overspend-
ing, corruption, and inflation as to make" it an empty promise.[10]
In the inflation, wages lagged behind profits and many illegal
strikes occurred.

In this situation, Vargas returned to office, winning the presidency as the candidate of the Labor Party. He now advocated
free institutions and democracy, and posed as the defender of
the common man injured by inflation. But during his return to
office the corruption and inflation which had begun before he
left in 1945 grew worse. Local government broke down until
there was no personal security in the large cities. Brazilian businessmen were unable to pay their foreign short-term debts. Only
a credit of $300 million from the United States prevented bank-
ruptcy. The cruzeiro was so overvalued by the official foreign
exchange rates that Brazilian exports fell off, making the foreign
trade deficit more severe. Strikes for higher wages continued.
Communists gained a strong foothold in the ministry of labor
and the armed forces.

In desperation, Vargas undertook an austerity program. The
parallel is obvious with Perón's last days in office. Vargas appointed Oswaldo Aranha finance minister who succeeded in
temporarily halting further credit expansion by business, and in
negotiating some favorable trade agreements. But the inflation
continued, and with it the strikes for higher wages. By 1954 all
blame for the wretched condition of the poor was being placed
on Vargas, and a great deal of anti-Americanism had also developed. Both Uncle Sam and Vargas were blamed for the sufferings
of the poor workers and farmers. But the immediate cause of the
fall of Vargas was the assassination of an air force major by the
bullets of gunmen intended for Carlos Lacerda, an ardent anti-
Vargas journalist. The air force and the army demanded Vargas'
resignation. Vargas was unwilling to resign, and for reasons
never fully explained he solved the problem by shooting himself.

The legacy of Vargas was thus the same as that of Perón, an
economy which had become seriously inflationary, an unbalanced

foreign trade situation, and a working class that had gotten out of hand. The differences are that Brazilian industry was still booming and was not hampered by too-high wages.

In the elections which followed the brief term of office of Vice-President João Café Filho, Jucelino Kubitschek was elected president. Café had attempted to restore order and introduce another austerity program. Kubitschek, however, largely rode with the waves. Corruption and inflation continued. There was no solution to the problems left by Vargas. In fact, they became worse as a result of Kubitschek's huge project, the building of a new capital, Brasilia, seven hundred miles from Rio de Janeiro in the interior. This was a giant public works, financed by inflationary measures, and justified on the grounds that it would provide more employment and open up the interior. Kubitschek, although sympathetic to the needs of the common people, really represented the business classes. He made no effort to curb inflation; he encouraged it and justified it as an instrument of economic growth.

Kubitschek is noted not only for Brasilia, but for his Operation Pan America, and his support of the Latin American Common Market. OPA was never a very specific concept. In general, it was a statement of the need for more rapid economic and social development in Latin America based on a large amount of aid from the United States. In a sense, it was a threat made to us: "If you do not provide billions in aid, Latin America will go communist." As a result of the rising popularity of the OPA idea, there was first the Act of Bogata, and later the Alliance for Progress. Perhaps Kubitschek can claim credit for having stirred up Latin America to demand large amounts of aid from the United States. But Fidel Castro can claim some of the credit, and has. As to the Common Market, some regard Kubitschek as the originator of this movement also, although the credit really belongs to Dr. Prebisch.

In 1960 Marshal Henrique Teixeira Lott was chosen as the candidate of the Social Democratic Party to follow the inflationary policies of Kubitschek, and he had as his running mate for vice president Goulart, the head of the Labor Party. Goulart had been the man chosen by Vargas to succeed him. Against Lott and Goulart, the opposition nominated Janio Quadros, the governor of São Paulo. Quadros soon became the champion of the lower classes who were suffering from the inflation of Kubitschek. For twenty years Brazil had been in a period of extreme inflation. The common man, who could not profit from the rise in prices through business and speculation, had had enough. He responded to the brilliant campaigning of Quadros. With the election of Quadros, hopes were high that his intelligent leadership would now solve the problems of Brazil in the interests of the majority. But these hopes were dashed when suddenly, in a quixotic reaction to criticism, and after only seven months in office, Quadros resigned.

Many people in both Brazil and the United States pinned their hopes on the brilliant, dramatic, and able Janio Quadros. He had a great and genuine concern for the poor of Brazil, and a strong dislike for privilege and corruption. Before he left office he made vigorous efforts to remove corruption in government against the opposition of Goulart, the recent president. Quadros was also firmly convinced of the need to halt the fantastic inflation, to restore foreign confidence and obtain foreign capital, to introduce sweeping tax and land reforms, to rehabilitate the northeast and the Amazon Valley, and to destroy the hold of the communists on the Brazilian labor unions. He met resistance from Lott, Goulart, Kubitschek and the upper classes of Brazil every inch of the way. His courting of Castro and his lieutenant "Che" Guevara was interpreted as pro-communism, as were his insistence on neutralism and his attempts to make trade pacts behind the iron curtain. Unable to withstand conservative criticism and the pressure of the right-wing elements in the army, he resigned.

But whatever interpretation we put on Quadros' foreign policies, his domestic policies seemed sound. The subsequent presidency of Goulart was checked by the right wing of the army because of his communist leanings. The constitution was amended to establish a parliamentary form of government which gave much of the power to a premier. The new premier, Tancredo Neves, was a complete compromiser, and the Congress which elected him followed conflicting outside pressures. But in the summer of 1962 Neves resigned, and a cabinet crisis followed. President Goulart, by refusing other prospective premiers, finally induced Congress to accept Francisco Brochado da Rocha, a leftist nationalist who followed Goulart's policies of relaxing austerity and of allowing the capture of the Brazilian labor movement by the communists. A Castro-like revolution thus be-

came a strong possibility.[11] Goulart's government lined itself
up with Latin Americans in other nations opposing the Alliance
for Progress. In 1962 one of the Brazilian states, Rio Grande do
Sul, was allowed to expropriate properties owned by the International Telegraph Company. A wave of anti-Americanism was
encouraged. The flow of American capital into Brazil dried up,
and a flight of American and other capital began. The struggle
against inflation started by Quadros was largely abandoned,
until near bankruptcy in foreign short-term credits forced
Dantas, Goulart's finance minister, to return to some measure
of austerity and plead for American loans.

The Current Economic Problems of Brazil

1. INFLATION

One is inclined to consider inflation as the main problem of
Brazil. Certainly the inflation there has been terrifying, but it
has not been as severe as the inflations of Bolivia and Chile.
However, prices increased 600 percent from 1948 to 1959. The
index of wholesale prices rose from 53 in 1948 (base 1953) to 305
in 1959, and the consumer-goods price index rose from 59 to 326.
The worst part of this inflation occurred under Kubitschek. The
tendency toward inflation had become so strong that even the
restrictive efforts of Quadros during his seven months in office
could only hold the price increase down to 45 percent. In some
months during these years of inflation, prices increased 10 to 15
percent, and a 50 percent annual price rise has been regarded as
"below normal." Wages have "normally" lagged 15 percent
behind prices, and inflation has amounted to a 15 percent sales
tax on labor each year.

Until 1961, inflation was not too great a problem for certain
groups in Brazil. Bankers, industrialists, and other businessmen
learned how to protect themselves and make large profits, and
enormous fortunes resulted. The technique of Brazilian business
was to plough back profits into business assets, so that with the
profits from the normal business activities and the inflationary
increase in business assets it was not uncommon to earn yearly
profits of 50 to 100 percent. Inflation apparently did not retard
business investment. On the contrary, it was an important stimu-

lating influence. Inflation was primarily a problem for the working class or for those with fixed incomes or investments. Assets in annuities and life insurance have been wiped out. As with every extreme inflation, grave injustices occurred for nonbusiness groups. After 1961, however, inflation even caused the stagnation of business.

The reason that inflation did not damage business or stop its growth in Brazil before 1961 is to be found in the government domination of labor established by Vargas. Even today a union cannot be started without permission from the Ministry of Labor. Wage increases are subject to government approval. Strikes are illegal, although they occur frequently. If wages had been pushed up faster than prices as in Argentina, inflation would have had retarding effects on Brazilian business. After 1961, however, the costs of labor began to rise, and business suffered seriously from the general disruption caused by the continuation of the inflationary spiral.

2. LOW AND UNEQUAL INCOMES

From one standpoint, the problem in Brazil is not so much the inflation as the low and unequal incomes created by it. In 1953 per capita income, according to Kindleberger, was only $215 per year. More recent estimates have set the current per capita income at $250 a year. But this is an average for the country. In the poverty-stricken northeast, incomes are as low as $50 a year.

A basic question naturally arises about the poverty in Brazil. If the country was growing at a rate of 6 percent for ten years or more prior to 1961, why are the people not better off? There may be several answers. For one thing, the people in São Paulo, Minas Gerais, Paraná, and Rio Grande do Sul *are* better off. Most of the growth has occurred in these southern states. But another answer is that incomes are very unequally distributed in Brazil. Taxes have been regressive, and the nation urgently needs tax reform through the adoption of progressive tax rates. Such a change need not cause fear that the rate of forced saving and investment will seriously decline. Unlike Argentina, Brazil has virtually irresistible growth factors. At least some increase in tax progressivity and the use of the proceeds to promote the welfare of the lower-income groups through social expenditures will not seriously decrease the rate of growth. Widespread tax evasion can be reduced also.

3. FOREIGN CAPITAL

Inflation may also be attacked as a probable deterrent to the inflow of foreign capital. In the early 1950s, at any rate, inflation did not reduce foreign investment. But Professor Johnson says that by the late 1950s "foreign capital showed great reluctance to enter the field in the face of economic uncertainties. . . . New United States private investment in Brazil in 1959 amounted to $218 million and to $95 million in 1960." [12] It can be argued, however, that the threat of communism in Brazil was a far greater deterrent than inflation. It is also true, as Professor Johnson indicates, that in recent years Brazil has become nationalistic. In Vargas' second term and under Kubitschek, there was much anti-Americanism. Under Goulart it had become extreme. To American businessmen this is a threat of expropriation. It happened in Mexico when Mexico became nationalistic even though the Mexican government was not communist. Today, Brazil seems to American businessmen both anti-American and communist and the investment "climate" has been ruined.

4. AGRICULTURAL PROBLEMS

Despite considerable progress toward industrialization, Brazil is still largely an agricultural country. As such, it not only shares with other Latin American nations the basic agricultural problems described in Chapter 8 but has them all in an extreme form. In the Amazon Valley and the great arid northeast there is a scarcity of good land. Both clearance and irrigation are needed. Methods of production are poor, fertilizer is scarce, and transportation and marketing facilities are inadequate.

In addition, there is the old problem of land concentration in large estates and the landlessness of the vast majority of the farm workers. Many of the northern estates are owned and operated by brutal and inconsiderate men. An ugly form of feudalism persists, giving rise to extreme poverty, disease, filth, and a Castro-like revolutionary ferment. Brazil is notable also for overproduction and overreliance on the foreign exchange earnings derived from coffee.

Conclusions

Brazil, in summary, reveals in an acute form the difficulties that plague most of Latin America. There is persistence of landed feudalism and cultural dualism. The rapidly developing south bears little resemblance to the north. In the south, the restrictive influence of the landlords was overcome. Now, however, resentment of the power and wealth of the United States threatens to retard growth by promoting acceptance of communism and a bootstrap anti-Yankee nationalism. Brazil, like Argentina, shuns the realities. It cannot progress rapidly if it forsakes both capitalism and American capital. It cannot progress through more inflation because it has carried it to the extreme where domestic saving, through the ploughing-back process, is finally being retarded and offset by the flight of capital. There is no way out for Brazil except domestic saving assisted by foreign capital.

The obstacles to planning for economic development in Brazil are cultural and political in the main, since the nation has a great industrial potential. It is not held back by lack of resources, but by the lack of political and cultural unity, by the failure of all parts of the nation to industrialize and grow simultaneously, by unwise inflationary government policies, by shortsighted antiforeignism, by illiteracy and disease, and by communist and other types of demagoguery. If these obstacles cannot be overcome, Brazil's growth will be seriously retarded. It has reached the end of the road as far as progress through inflation is concerned. In 1963 there was low morale in both Argentina and Brazil. It was reflected in a sharp decline in incentive, an increase in graft and corruption, and the collapse of both personal and business morality.[13]

References

1. Williams Benton, *The Voice of Latin America*, Harper and Brothers, New York, 1961, p. 11.

2. Alexander, *Labor Relations in Argentina, Brazil and Chile*, McGraw-Hill, New York, 1962, p. 25.

3. *Ibid.*

4. *Ibid.*, p. 29–30.

5. Cf. Alexander, *op. cit.*, pp. 44–45.
6. Cf. Alexander, *op. cit.*, pp. 45–46.
7. Cf. Alexander, *op. cit.*, p. 58.
8. Reconstruction Finance Corporation.
9. Cf. Herring, *op. cit.*, pp. 729–731.
10. *Ibid.*, p. 731.
11. John J. Johnson, "Politics and Economics in Brazil," *Current History*, February, 1962, p. 89.
12. Johnson, *op. cit.*, pp. 93–94.
13. As this book went to press, President Goulart was overthrown in a rebellion led by Dr. Carlos Lacerda and Generals Kruel and Mourao. Goulart was going too far to the left and there was serious danger of a communist revolution.

CHILE AND THE ANDEAN COUNTRIES

FROM THE ISTHMUS OF PANAMA SOUTHWARD ALONG THE WEST coast of South America to the Straits of Magellan and Tierra del Fuego are five nations—Colombia, Ecuador, Peru, Bolivia, and Chile. Each country contains part of the Andean mountain chain. Except in the case of Chile, a considerable proportion of the population lives in the mountains. With the exception of Chile also, these countries consist to a large extent of *mestizos,* or people with mixed white and Indian blood. The Indian influence not only differentiates them from Argentina, Brazil, and Chile, but makes them resemble Mexico. Like Mexico also, they have a weak agricultural base and they have attempted to develop their economies through the exploitation of mineral deposits.

In 1961 the Pan American Union estimated that the population of Bolivia was 3,462,000, that of Chile, 7,551,000, of Colombia, 14,132,000, of Ecuador, 4,298,000 and of Peru, 10,857,000. Colombia was the largest in terms of population, but Peru had the largest land area, and Chile the highest per capita income. The International Monetary Fund has estimated that the per capita income of Chile in 1959 was $500, of Bolivia, $126 and of Peru $119. The United States Department of Commerce, however, estimated the 1958–59 per capita income of these countries as follows: Chile (1959) $343; Colombia (1959) $250; Ecuador (1959) $167; and Peru (1958) $111.[1] The per capita income in Bolivia is very uncertain. In 1959 it may have been as low as $60, or as high as $130. It is generally believed to be lower than that of Peru. In 1953 Kindleberger estimated that it was only $55 per capita, the lowest in Latin America.

The Characteristics of Chile

The most advanced of the Andean nations is Chile. It was growing in the 1950s at a rapid rate. Its real gross national product rose 3.5 percent a year between 1948 and 1959. In 1953 it ranked sixth in per capita income. Average incomes were higher in Venezuela, Uruguay, Argentina, Cuba, and Panama, but it was better off than any other Latin American nation on the west coast of South America. In recent years, however, Chile has forged ahead while other nations have fallen behind. Because of the economic difficulties of Argentina and Uruguay and the adverse conditions in Cuba since the advent of Castro, Chile probably has the third highest per capita income in South America. Only Venezuela and Argentina exceed it.

Chile has a considerable economic potential. It can industrialize more successfully than Argentina because of its mineral resources. It is rich in copper and nitrate. But there are also deposits of borax, manganese, molybdenum, sulphur, iron, coal, and oil. Except for copper and nitrate, however, these deposits are not large. Yet the diversity of the mineral resources, and their greater accessibility to the centers of manufacturing in Santiago, Valparaiso, Valdivia, and Concepcion make Chile more suitable for industrialism than Argentina. In fact, at one time it was seriously proposed that Argentina and Chile unite as one country. The industrial resources of Chile were to be complemented by the agriculture and commerce of Argentina. National pride and independence, and the difficulties of linking the two nations by transportation over the Andes, prevented their union. A railway line, however, connecting northern Chile with Salta in Argentina was completed and has provided Argentina with some of Chile's minerals.

Although the average per capita income in Chile is high, it is very unequally distributed, and a large part of the Chilean population is very poor. The agricultural workers on the *Fondos* of the *Valle Central* are especially poor, and the urban industrial workers are worse off than those of Argentina. As in Brazil, the standard of living of the workers has not risen in proportion to the general rise in the national income.

Geographically, Chile is a monstrosity. It extends southward 2,600 miles, but at no point is it wider than 100 miles. The mountains encroach upon the sea. Northern Chile is an arid region which contains most of the minerals, but nothing grows in some parts of it without irrigation—not even a blade of grass. The central region of Chile contains most of the arable land, most of the population, the capital, the leading seaport, most of the industry, and the Valle Central. In the upper two thirds of this valley are the great landed estates, or *Fondos,* which are owned by descendants of the Basques who originally settled Chile and controlled its government until 1920. About 87 percent of the arable land is in units of 1,000 or more acres, and only 26 percent of this was cultivated in 1961. As a result, Chile still imports food. The southern part of the Valle Central contains small farms, the *chacras* and *parcelas,* which are operated in many cases by descendants of German and Italian immigrants. The southern third of Chile is a cold and rainy area extending down to the Straits of Magellan and Tierra del Fuego. Sheep raising has developed in this region. Oil has been located near the straits. Punta Arenas on the northern side of the Straits is the southernmost city in the world. It has a population of 40,000.

Unlike the rest of the Andean nations, Chile is racially very homogeneous. There were virtually no Negroes and few Indians in Chile. There has also been little immigration. The present population consists of the descendants of the Basques and other Spanish people who originally inhabited the country with some intermixture of Indian, German, and Italian stock. The Araucanian Indians, the only Latin American Indians who were never subdued by the Europeans, largely remained apart from the rest of the population until the 1880s, when they formally accepted a treaty which included them in the nation. Chileans, moreover, are not only racially homogeneous, but nationalistic. Unlike many Argentinians and Brazilians, they have no strong ties with Italian, Spanish, or Portuguese culture. Chile is not another Italian or Spanish nation. In Western Latin America, especially in Chile, Colombia, and Mexico, there is a firm *indigenous* nationalism.

Before World War I Chile was a nation governed by the great landowners, and had little industry. American and British capital was welcomed to exploit the nitrate in the north. Heavy export taxes were levied on nitrate which supplied 60 percent of the Chilean budget revenues. As a result, the landowners could be virtually free of taxes. But in World War I the Central Powers began to produce synthetic nitrates, and the nitrate monopoly of Chile was broken. Copper became a more important mining export and a greater source of revenue. The Guggenheim interests, however, succeeded to some extent in reducing the cost of extracting nitrates so that Chile could continue to compete in the world market against the cheaper synthetics. Today, Chile provides 16 percent of the world's nitrates, a material greatly needed for fertilizer and explosives. A government corporation has been established to monopolize the sale of nitrate and organize the industry which now consists of the Guggenheim companies at Pedro de Valdivia and Maria Elena, the large Chilean company (*Compania Salitreva de Tarapaca y Antofagasta*), and some small Chilean firms.

Copper has also been exploited through American interests. The Anaconda Copper Company has a huge deposit at Chuquicamata and a smaller deposit at Potrerillos. A third large deposit is controlled by the Kennecott Company at Rancagua in Central Chile. This was formerly owned by the Braden Company. Copper now supplies 56 percent of the exports of Chile. Other mining operations of importance are the iron mines owned by Bethlehem Steel near Coquimbo which produce four million tons of ore annually, the coal mines at Lota in the Central area, and the oil in the Magellan area.

As a result of the two world wars and the depression, and also as a result of the political influence achieved by the middle classes and workers in the election of Arturo Alessandri in 1920 and of Pedro Aguirre Cerda in 1938, Chile has made considerable progress in industrialization. The industry developed is diversified. In the wars and the depression of 1929, Chile could not obtain manufactured goods which it had formerly imported. As a result, a large textile industry grew into being. In addition, food products, shoes, clothing, paper, porcelain, glass, edible oil, and wine are manufactured. The wars and the depression were Chile's protective tariffs.

The Economic Problems of Chile

Despite Chile's natural advantages for industrialism, it has many serious economic problems. Some of these are similar to those of Argentina and Brazil, but they are cast in the mold of Chile's own peculiar economic conditions.

Five Chilean problems stand out: overdependence on the export of copper, extreme inflation, great population pressure, the need for land reform, and the need for further industrialization. In the years 1957 to 1959, copper constituted 66 percent of the export earnings of Chile. As a Latin American nation, Chile is not unusual in its excessive dependence on one export. But in view of the fact that Chile has achieved greater industrial self-sufficiency and diversification than some of the other countries, it is doubtful that the copper problem is as serious for Chile as the coffee, banana, petroleum, and tin problems are for the other countries. At any rate, the solution lies in the further expansion and diversification of the economy and still greater production for the home market. This was the solution forced on Chile during the depression of 1929 and led directly to the formation of the Corporacion de Fomento,[2] and other efforts to promote industrialization. Like Brazil, Chile accepted some of the features of the economic policy revolution. In promoting industry, however, Chile did not emphasize tariffs and exchange control, but the internal promotion of industry through the extension of credit to business.

It was the latter which led to serious inflation. Except for Bolivia, no country in Latin America has had a worse inflation. Between 1948 and 1953 when the inflation was relatively slow, both consumer and wholesale prices rose 300 percent. But between 1953 and 1959, when the inflation got out of hand, they rose 700 percent, making the rise for the whole period, 1948–59, 1,000 percent!

Inflation came about in Chile because of continuous deficit spending. It began as early as 1930, and continued steadily thereafter. Liberal bank credit added to the inflationary influence of the unbalanced budgets. We have seen that in Argentina inflation was induced by wage increases as fast and faster than the rise in the cost of living, and by deficit spending for an overliberal social security program. In Brazil the major influences, apart from an increase in government expenditures and liberal loans to business, were speculative spending on consumer goods and real estate, and the subsidies to farmers. In Chile, however, inflation was due in large measure to the great loans made to business and government enterprises. Wages were not forced up faster than prices, social security expenditures were not excessive, and there were no considerable subsidies to farmers.

Speculation was a factor, but it is not possible to say whether it was more or less severe than in Brazil.

Until inflation became so very extreme and rapid after 1955, the growth of Chile was not retarded. Like Brazil, Chile made considerable progress. But the inflation got out of hand, and economic stagnation resulted from it. Moreover, even before this happened Chile's average rate of growth was exceeded by Brazil, Peru, Mexico, and Venezuela—countries in which inflation was less severe. It should be pointed out also that, in its more moderate stages, inflation in Chile promoted saving and investment. This forced saving substituted for insufficient voluntary saving. But inflation went too far. By 1959 it could no longer serve as a device to force saving.

Chile needs some alternative to inflation as a means of obtaining the capital required for further industrial growth. Inflation should at least be held down to a level that will not disrupt industry. Outside sources of capital should be sought such as foreign-government loans. Internal saving must somehow be encouraged. Industrial growth must not be allowed to stagnate for want of capital. Further industrialization will be even more urgent in the future because of the rapidly rising rate of population growth.

Chile has a serious population problem. Its population is growing at 2.3 percent a year. However, Chile is the only Latin American country that has taken steps to face the population problem squarely. A National birth-control committee was established in 1962 to investigate the effects of the high birth rate. Some progress may be made in birth control in the next few years.

It is extremely important for Chile to curb the growth in population. It has enough resources for a high standard of living with 8 to 16 million people, but not with 24 million. At the present rate of growth there will be 24 million Chileans in 50 years. In the meantime, the actual per capita rate of production growth will be reduced to 1 percent a year or less by allowing the population to expand rapidly. Chile is one of the countries of Latin America in which the pressure of population is a real problem. Although a rapid rate of production growth was sustained until 1957, the growth of population absorbed most of the gains made in production. A similar problem exists in Costa Rica and El Salvador, and to a lesser extent in Colombia and Mexico.

Chile also seriously needs land reform. The land system is largely feudalistic. The land is worked by the *inquilinos,* who make contracts with the landowners or their managers which commit them to a certain amount of labor in return for a poor dwelling, a small plot of land to work for themselves, grazing rights, small food rations and very small wages, the equivalent of 30 cents or less a day in 1960. The workers have virtually no chance of ever owning land. The exception to this system consists of the small farms in the south of the Valle Central owned by independent farmers of Italian and German origin. These farmers are relatively well off. They are also more progressive than the large landowners to the north who still employ a great deal of hand labor, and, instead of using fertilizer, allow land to lie fallow and uncultivated. Agricultural productivity is very low on the large estates. With only 26 percent of the land cultivated in a country where only 7.5 percent of the total land is arable, and with some of the produce from the *fondos* intended for export, there has never been enough food even for the small population of Chile.

The land problems in Chile cannot be solved until the political power of the landowners is reduced or the landowners become enlightened. The landowners of Chile are still a very powerful political element and they obstruct not only land reform but tax reform and social development. Chile, for this reason, has not been able to carry out its agreements under the Charter of Punta del Este. Chile resembles Uruguay in that a deal was made between the landowners and the businessmen. It was made when Arturo Alessandri came to power in 1920. The landowners allowed the businessmen to industrialize and control labor in the cities provided the liberals who supported Alessandri would not interfere with the landowners or threaten their system of land tenure.

The future of the poor farm worker in Chile lies in the growth of industry. He cannot hope for land reform in the near future unless there is a revolution. As industrial jobs increase in the cities, he may be able to leave the life of extreme poverty he now lives on the large estates. The urban migration of labor would have two desirable results if real wages rise in the cities. On the one hand, the farm workers who migrate to the urban centers will have higher incomes. On the other hand, loss of labor in the country may cause higher wages, the use of machinery and fertilizer, and reforms in land tenure in the country. It would appear that Chile's feudalism will only be destroyed by industrialization.

Chile has made conscious efforts to promote diversified industrial growth. Perhaps the most important step in the promotion of industry was the formation of the government planning and industrial development corporation, the *Corporacion de Fomento de la Produccion* in the administration of President Cerda. Brazil and Puerto Rico have established similar corporations. But the Chilean development corporation more closely resembles that of Puerto Rico. Not only can it lend large sums to business enterprises through the Central Bank, but it can also engage in enterprises on its own. Thus it combines planning, financing and state enterprise. The financing may be in the form of loans, grants-in-aid, or direct investment. It seeks not only to increase the amount of industry, but to diversify it, and fill gaps in the economy.

Among the leading achievements of the Corporacion de Fomento are the establishment of the *Empresa Nacional de Electricidad, S.A.,* the *Empresa Nacional de Petroleo,* and the *Cia. de Acero del Pacifico.*[3] A national electricity corporation (ENDESA) rapidly expanded power facilities after World War II. The consumption of electricity increased 150 percent between 1946 and 1956.[4] The National Petroleum Enterprise (ENP) bought oil and gas wells and prospected for more oil. It established a refinery near Valparaiso. Ultimately, Chile hopes to be independent in oil. It has already exported oil, mainly to Uruguay, and its refinery was producing 60 percent of the nation's oil product requirements by 1956.[5]

But of greatest interest to Chileans was the establishment by the Corporacion de Fomento through the Pacific Steel Company of an integrated steel plant at Huachipato not far from Concepcion. Chile uses its own iron ore from Coquimbo and its coal from Lota. It became self sufficient in steel through this plant and was able to export steel to Peru and Ecuador. The steel plant had nationalist significance similar to Volta Redonda in Brazil, and its stock is widely held by the public. It differs from most Chilean corporations which, like those in other parts

of Latin America, consist either of family or individual holdings.

Labor, Society and Government in Chile

Chile has always been one of the most class-structured countries in Latin America. It has consisted of farm workers (inquilinos), mine workers and urban unskilled workers (rotos),
the landowners (hacendados), the skilled workers, and the middle
class consisting of professional people, bureaucrats, small farmers, military men, and owners of businesses and industries.[6] A
strong distinction still exists between obreros or ordinary workers, and empleados, or white-collar workers. The largest part of
the population has consisted of the obreros on the farms, in
city factories and in the mines. All these were in a wretched
state in 1920, yet unionization was strongly opposed. Alessandri
came to power vowing that he would better the lot of the
Chilean masses.

After Alessandri, labor became increasingly organized. As in
Brazil and Argentina, the government largely controlled the
unions so far as their ordinary trade union activities were concerned. It exercised a paternalistic role, entered into labor
negotiations, and compelled the use of government mediation.
Unions, on their part, exercised control over the government
through the political parties with which they were affiliated.

Despite the paternalism of the government, the labor movement in Chile has been very influential politically, and it is extremely leftist. The original Gran Federacion Obrero de Chile,
organized among the railroad workers in 1909, was captured during the first world war by supporters of the Third International,
and changed its name to the Federacion Obrera de Chile. An
IWW was also established with anarchosyndicalist doctrines.
After various vicissitudes, the communists captured the labor
movement from the socialists and the IWW. In 1947 they engaged in numerous disruptive strikes. President Gonzalez Videla,
who had accepted communist support, turned against them, and
got Congress to outlaw the Communist Party in 1948.[7] But the
communists are still very active in both government and labor
circles. Labor is restive and might easily turn again to the communists.

Conclusions

One may conclude that the economic problems of Chile are partly social and political. There are three distinct power groups in Chile—landowners, businessmen and organized labor. Each causes economic problems in its own way. The landowners will not allow tax and land reform. This leads to lack of self-sufficiency in food, overreliance on the earnings from copper exports, and inflation. Business, as in Brazil, will not promote saving and investment for economic growth through austerity. Hence the use of credit and the problem of inflation. Organized labor threatens communism. Hence the unholy alliance between business and the landlords. This prevents tax reform and land reform.

The Characteristics of the Andean Countries

Bolivia, Ecuador, Colombia, and Peru constitute an important section of Latin America with characteristics which, as we have said, resemble those of Mexico. They have a strong Indian influence and a mountainous terrain rich with minerals, but providing only a weak agricultural basis for their growing populations. Together with Chile, they possess one-fifth of the population of Latin America. Almost half of the Indians of Latin America live in this area. The social revolution in Latin America is acutely manifested by the Andean Indians and the *mestizos* of the lower middle class. There is much unrest. These people, like many others in Latin America, believe that "their time has come." They are unwilling to wait any longer for social betterment. They may become the spearhead of a communist revolution. Although the workers of the ABC countries have actually been more seriously damaged by inflation than the Andean workers, the latter are more incensed by it. They are also extremely bitter because of the lack of land reform. In short, the Andean lower classes, together with those of Cuba and the Dominican Republic, are the powder keg of Latin America which threatens at any moment to ignite and cause a violent explosion. Radical revolutions have already occurred in Bolivia and Cuba. A long-drawn-out undeclared civil war, which has caused the loss of thousands of lives, was still active in Colombia in 1962.

The Andean countries have low per capita incomes, and in some of these, incomes have declined since 1954. Professor E. S. Urbanski, citing the data of the United States Department of Commerce, reveals that the per capita income of Colombia fell from $282 in 1954 to $250 in 1959, and that of Peru from $118 in 1955 to $111 in 1958.[8] Three of these countries had a fairly high rate of growth until 1955. The growth in per capita income in Colombia between 1945 and 1955 was 4.5 percent a year. Industrial production grew 3.6 percent a year. In Ecuador the corresponding growth rates were 3.8 and 6.0, and in Peru, 3.1 and 4.6.[9] The International Monetary Fund, moreover, estimated that the growth in gross income in Peru was 6.2 percent between 1948 and 1959.

The failure of per capita income to rise in some of these countries may be attributed to a number of factors, the inflation, the rapid growth in population, the failure to increase agricultural production through agrarian reforms, the lack of capital, the disastrous economic effects of the revolution in Bolivia, and the decline in the export earnings of copper, tin, and coffee. Some of the cities are flourishing, such as Lima and Medellin. But the growth of population, and the depressed state of agriculture, go far toward offsetting the growth of industry in the cities. As a result, per capita incomes for these nations as a whole do not rise rapidly, and national income is very unevenly distributed as between rural and urban areas.

Land Reform in the Andean Countries

Actually, although the need for land reform arouses more bitterness in the Andean countries, and is a more urgent political issue than in Brazil and Chile, the land problem is farther along toward a solution. These were the nations most characterized by great latifundias. But the revolution in Bolivia redistributed part of the land among the Indian peasants. In Ecuador the estate system has partly collapsed for economic reasons. The Indians and mestizos are being assimilated into banana culture in which the agricultural worker is somewhat better off. In Colombia there is a great deal of *minifundism,* and both Colombia and Peru have new plans for agricultural resettlement. Former President Camargo of Colombia maintained that Colombia had plenty of unused land to meet the needs of the landless. The problem was to obtain the capital for transportation, seed, housing, and machinery.

In fact, it may be that the real problem in the Andean countries is not so much latifundism as minifundism. Professor Urbanski cites data which show that there were in Bolivia 61,704 farms between 1 and 10 hectares, and 24,756 below 1 hectare. In Colombia, the corresponding figures were 486,337 and 161,778. In Ecuador they were 195,549 and 92,387.[10] On farms of this size, not much can be done to raise farm productivity. They are too small for machinery. They are not even large enough to sustain the owner and his family even with the use of better seed and fertilizer. Many of these farms are becoming even smaller as a result of division at the death of the owner among members of his family. About all that is accomplished by this minifundism is to give the poor farmers pride of ownership, and a certain independence on a semistarvation level. To break up the large estates might increase the size of farms somewhat, but not enough to put agriculture on an economic basis. Camargo and others in this area are probably right in thinking that the realistic solution consists of resettlement on unused land of which there is a good deal on the eastern slopes of the Andes. However, the fact remains that most of the land used belongs to the owners of large estates. This creates a political situation which on the one hand needs to be met quickly, but on the other hand is hard to cope with because of the political power of the great landowners.

In the past it was possible to thwart the demand for reform through military dictatorship. Three changes make this increasingly difficult. In the first place, the awareness of the need for reform has spread throughout the lower levels of the population, and they are not willing to accept fate or religion as answers to their impoverished condition. Second, the area is rife with revolutionary propaganda among the lower classes which is by no means entirely communist. Third, radically oriented unions and political parties have grown stronger.

The Andean Labor Movement

A prime difference between the Andean countries and Argentina, Brazil, and Chile is that the governments have not been able to establish a cooperative or paternal relationship with the labor unions. In Brazil and Chile, as we have seen, real wages were actually kept down, and the governments of Vargas, Dutro, Kubitschek, Alessandri, and Cerda had the political support of the labor movement. Labor, in a sense, was inside the government and controlled by it. The same thing can be said of Mexico under Mateos and of Cuba under Castro. But the labor movements of Peru, Ecuador, Colombia, and Venezuela have grown in recent years and are largely *outside* the governments. They are also much affected by the *Confederacion de Trabajadores de la America Latina,* the international body of the Latin American labor movement which has fallen under the Marxist leadership of Lombardo Toledano.

The labor movement has assumed various roles in Bolivia, Peru and Colombia since 1950. In Bolivia it backed MNR (*Movimiento Nacional Revolucionario*) and PIR (*Partido Izquierdista Revolucionario*). The former was the party of Victor Paz Estenssoro. MNR staged the revolution in 1952 which placed Professor Estenssoro in the presidency. Following the expropriation of large estates and the nationalization of tin, labor has felt it had a right to meddle in Bolivian economic policy. The Bolivian miners and the peasants' unions are particularly strong. Bolivian labor is organized in the *Confederacion de Trabajadores Bolivianos* which has Marxist leanings. Its overoptimistic efforts to improve the condition of the workers and peasants have forced the government to adopt ill-advised measures. Urbanski concludes that ". . . the CTB brought the 'shaky' Bolivian economy to a deplorable level, unjustifiable in view of certain progress in the agrarian rehabilitation of the indigenous population."[11] *Fidelistas* are very active in CTB and MNR. Because of the virtual collapse of the economy in 1960, they might have sparked a revolution similar to those which occurred in Guatemala and Nicaragua in that year.[12] Fortunately, President Estenssoro, despite his fascist beginnings, now has democratic leanings, and is not anti-American. He has accepted our financial and technical aid without which revolution would have been a certainty.

The Peruvian labor movement also has considerable power. It has become associated politically with APRA (*Alianza Popular Revolucionaria Americana*), which was originally communist. This party, which was officially banned and is under the leadership of Victor Haya de la Torre, has as its chief objective the expropriation of the great estates and their distribution among the impoverished Indians. The *arpistas* supported the election of President Prado on the assumption that he would introduce land reforms. The unions are therefore primarily a powerful force for land reform in Peru at the present time. But in July, 1962, the *arpistas,* who had been legally reinstated, received the highest votes for their candidate, Haya de la Torre, in the presidential election. This prompted an army junta to take over the government, claiming election fraud.

It is not much wonder that the labor movement in Peru has become concerned about the landless Indians. They are 80 percent of the population. They are actually living outside the advanced Peruvian economy. Some of them come down from the mountains in desperation to live in some of the worst slums in the world—those of Lima. There they sit in unbelievable squalor and filth only a short distance from the homes of some of the wealthiest people in Latin America. These Quechua Indians, like those in Ecuador, have no right to vote, since voting requires a literacy test. Some progress is being made in both Peru and Ecuador in teaching them to read and in providing them with public land, seed, and fertilizer. But the landed Peruvians are indifferent to their problems. The labor movement is their only real spokesman. Communist "shock troopers" from Cuba and Mexico have been making headway in winning over the Indians in the Andean countries to a policy of revolution.

In Colombia the labor movement has never been as strong as in Chile, Bolivia, or Venezuela. The political struggle in Colombia has centered on the issues of democracy versus dictatorship, and liberal versus conservative policies. The coalition of liberals and conservatives which has backed the governments of Camargo and Valencia would benefit from labor support. Camargo encouraged the organization of unions, not merely because he was strongly democratic but because, in that way, the labor movement can become more representative and less of an opposition force under the tutelage of leftists.

The labor movement of the Andean countries has often defeated its own best interests. Instead of working for collective bargaining and social security it has become involved in national policy beyond the scope of organized labor. It has been essentially syndicalist. Andean unions believe that the interests of labor and business are irreconcilable. Thus they are militant and class-conscious. Instead of attempting to breach the gap between the *obreros* and *empleados,* they make it wider.

The labor movement in the Andean countries exemplifies a basic cultural dualism or, more exactly a "quadralism." There are the landless, penniless, illiterate, coca-chewing Indians of the sierra (*serranos*) who are outside the actual economy; the leftist, often-communist *obreros* of factory and farm led by politically minded intellectuals, often Marxist in ideology; the growing, progressive, enterprise-minded middle class of the cities; and the anachronistic, conservative *hacendados* who oppose progress and seek to maintain the status quo by influencing the army generals. Both economic and political progress depends on some formula by which these four groups can work together under democratic institutions. In the past, dictatorship was the only answer.

1. LAND PROBLEMS

The economic problems of the Andean region follow, for the most part, the general pattern of Latin American problems. There are the usual problems such as latifundism, insufficient industrialization, inadequate power resources, scarcity of capital and inflation. There are important differences, however. Although land ownership is highly concentrated in Peru, Ecuador, and Colombia, there is also a serious problem of minifundism. Also, due to the concentration of population in the mountainous regions, there is a greater need than elsewhere in Latin America for the relocation of the farm population on new land, and the opening up of this land for cultivation. In fact, it appears that a land redistribution which would break up the large estates could accomplish little. Land is too scarce, and there are too many people on the land. The mountainous parts of the Andean region are ill-adapted to agriculture.

2. INDUSTRIALISM

As in other parts of Latin America, industrialism is the primary need. Peru, Ecuador, Colombia, and Bolivia need greater industrial growth. But none of these nations, except possibly Bolivia, is endowed with a sufficient supply of raw materials. Industrialization will have to stress the light industries. Peru, Colombia, and Ecuador are now producing food products, pharmaceuticals, chemicals, textiles and clothing. Colombia produces auto tires. Many machine parts, mechanical devices, and electrical products are also made. But the development of integrated steel, as in the Colombian plant at Belencito and the Peruvian plant in Chimbote, is uneconomical. There is enough iron ore for further expansion, but virtually no coal.

3. PLANNING AND POWER DEVELOPMENT

As a result of these resource limitations, the Andean region urgently needs careful economic planning to provide for economic diversification and balanced growth. Only Chile has made considerable progress in this direction. The future of the Andean countries lies in new domestic markets and light industries to supply them. These nations must greatly reduce their dependence on export markets for copper, tin, coffee, and bananas. Granted their backwardness, government planning is essential both to direct and speed diversification. Also, wages must be allowed to rise, thus providing the purchasing power needed for the growth of the domestic markets. Lacking coal and oil, the governments must step in to provide a substitute in the form of electric power. The Andean countries require TVAs such as the great project planned in the Cauca Valley in Colombia.

4. CAPITAL AND INFLATION

As in the rest of Latin America, the Andean region lacks capital. Domestic capital accumulation has not gotten under way anywhere on the west coast of Latin America except through the process of inflationary forced saving. In Chile, Colombia, and Peru domestic saving increased through inflation when the price rise was not extreme. But in Chile and Bolivia, inflation went too far. It threatens to go too far in Colombia and Peru. Only

Ecuador succeeded in curbing inflation in the years after World War II.

Fortunately, most of these countries have received a good deal of foreign capital. American capital has poured into Peru especially. None of these countries has been strongly or permanently anti-Yankee. But the threat of communism and the extreme inflation in Bolivia and Chile have greatly reduced the inflow of American capital in these two countries. If Chile and all of the Andean countries could maintain political and economic stability in the future, it is probable that they could count on a great deal of American direct investment. This is an essential need to bring them to a take-off point in their economic development.

5. SOCIOECONOMIC FACTORS

Perhaps the most threatening aspect of the economic situation in the Andean region is the failure to unite organized labor and the poor farm population behind liberal industrial leadership. Part of the failure is due to the weakness and ideological character of the labor movement, and the dangerous Marxist influence of the Latin American Confederation of Labor. Part of it is also due to strong communist penetration and the weakness of pro-capitalist American propaganda. Last but not least is the stultifying influence of the landlords and the military who will not compromise or make concessions to the economic needs and psychology of the poor farmers.

References

1. The estimates of the Chase-Manhattan Bank for the countries in 1960 in terms of GDP per capita were as follows: Bolivia, $100; Chile, $375; Colombia, $325; Ecuador, $180; Peru, $240.

2. The Development Corporation which lends large sums to private and public enterprises.

3. *Empresa* means "enterprise." *Cia.* and *S.A.* mean corporation (*sociedades anonimas*).

4. Cf. Alexander, *op. cit.*, p. 240.

5. *Ibid.*

6. Cf. Donald Beatty, "Middle Class Government in Chile," *Current History*, February 1962, p. 110–111.

7. Cf. Alexander, *op. cit.*, p. 260.

8. Urbanski, E. S., "The Development of Andean America," *Current History*, February 1962, p. 99.

9. *Latin American Business Highlights*, Chase-Manhattan Bank, September 1956.

10. Urbanski, *op. cit.*, p. 102.

11. Urbanski, *op. cit.*, p. 98.

12. Agricultural output dropped so badly that even basic food products had to be imported.

MEXICO

MEXICO AND URUGUAY WERE THE LEADERS IN THAT COMBINATION of statism, socialism, economic nationalism, and the encouragement of industrialism through private as well as public investment which has been called the economic policy revolution.[1] As a leader in this movement, Mexico is of greater significance than Uruguay because of its size, moderation, gradualness, and economic balance. Also, as Professor Teichert points out, "economists generally agree that patterns developed following the Mexican Revolution of 1910 provide a formula for the solution of basic problems common to the rest of Latin America."[2] Consequently, it has often been suggested that Mexico assume the role of leadership in Latin America. But for a variety of reasons Mexico does not want to lead at the present time.

Mexico stands out, however, as the natural leader of Hispanic America. It has the largest Spanish-speaking population and the second largest land area of any Spanish nation. In 1962 there were 37 million people living in Mexico's vast region of 760,000 square miles with a coastline of over 4,000 miles. Mexico is also the nation with the most homogeneous *indigenous* population in Latin America. It is not composed largely of second and third generations of European immigrants because it has discouraged immigration and has been most unwilling to grant citizenship to foreigners. As a result, its population is largely native. In this respect, it has a close kinship with Colombia, Ecuador, Peru, and Bolivia and is a genuine "American" nation. There is one great difference, however. The Indian population is not as isolated from the modern development of the country as in the Andean region.

218

General Characteristics

The natural endowment of Mexico is puzzling. In some respects it is great; in others, meager. Mexico is ridged with high mountains which make transportation difficult and greatly reduce the amount of land suitable for cultivation. Only 57 percent of Mexico's land is even classified as agricultural, and only 8 percent was actually cultivated in 1960. Some have estimated the amount of arable land as less than 10 percent of the total. In the north and northeast there is a great arid region resembling in some respects northeastern Brazil.

The great assets of Mexico are its diversity in resources and climate and its growing population. Although the supply of land is scarce, all climate conditions are present, making it possible to produce tropical, semitropical and temperate crops. Moreover, although Mexico does not have a great quantity of coal or iron, it has a sufficient amount of each, located in reasonable proximity, to make an efficient steel industry possible. In this respect it is much more fortunate than Argentina and the Andean nations. The coal of Lampazos can easily be combined with the iron ore of Durango. This union accounted for the original growth of the industry in the city of Monterrey.

Mexico is well supplied with minerals other than coal and iron. There is, for example, a considerable amount of oil. Many of the wells that were active in the 1920s when Mexico was a leading oil exporter have run dry, but even today Mexico produces 91 million barrels of oil annually, and large additional new reserves exist which have not yet been exploited. There is also a great quantity of other minerals, including copper, silver, zinc, lead, antimony, mercury, molybdenum, and sulphur. In addition, Mexico has much natural gas and water power. These many different resources give Mexico a considerable industrial potential.

After World War II the population of Mexico began to grow rapidly. The increase has been at a rate of over 3 percent, or an addition of about a million people annually. At this rate, Mexico will have 45 million inhabitants by 1970. This rapid growth rate would cause serious problems in a country already having great population density, such as Haiti or Cuba, but the density in Mexico is relatively low. Rapid population growth is also a serious matter for countries without ample resources or with low rates of economic growth. But Mexico can continue to progress because of its large resources and because the growth of production exceeds the growth of population. Production had been growing until 1955 at a rate variously estimated as between 4.5 and 8 percent a year.[3] A slump developed after 1955, and by 1962 the growth rate had fallen to only 3.5 percent— barely enough to offset the growth of population. In 1963, however, Mexico was one of the few Latin American nations that returned to the boom level of growth. The growth rate rose again to 6 percent.[4]

The population of Mexico is not only growing rapidly, but continues, as in the past, to be centered in and around large cities. Mexico City and the Federal District are becoming very large. In 1962 the capital had 3,302,000 people and *Distrito Federal,* including Mexico City, has a population of almost five million. Guadalajara had 734,000 and Monterrey 615,000. Puebla and Orizaba, leading textile cities, had populations of almost 300,000. Since 1940 the Mexican government has become increasingly concerned about the centralization of population and manufacturing. It has made an attempt to decentralize, but without marked success. Mexico is not only rapidly becoming urbanized, but the leading urban centers have the most rapid rate of growth. There are now fourteen cities with a hundred thousand or more people. Within another decade, well over 50 percent of the Mexican population will be urban.[5]

The composition of the population racially is changing also. The pure whites have never exceeded 10 percent. But in the early history of the country, the remainder of the population was largely pure Indian. Much racial intermixture has occurred over the years, however, and the pure Indians have declined to 30 percent. The majority of Mexicans are *mestizos.* They will continue to increase. Although Mexico has been referred to by the supercilious as "those Indians," it is more correct to say, "those *mestizos.*"

In addition to advantages from the diversity of climate and resources and the growth and integration of the population, Mexico has benefited enormously from the revolution of 1910–17. It started Mexico on the road toward the solution of the typical political and economic problems of Latin America ten to twenty years in advance of most of the other countries. Not only did

Mexico get a "head start," but the revolution helped it to develop in a gradual, stable and balanced fashion.

One of the leading requirements for Latin American progress is to break the political and economic power of the *hacendados*. In Mexico, this had been accomplished by the early 1930s. No longer could great landowners restrain the growth of industry or the improvement of agricultural methods. Also, political unrest among the poor farmers was largely quieted by the widespread redistribution of the land that occurred after 1933. Mexico had had its revolution. It did not need a new one of a Soviet-Marxist character. Most Mexicans wanted to be left alone to carry out the principles of the revolutionary constitution of 1917. Thus the revolution made for stability. Mexicans were proud of the revolution and wanted to see it completed without foreign interference, either capitalist or communist. But the situation in Mexico which gives it greater stability than other Latin American nations can best be understood by returning to the history of the years following the revolution.

Completion of the Revolution

As was pointed out in Chapter 3 the chaotic period, 1910 to 1917, saw the overthrow of Diaz, the temporary regime of Huerta, the triumph of Carranza and the politico-businessmen, and the adoption of the constitution. With the elimination of Carranza by Obregon who really believed in the revolution, a relatively stable government was established which eventually supported and developed a new economic policy. Fortunately, Obregon was a realist and believed in gradualism. To him goes the credit of having started Mexico off after the revolution in a sensible direction.

Obregon feared that the rapid elimination of the system of *haciendas,* called for by the revolutionists, would destroy the economy. Thus he concentrated on the improvement of education by the establishment of rural schools under his able Minister of Education, Vasconcelos, rather than on land reform. Calles, Obregon's successor, went much farther in aiding the peasants, and styled himself the "heir" of Zapata, the great peasant leader. Seven and a half million acres were expropriated during his presidency. But Calles, like Obregon, believed in improving agricultural productivity more than he did in land redistribution. Seed, tools, and fertilizer were given to small farmers, irrigation projects were begun, and agricultural credit banks were established. In addition, Calles in 1925 began the expropriation of foreign oil interests by decreeing that the oil companies no longer owned their land and must accept fifty-five year concessions in place of ownership. This change, and his violent treatment of the Church, caused a wave of anti-Mexican sentiment in the United States.

Calles also promoted the power of organized labor. This was true to such an extent that his regime was referred to as a "labor government." The 300-pound Luis Morones, head of the federation of labor, CROM,[6] became, with the aid of Calles, the dictator of over two million organized workers, and badly tyrannized employers. Every businessman had to cooperate. The glorification of the worker was almost as great in Mexico as in the Soviet Union, and Samuel Gompers and other American labor leaders were invited to Mexico and lavishly feted. Had Calles continued these policies, economic growth would have stagnated as in Argentina through the excessive power of the unions.

After his presidency, Calles moved to Cuernavaca with many of his political followers. There they built beautiful villas and conferred daily with Calles, who named and controlled two subsequent presidents, Portes Gil and Ortiz Rubio. Calles was an unofficial dictator, controlling not only the presidency but a united Mexican party (PNR, *Partido Nacional Revolucionario*) under what amounted to a one-party system of government. But the period of his dictatorship, which ended in 1934, revealed a gradual rise in power of the new businessmen and the decline and subordination of organized labor which he had made all-powerful in 1925. As Herring says, "Despite fine words about democracy and the rights of man, Mexico's political and economic life was ruled by a small group around Calles—a new band of *cientificos* whose science was that of business enterprise. These men were suave and astute, possessed of a good economic sense, and, paradoxically, they combined ability to seize private profit from the Revolution with a measure of loyalty to the interests of the nation."[7]

A fundamental change in Mexican economic policy was made by Calles in 1930. At this point the agrarian equalitarianism was abandoned as the solution to the agricultural problem. Calles stated that the redistribution of land to the peons had failed because it had resulted in a sharp decline in the production of food. From this time on, Mexicans assumed a sophisticated attitude toward land reform, asserting that redistribution of land was not the solution for the low standard of living. Industrialization, both in manufacturing and agriculture, was the answer. Excess farm labor had to be drawn off to the cities in industrial employment, and farm productivity increased through irrigation, better seed, and better farming methods. Cardenas, who followed Calles' puppet presidents, proceeded on the broad basis of an over-all Six-Year Economic Plan which, although calling for more land redistribution, emphasized education, land reform, and industrialization.

Real progress in Mexican economic life began with Cardenas. By his time the foundation for it had finally been laid by a protective tariff system, the rise of a new business group, the beginnings of land reform, the creation of 12,000 rural schools, and the beginnings of domestic manufacturing. Cardenas also completed the expropriation of the British and American oil interests by making them government enterprises in 1938. Cardenas ended the personalized dictatorship of Calles, which threatened to become a German type of fascism. When Calles was forced out of Mexico by Cardenas, he was carrying under his arm a copy of *Mein Kampf*.[8] Cardenas, who had campaigned for election all over rural Mexico, had the full support of the common people and united Mexico in favor of a socialistic reform program to an extent greater than anyone before him.

World War II and the election of Camacho in 1940, however, resulted in rightist tendencies. There was decreasing emphasis on institutional changes and reform and increased emphasis on raising the level of production and income.[9] Moreover, the war and Mexico's actual participation in the fighting on the side of the Allies not only reduced Mexico's isolationism but aligned Mexican politics with the democracies. Beginning with the influence of Dwight Morrow as ambassador, relations with the United States had become more friendly, the oil dispute had been settled by a promise to pay for the oil lands, and Mexico began to invite and receive American capital for internal development. The economic stimulation of the war, and the foreign capital, started a phenomenal economic boom in Mexico with growth rates in some industries exceeding 100, 200, and even 500 percent over the ensuing ten years. From an average income of less than $50 a year in 1930, Mexican per capita income increased to $320 a year in 1960.

Much of this rapid growth was self-achieved. Mexico received proportionately less foreign capital than Argentina, Brazil, and Uruguay. Most of the rapid increase in investment that made the general economic growth possible was domestic. Rates of domestic saving exceeded 14 percent a year. (Americans have saved about 7 percent.) The vicious circle of poverty was being broken by *domestic effort* through a combination of tariffs, economic nationalism, a program of public works, a Mexican RFC to loan to industry known as *Nacional Financiera,* socialism in oil, railroads, the utilities and a few manufacturing fields, greater education, and the simultaneous rapid growth of private domestic enterprise, both commercial and industrial. Thus Mexico, in a somewhat different way, repeated the pattern of development of Uruguay—a combination of economic nationalism, socialism, planning, and the stimulation of private industry. Under Camacho, Alemán, Courtines, and Mateos, Mexico restrained its socialism, held inflation to lower levels than Bolivia, Peru, and the ABC countries, maintained free-exchange rates, curbed the wage demands of organized labor, and preserved political stability under a semidictatorial government with a one-party system. In 1964 the same political party had been in power 44 years.

The Nature of Mexico's Economic Growth

More than any other Latin American nation, Mexico follows the precepts of Rosenstein-Rodan and Nurkse. Social investment has accompanied, and to some extent preceded, business investment. Saving has also increased as investment increased. Investment has been diversified in various industries, so that the supply created by one industry becomes the demand for the others, Nurkse's precept of balanced growth. Mexico has, moreover, not been overdependent on any one export, unless it is tourism. Mexico's most valuable commodity export, cotton, accounted for only 25 percent of its export earnings in 1959.

1. AGRICULTURE

The emphasis on agricultural growth is especially significant. In the period of rapid industrial growth between 1947 and 1962, agriculture did not fall behind, but advanced. In 1947, 17.5 percent of the national product of Mexico was created by agriculture, but in 1962 agriculture accounted for 20.4 percent of a much larger national product.[10] As we have pointed out, beginning with Calles the growth of agricultural productivity was emphasized. Better seed and fertilizer and the use of machinery raised productivity. Huge irrigation projects in northern Mexico made possible the growth of cotton farming. Mexico is now exporting considerable quantities of cotton, sugar, and coffee. The production of corn has grown until Mexico is virtually self-sufficient in this basic staple of the Mexican diet. Agricultural progress has occurred simultaneously with the reduction in the size of farms and the distribution of 125 million acres of land among the landless peasants. Unlike Bolivia and Cuba, land reform has gone far beyond the more distribution of land among the landless.

It must be pointed out, however, that agriculturally Mexico still has many problems. More land needs to be brought under cultivation through irrigation. The transportation system of Mexico is inadequate for farm needs. Corn is being raised in the central highlands which would be much more suitable for cattle and dairying. Greater emphasis on meat and dairy products would not only provide a better diet but would result in a more efficient use of the available land. Finally, Mexico has serious problems of erosion, and like most Latin American nations, has not made sufficient use of fishing as a source of food.

2. INDUSTRY

Industrially also, Mexico can point to great accomplishments. The per capita income of Mexico as a whole has been increasing at the rate of over 3 percent a year despite the very rapid growth in population. But the urban and industrial per capita income has probably grown at a rate of over 4 percent a year. The rate of growth of per capita income in both the industrial sector and in the country as a whole was 50 percent greater between 1939 and 1955 than the growth in Argentina, and 10

percent greater than that in Brazil.[11] Economic growth was twice
as fast as the growth of population, even though Mexico has
one of the fastest growing populations in the world.[12]

3. THE COMBINED MEXICAN WORKING PARTY REPORT

The most comprehensive investigation of Mexico's economic
development after 1939 was made under the auspices of The
Combined Mexican Working Party for the International Bank
for Reconstruction and Development. This report was the work
of Raoul Ortiz Mena of *Nacional Financiera*, Victor L. Urquidi
of the Banco de Mexico, and Albert Waterston and James H.
Haralz, both of the International Bank.[13] Unfortunately, the
study covers only the period from 1939 to 1950. Data for subsequent years must be obtained from the Banco de Mexico and
other sources. According to the basic study, the following percentage increases occurred in the real net national domestic
product in the various parts of the Mexican economy between
1939 and 1950 based on the price level of 1939.[14]

Agriculture	83.8
Livestock	37.5
Forestry	− 0.6
Fisheries	204.0
Mining	− 2.2
Petroleum	71.2
Electric power	79.7
Building and Construction	54.8
Manufacturing	128.2
Transportation and communications	106.1
Government services	85.1
Rents	56.9
Commerce and Private Services	150.7
Total	114.4

The combined Working Party report sums up these changes
as follows: "The real net domestic product more than doubled
over these years and . . . on the average the annual increase exceeded 7 percent. . . . Output increased in almost every sector of
the economy . . . between 8 and 11% in commercial and other
services, industry, and fisheries; from 5 to 7% in transportation
and communications, agriculture, electric power, petroleum and
government services."[15] In 1940–50 the average annual increase

in real net domestic product of 7.2 percent yielded an average annual rise in net product per capita of 4.5 percent. As the growth of domestic product slowed down "from 8.2% yearly in 1940–1945 to 5.9% in 1946–1950, the growth of population reduced the rate at which per capita income was growing from 5.9% to 2.9%."[16]

4. AFTER 1950

It is difficult to obtain an accurate picture of what has happened to net product and per capita income since 1950. Perhaps Dr. Navarrette's optimistic estimate of a growth rate of 6 percent between 1945 and 1955 can be accepted. Data presented by the Chase-Manhattan Bank in 1963 for the period 1950–60 place the growth rate at 5.8 percent a year in terms of GDP. There is no doubt that Mexico's growth in total product slowed down after 1945, but that it held up to somewhere near 6 percent a year until 1955.

Financing Economic Growth

Of perhaps greater significance than the rate of economic growth in Mexico is the way it was financed. As Professor Teichert has pointed out, ". . . most of the investment funds needed for Mexico's spectacular growth were obtained from local sources. Mexico has literally lifted itself by its own bootstraps."[17] In the author's opinion, not only is this conclusion of Professor Teichert correct, but in this respect Mexico is almost unique in Latin America. Mexico may have a lower average per capita income than Venezuela, Colombia, Chile or Argentina, but it has reached the "take-off" point where it can grow largely by itself. If this trend in Mexico continues, its ultimate prospects are great. The low level of domestic capital accumulation in some of the other Latin American countries holds them back, and will offset their "head start," or the fact that they have greater resources than Mexico.

Since World War II, direct investment by the United States in Mexico has amounted to only $1 billion, and aid only to $900 million. The great growth of Mexico is based on the unprecedented period of domestic capital accumulation between 1939 and 1950. The volume of investment in real terms increased almost three times, but *the volume of consumption during the same period only doubled.*[18] The volume of real investment had reached 14 percent a year by 1947. The capital investment of Mexico, moreover, is now great in the industrial fields. Industrial investment by 1947 had become 30 percent of total investment. Mexican investment in industry was also highly diversified. This is as it should be. Investment was not going unduly into real estate as in some of the other nations.

Investment, when domestic, must be based on saving. As a poor country, Mexico found it difficult to save enough voluntarily for the great growth of the economy. But the report of the Combined Mexican Working Party says, "Economic conditions in Mexico encouraged voluntary domestic saving in 1939–1950. An increasing amount of savings found their way into securities like certificates of participation of Nacional Financiera. Nevertheless, the high rate of savings in this period was also the result of a much higher rate of investment than voluntary domestic savings and capital imports could support. The difference was financed by government deficits and an increase in bank credit."[19]

Thus, as in other Latin American countries, Mexico resorted to forced saving through inflation. But in contrast with such countries as Argentina, Brazil, and Chile, a large amount of the Mexican saving was voluntary on the part of consumers. Another basic difference is that unlike Chile, Mexico kept inflation low enough to provide forced saving without disrupting business or choking off development. Also, the control of the labor movement by the government prevented a rise in wages which would have reduced forced saving, made the inflation worse, and discouraged business and economic development generally, as in the case of Argentina.

In mobilizing the nation's funds for economic development, three institutions have played leading roles—the Central Bank (Banco de Mexico), established in 1925, the national bank for agricultural credit established in 1926, and the Nacional Financiera, established in 1934. Of these, the latter is the most important. The role of the government in promoting industrial development has been exercised mainly through Nacional Financiera, although tariff policies, tax exemptions,[20] and the encouragement of foreign investment have also been used by the government as promotional devices.

Nacial Financiera began definitely to devote its resources to economic development after 1941. It sponsored projects in fields where there were wartime shortages. Lack of machinery for new factories prevented it from making much headway, but after 1945 large projects were undertaken in the iron, steel, textile, pulp, paper, cement, electrical, and chemical industries. Between 1949 and 1950 it began to promote new industries such as the fertilizer industry. Nacional Financiera does not have the power to operate its own businesses as do the development corporations of Chile and Puerto Rico. It does not even closely resemble the development corporation of Brazil. It is essentially a bank rather than a planning agency, and most of the new industry financed by it is privately owned or owned by the government rather than by it. Of the development agencies thus far discussed, it most resembles the American RFC. It is a large public investment bank, making loans to and holding the securities of the many enterprises that it desires to promote.

To a considerable degree Mexico remains capitalistic. Although the railroads, telegraph, harbors, highways, many transportation lines, public utilities, and the oil industry are government owned, most of the economy is private. The leading industry of Mexico, textiles, is small-scale and private. Of the two leading steel companies, *Cia. Fundidora de Fierro y Acera de Monterrey, S.A.* and *Altos Hornos de Mexico, S.A.*, the former is private. Much of the rest of Mexican industry is private. In addition to having a large amount of private ownership, economic planning and control by the government has been less extensive and rigid than in Uruguay and the ABC countries. In fact, Mexicans have complained that their industrial growth has been unbalanced because Nacional Financiera was not given broad planning powers. There is, however, a large socialistic element in the Mexican economy. In 1955 public investment had become 55 percent of all investment.

The Large Mexican Middle Class

The development of a large middle class has often been regarded as the best insurance against communism. If this is true, Mexico is well insured. According to Daniel James, the middle class in Mexico now consists of 10 million people or 30 percent of the entire population.[21] This group is larger proportionately than the middle class of any other Latin American nation with the possible exception of Chile. It consists of many small businessmen, government employees, business executives, managers, foremen, skilled workers, professional men, and people in the service trades. At the top is a ruling hierarchy of politicians, big businessmen, and bankers. This group, which combines politics with business, controls the dominant party, PRI, and both the government and the economic life of Mexico. It determines the direction and the rate of growth of Mexican industry, and the amount of investment and forced saving. It has held together well, and has created a stable "disciplined democracy," to use the phrase coined by Getulio Vargas. Unlike the Vargas regime, it is less brutal to its opponents, economically and politically more realistic and intelligent, and not centered around any one personality. It is ruled by a clique rather than by one revered dictator who has tried to become the permanent paternalistic leader. Ideologically, it is revolutionary and supports public welfare goals achieved through statism, but in practice it is largely capitalistic.

The Economic Problems of Mexico

From a broad economic standpoint, Mexico has three main economic problems: (1) to discover and develop more of its natural resources; (2) to win in the race between a too rapidly growing population and the growth of production; and (3) to maintain a degree of inflation which is great enough to provide domestic capital for internal development, and not so great that it disrupts business and economic growth.

Mexico resembles Brazil in that government control of the oil industry has not resulted in enough discovery and exploitation of new oil reserves. Also, the rate of extraction of oil has been so rapid that the amount of oil derived from the existing reserves will be prematurely depleted. This is the case especially in the largest field, Poza Rica. When this field was privately owned before expropriation, Mexico could justly complain that it was not being developed rapidly enough. Under government control, the opposite is true.

Other important reserves in Ebano-Panuco, Faja de Oro, and the Isthmus have already been largely depleted. There is much oil in Mexico, but the government needs to devote more effort to the discovery of new reserves. This same problem exists with other resources. Much more land needs to be opened up for cultivation in the north through irrigation, although Mexico has already made great progress in this direction. Possibly there can be some shift of corn growing northward, leaving the central highlands free for more cattle raising and dairying.

The race between population and production will eventually be solved as urban life increases and the standard of living rises. With greater urbanization, the birth rate usually falls. But in the meantime, either the birth rate must be reduced, or the high rate of growth sustained. Perhaps Mexico should follow the example of Chile, and set up a national committee to consider the serious problem posed by the high birth rate.

In the 1950s, inflation threatened to get out of hand in Mexico.[22] It was due to the heavy loans to industry made by the government and the expansion of social investment. These expenditures caused inflationary government deficits which the government would not reduce either by cutting expenditures or raising taxes. In 1960 and 1961 an effort was made to curb inflation by reducing government loans to business. Inflation stopped, and prices began to fall. But the slump continued also. Lacking the annual increase in public investment which had occurred in the years after World War II, the economy failed to recover rapidly and resume its high growth rate. In 1963 government spending increased, prices rose, but the economy recovered.

Thus Mexico faces a dilemma. If inflation is not used as the device for high saving and investment, other means of increasing saving and investment must be found. One possible solution is to make greater use of foreign capital. In addition, wages may have been kept too low. The rate of consumption may not be high enough to cause "induced" investment. A capitalist economy, which Mexico essentially is, must ultimately rely on a rise in consumer demand to increase investment. In 1963 Mexican economists began to worry over the failure of domestic purchasing power to provide full employment of capital and labor in the cities. Tariff reductions and further increases in foreign trade were suggested as the solution. But higher wages might also be a way out.

This need points to another serious economic problem in Mexico—the very unequal distribution of wealth and income. In the early stages of economic growth, an unequal distribution of income is not only normal but desirable. It increases the saving and investment need for capital accumulation, the basis of growth. But the inequality can be too great, not only for humanitarian but for economic reasons. As productive capacity grows, buying power may not grow fast enough. Higher wages may now be desirable in Mexico. They might increase buying and cause still greater saving and investment by the middle- and upper-income levels to meet the rising consumer demand.

Another savings device to consider is taxation. Mexico has income, excess profits, and export taxes, as well as a great variety of indirect taxes such as customs duties, sales, and excise taxes. From 1939 to 1950, the yield from direct taxes increased, but total taxes were a smaller percentage of the gross national product. If inflation is not to be used as a means of saving, the proportion of taxes to total income should rise. But the rise should be in direct taxes. This would increase the funds available for loans to business while not reducing the growth in buying power of the lower income groups needed to encourage further investment. How an increase in saving and buying power can be brought about simultaneously is not clear. But many believe that the main current problem lies here.

Another basic problem in Mexico is low productivity. It exists in both agriculture and industry. Although great progress has been made, Mexican agriculture still has a long way to go in increasing productivity so that a high food standard can be provided and at the same time release 60, 70, or even 80 percent of the labor force for nonagricultural employment. In industry also certain fields are producing at much too high a cost. Mexican steel prices are far higher than the prices of imported steel. Local steel production would be wiped out by competition if it were not for the high protective tariff on steel. Mexico now produces most of its steel requirements, but at too high a cost.

Some economists have claimed, however, that one of the main reasons for Mexico's success is its greater industrial efficiency as compared with other Latin American nations. There are supposed to be more trained technicians and more trained and energetic managers. Even though Mexico may surpass some Latin

American countries in these respects, it still has serious managerial and efficiency problems.

Conclusions

One is tempted in analyzing Mexico's economic problems to conclude that what has led to success in the past should be continued in the future. This means that if no other way except inflation can be found to maintain a high rate of saving, inflation should be continued at a restrained rate. Mexico could use more foreign capital, but internal saving and investment has been and should remain its principal means of economic development. Inflation has been largely instrumental in causing this high domestic saving and investment.

It may be concluded also that, unlike most other Latin American nations, Mexico reveals few obstacles to sound planning for economic growth. It is the ideal which other Latin American nations should follow. It approximates the conditions, theory, and policy advocated for Latin America in this book.

References

1. Cf. Chap. 3.
2. Pedro C. Teichert, *Economic Policy Revolution and Industrialization in Latin America,* University of Mississippi, University, Miss., 1959, p. 153.
3. One authority, Dr. Alfredo Navarrette, has estimated that the growth was 8 percent between 1939 and 1945, and 6 percent between 1946 and 1955. Cf. Higgins, *op. cit.,* p. 68.
4. *New York Times,* Jan. 17, 1964.
5. The United Nations has estimated that Mexico will be 62 percent urban by 1980. Cf. Daniel James. "Kennedy visits the 'New' Mexico," *New York Times Magazine,* June 24, 1962, p. 24.
6. *Confederacion Regional Obrera Mexicana.*
7. Hubert Herring, *History of Latin America,* A. Knopf, New York, 1960, p. 373
8. Herring, *op. cit.,* p. 377.
9. Some believe that the stress on production was due to a recognition of the failure of the program of dividing up the landed estates into smaller farms. Productivity had declined. Mexicans wanted to turn away from their land division program and seek greater productivity. Cf. Teichert, *op. cit.,* p. 154.
10. Cf. James, *op. cit.,* p. 24.

11. Teichert, *op. cit.*, p. 155.

12. United Nations, *Economic Survey of Latin America*, 1955, p. 4.

13. Combined Mexican Working Party, *The Economic Development of Mexico*, Johns Hopkins Press, Baltimore, 1953.

14. Combined Mexican Working Party, *op. cit.*, pp. 176–177.

15. *Ibid.*, p. 3.

16. *Ibid.*, p. 7.

17. Teichert, *op. cit.*, p. 153.

18. Combined Mexican Working Party, *op. cit.*, p. 9.

19. Combined Mexican Working Party, *op. cit.*, p. 13.

20. Tax exemptions are granted for ten years for new industries from all principal federal taxes.

21. James, *op. cit.*, p. 24.

22. Wholesale prices rose 43 percent and retail prices 54 percent between 1950 and 1959.

SEVENTEEN

VENEZUELA

VENEZUELA IS ONE OF THE RICHEST, IF NOT THE RICHEST, NATION in Latin America. The per capita income was $1,080 in 1959 according to the International Monetary Fund. But this figure is deceptive because it is partly a result of the high earnings of petroleum production, 35 to 40 percent of which go to the foreign corporations that own the oil fields. The figure is also deceptive because not enough account was taken of the high level of Venezuelan prices. The mission sent to Venezuela by the International Bank for Reconstruction and Development estimated that the *real* per capita annual income was more nearly $600.[1] In addition, one must recognize the fact that income is very unequally distributed in Venezuela. The upper classes in Caracas have high incomes, but the rural population is very poor. Three fourths of Venezuelans have a per capita income of $200 or less. Both the peasants and working class are worse off than those of Argentina and Uruguay.

As a result of the great backwardness and poverty of parts of the population, and the underdeveloped and unexplored character of most of the land, Venezuela has been called "the richest undeveloped country in the world." It has begun to grow rapidly since the regime of the dictator, Marcos Perez Jimenez (1948–1959). But Venezuela must still import food, machinery, and consumer goods. Industrialization has grown only in the last two decades, and there is a great problem of agricultural reform yet to be solved. Before the discovery of oil in 1917 and its subsequent development, Venezuela had been for 400 years a poor country exporting cattle, coffee, and other food products.

General Characteristics

Venezuela is one of the largest nations in Latin America in terms of area (352,000 square miles), and one of the smallest in terms of population (7.6 million in 1962). It is larger in area than France and the United Kingdom combined. Its climate ranges from the great heat of the swamps in the delta of the Orinoco to the frigid climate of the Andes which rise in Venezuela to 16,000 feet. The country consists of four parts—the Andes highlands running from San Cristobal to the Paria peninsula, the Maracaibo area consisting of lowlands which are hot and humid and border the great lake, the *llanos* or plains extending from the Andes to the Orinoco, and the Guayana highlands south and east of the Orinoco. Its climate varies from temperate to tropical. It contains the second largest river in Latin America and the highest waterfall.[2]

The density of population is very low, only 17 per square mile. The population is concentrated in the Andes highlands and in the region around Lake Maracaibo. The rate of population growth is one of the highest in Latin America. There were only 2.4 million people in Venezuela in 1900, but by 1941, the population had grown to 3.8 million, and in 1950, to 5 million. The annual rate of growth has been between 3 and 4 percent. It is the result of a 50 percent fall in the death rate and the continuation of a very high birth rate. The urban areas are growing more rapidly than the rural areas, and since the great oil and building booms of the 1950s, thousands of poor farm workers have migrated to the cities, principally Caracas. The latter now has over 1.3 million people, of which 300,000 were unemployed in 1961. As in the case of other large cities in Latin America, Caracas has wretched slums. Racially, Venezuela consists of 20 percent whites, 65 percent *mestizos,* 8 percent Negroes, and 7 percent pure Indians. It is essentially a *mestizo* country like Mexico.

Venezuela has a great economic potential because of its low population density, unused land, and rich resources. It is also strategically located in a direct line from North to South America and in the middle of the Gulf of Mexico. It is near enough to the United States and Brazil to allow profitable trading in both directions. The great oil field of Lake Maracaibo is its leading natural resource, and as a result, Venezuela accounts for about a third of all the oil exports in the world. Its known reserves of oil, however, amounted in 1959 to only 18 billion barrels.[3] In addition to oil, Venezuela is rich in other resources. Its iron ore deposits in the hinterland of Puerto Ordaz and near the mouth of the Orinoco are among the largest in the world. It has considerable amounts of gold, copper, salt, tin, manganese, diamonds, and mica, and it also has some coal, and a great water-power potential. Its first hydroelectric power plant was inaugurated in 1959 and has a capacity of 400,000 kilowatts. The plant, located on the Caroni River, supplies power to Venezuela's new integrated steel mill which has an annual capacity of 750,000 tons of steel ingots.

But despite its wealth of resources, Venezuela has serious weaknesses. They consist of governmental instability, considerable illiteracy (over 40 percent), lack of general and technical education, and overdependence on oil exports for capital to develop the country, and the great need for land reform.

The History of Venezuela

The history of this Latin American country is perhaps not as important in determining its development as the history of Mexico and the ABC countries. But its current problems cannot be understood without some knowledge of its historical background. Venezuela was discovered by Columbus on his third voyage to America in which he found the mouth of the Orinoco. Subsequently, Alonzo Ojeda discovered Lake Maracaibo, and named the country "Little Venice" because he found the natives living in houses built on stilts. Venezuela was later colonized by Spain, but was considered one of her least prized possessions. In the period of revolution from 1810 to 1830, Venezuela furnished the great leader of the movement in northern South America, Simon Bolivar. It also supplied many of the men who followed Bolivar, and the population of Venezuela was reduced by 25 percent as a result of deaths among the men who served with him.

After 1830, when Venezuela became an independent nation by secession from Gran Colombia, the country went through twenty "new" constitutions, fifty armed revolts, and many dictatorships. Before the election of Betancourt in 1958, Venezuela

had scarcely more than a year of consecutive democratic government in its long hectic political history. *Caudillos* had dominated
almost continuously. Among the great caudillos or outright dictators were Jose Antonio Paez, Antonio Guzman Blanco, Cipri-
ano Castro, Juan Vincente Gomez, and Perez Jimenez.

The most vicious of the dictators was Gomez, who ruled
from 1908 to 1935. He had started life as a cattle hand in the
Andes, and succeeded in becoming a large rancher before he
seized the presidency. Like those who preceded him, he ruled in
the interests of the large landowners through his control of the
army. But in 1917 oil was discovered, and Gomez began to make
shrewd bargains with foreign interests over concessions to exploit
the oil. He played off American against Dutch and British businessmen to the benefit of Venezuelan tax receipts and his own
personal enrichment. Gomez, despite his personal faults[4] and
his brutal suppression of all opposition, began the modernization
of Venezuela. Its advancement through capital derived from oil
earnings started under Gomez. He used these earnings to pay off
the external public debt completely, built roads and public
works, improved sanitation, and increased public education. He
was an excellent administrator and gathered around him able
men.[5]

In 1935 Gomez died, and the long pent-up resentments against
El Benemerito, as he was called, broke loose. But Venezuela was
without strong parties or able leaders. For eleven years it was
governed by semidictatorships under army tutelage. First Lopez
Contreras, then Medina Angarita, both army officers, held the
presidency. Under the latter, opposition parties were finally
allowed to organize. The largest of these was the mildly leftist
Accion Democratica. Afraid that Medina would hold an unfair
election in 1945 and return General Lopez Contreras to the presidency, the Accion Democratica organized a successful coup and
made Romulo Betancourt provisional president. It was the first
triumph of civilians and the middle class over the military men
and the landowners.

The provisional government adopted a new constitution
providing for social legislation, the right to expropriate the oil
lands, and the election of the president by popular vote. It began
to remove corruption in the army and to recover the ill-gotten
wealth obtained by Gomez while president. By planning to

break up the large estates and distribute the land among the landless, the Accion Democratica was attempting to repeat the Mexican revolution of 1910–17. The first free election in Venezuelan history was held in 1947. Romulo Gallegos, the candidate of Accion Democratica, and a famous popular novelist, was elected president by a four-to-one vote. But Gallegos lasted in office only ten months. Although he moved slowly and moderately in carrying out the program of Accion Democratica, the conservative opposition, consisting of the irate generals, the landowners and those supporting the foreign oil interests, engineered a new military coup. Gallegos and Betancourt were exiled, and democracy came to an end. It has been charged that the Standard Oil Company of New Jersey and the other concessionaires were actively back of the coup, and Perón was also blamed. But Professor Herring believes that the oil companies were not involved.[6]

The new regime, consisting of a three-man military junta, came to power late in 1948; declared that it was the true defender of democracy; stated that it had saved Venezuela from communism; censored the press; and jailed its opponents including the labor leaders. The Accion Democratica was outlawed, and "went underground." It organized in secret cells among the farmers and workers. In order to obtain recognition from the United States, however, the junta agreed to hold a free election in 1952. The government party, a conservative democratic party (URD) and a clerical party (COPEI) were allowed to present candidates. Through foreign instruction from Betancourt, the Accion Democratica voters cast their ballots for the democratic and clerical parties, and the government party lost the election. But Marcos Perez Jimenez, one member of the three-man ruling junta, censored the election returns, announced that the government had won an overwhelming majority, and took office as provisional president. In 1953 a constituent assembly named him president. The dictatorship was thus continued.

The period of Jimenez was one of boom and rising prosperity, and it converted many of the common people into supporters of the dictatorship. Oil production increased and added much revenue to the Venezuelan budget. Some of these funds were used to build roads and public works, and to increase public health facilities and education. A great building boom occurred in Caracas, and it became a clean handsome city with fine hotels and public buildings. Job opportunities increased, and thousands of peasants migrated to Caracas in the hope of finding work. The government subsidized those who remained unemployed with security payments that often exceeded what they had earned on the farms. The city and the countryside were well policed, and the standard of living of the poorer people in Venezuela rose. Jimenez became increasingly popular.

The dictatorship strongly encouraged the influx of foreign capital. The Bethlehem Steel Company opened iron mines near Puerto Ordaz, and began to ship two million tons of ore a year to the United States. The great ore deposits were discovered in the Cerro Bolivar, southwest of the mouth of the Orinoco, and were developed by the United States Steel Company under a contract with the Venezuelan government. About 5 million tons a year were shipped to the United States from this great ore mountain which contains one of the largest ore reserves in the world. But no domestic steel industry was developed under Jimenez. American capital flowed into the country in large volume for a variety of other purposes, such as the building of pipe lines, refineries and assembly plants for automobiles. It cannot be denied that American business felt safe under Jimenez.

In 1957, however, Venezuela encountered economic difficulties. The Suez crisis which had boosted Venezuelan oil exports was over and tax receipts declined. In addition, building declined with the collapse of the land boom in Caracas. Construction machinery became idle and contractors began to seek work abroad. Unemployment in various types of work increased. The decline in oil exports also began to cause foreign trade balance problems. These economic difficulties strengthened the hand of the underground Accion Democratica, and opposition to the dictatorship grew until the armed forces with the overwhelming support of the people removed Jimenez in January, 1958. A junta was formed, consisting of three military men and two civilians. Civil liberties were immediately restored, and a free election was held in December, 1958. The Accion Democratica, supporting Betancourt for president, obtained almost a majority of the votes over the entire opposition of URD, the Democratic Republican Union, the Christian Social Party, COPEI, and the communists. Betancourt assumed the presidency for a five-year term.

Economic Consequences of Venezuelan History

In perspective, certain economic consequences of Venezuelan history stand out. In the first place, it is evident that Venezuela was one of the last of the Latin American countries to achieve middle-class government and to challenge the power of the landowners and the military forces. The challenge is still in doubt. But should the Accion Democratica continue in power, the triumph of the middle classes will date from the election of 1958. In Mexico, this victory was achieved in 1920, in Chile in 1925, in Brazil in 1935, and in Argentina in 1943. Colombia had attained middle-class control between 1930 and 1946, although it suffered a temporary setback in the presidency of the reactionary Gomez (1949–1953).[7]

The power of the landowners would have retarded industrialization in Venezuela had it not been for the fact that the dictators favored the inflow of foreign capital, especially American. But the industrialization that occurred under Gomez and Jimenez was very unbalanced. Mining was expanded and manufacturing and agriculture neglected. Venezuela became unduly dependent for its growth on oil and iron exports. Social overhead capital, however, was advanced to some extent as a result of the export earnings from oil and mining. Lastly, with the increase in production, wealth flowed into the hands of the few, and wealth and income were very unequally distributed. The upper cliques in politics and the armed forces, moreover, did not devote their earnings to investment in domestic enterprise and much of the new wealth flowed abroad.

Thus Venezuela is at the very threshold of such basic changes as internal industrialization, middle-class control, domestic investment, land reform, and government stimulation of enterprise through private and public investment which began long ago in other Latin American nations. It is both politically and economically immature, an odd situation for a country which is probably the richest in Latin America. It has not followed the Latin American economic policy revolution, and there is very little socialism. Until 1958 there was little national economic planning. But more than in most other Latin American nations, there is acceptance of free enterprise.

The history of Venezuela reveals also the gradual rise of a

strong mass sentiment, not only favoring civil liberty and democratic government, but rapid industrialization, a more equal distribution of the income derived from economic progress, honesty and efficiency in government administration, and extensive land reform. Perhaps more than anything else, the ability of the government to provide land reform will determine its tenure of office.

Land Problems and Reform in Venezuela

Although the upper classes in Venezuela were not happy about the Betancourt regime and the triumph of Accion Democratica, they seemed to think that a new military dictatorship would lead to revolution of a Castro-like character. Some of the supporters of Accion Democratica would certainly turn to the communists. The demand for land reform is too great to be denied. The only hope of the landowners is that land reform can be achieved to the satisfaction of the landless without undue disturbance of the large estates, and they are fortunate in that Betancourt tried to do just that.

In Venezuela, 10 percent of the landowners owned 85 percent of the arable land in 1958.[8] Earlier data for 1956 reveal that about two-thirds of the farmers, whether owners, tenants, or squatters, operated farms smaller than 5 hectares. A quarter of the farmers operated farms of less than one hectare.[9] Only a quarter of the farmers who lived on the land owned their farms, small though they might be. Another quarter were tenants. But half of the farmers lived on the land in a semilegal fashion. They were not owners, tenants, or paid workers. They were mere squatters with no legal status and operated the land on the sufferance of the owners who did not want to cultivate it themselves.

The fact that most of the Venezuelan farmers were squatters cultivating land on a subsistence basis is one of the reasons for the land policy adopted by the Betancourt government. The other is the existence of a large amount of unused land. In both the highlands and the *llanos,* there are many acres which could be used, if they were cleared or irrigated. There is much publicly owned land. No actual shortage of land exists although few own land. Consequently, the policy adopted by the government in the beginning of the land reform did not stress redistribution but cultivation. It is summed up in the statement, "the land belongs to those who cultivate it." As a result, no cultivated land, however large the tract, was subject to expropriation. But some land not cultivated by the owners has been expropriated and given to the squatters who lived on it and grew crops. Even *campesinos* who live on the land and are not now cultivating it but intend to do so can obtain ownership. The legal owners, however, are being compensated by the issue of government securities. There is no outright confiscation.

From 1958 to 1962, therefore, the policy was not to break up large estates if they were being cultivated and to compensate landowners when the land was expropriated. Moreover, not much private land was taken by the government. Its major efforts were directed toward the resettlement of farmers on new land. Venezuelan land reform followed the pattern originally adopted in Uruguay and now followed by Colombia and Peru rather than the policy of Mexico and, more recently, that of Bolivia and Cuba. In 1962, however, there was an important change. The government decreed that no estate should exceed 500 acres. Whether larger estates will be broken up remains to be seen. But this upper limit far exceeds the limits set in Cuba, Bolivia, and Mexico.

Land reform in Venezuela is broadly conceived. It does not end with the redistribution of land. One of the principal objectives of the government is to increase productivity. As the mission of the International Bank points out, the agricultural problem in Venezuela has two separate aspects, "the problem of increasing the production and efficiency of the commercialized sector, and the problem of raising the income and living standard of the subsistence farmer."[10]

In its attempts to increase productivity, the government has (1) resettled farmers on better land which is not on hillsides and already badly eroded. (2) provided seed and fertilizer, (3) established a large agricultural extension system, (4) provided credits and subsidies, (5) built new roads, (6) engaged in irrigation projects, (7) provided disease and pest control, and (8) engaged in agricultural research. By 1961, 30,000 farm families had been resettled on new farms. Over a half billion *bolivares* had been spent on the agricultural program as a whole. Farm prices had been stabilized at minimum levels by government buying and price fixing in product markets for corn, rice, cotton, sisal, potatoes, onions, coffee, cacao, and sugar. One government agricultural extension station had been set up for every 400 farm families. Between 1959 and 1961 the production of rice, potatoes, and eggs doubled.

Certain problems peculiar to Venezuela make the improvement of the state of the impoverished farmer difficult. In the first place, about 400,000 migrated to Caracas to find work. Some did, but most of them remained unemployed. They were supported by security payments initiated by Jimenez and increased in amount under Betancourt. These payments are a heavy drain on the national budget. Politically, it is dangerous to eliminate or reduce them. The unemployed workers are unwilling to move back to the country, and yet there is no industrial employment suitable for them. They have become an unproductive burden on the economy. No lure seems sufficient to get them to return to the country, even on new land. In addition, many poor farmers remaining in the country and farming very poor land seem unwilling to leave the exhausted and impoverished land on which they have always lived. Re-education in better farming methods is also proving difficult. With the present poor technology, farmers often cannot farm more than two hectares (about five acres).

Oil and Industrialization

As in most Latin American countries, the long-run solution for Venezuela's problems consists of industrialization. But Venezuela in the period from 1917 to 1957 largely followed the policies of Chile in an earlier period (1870 to 1920). The landowners wanted foreign capital to exploit the great natural resource, oil, so that they could avoid taxation. As a result, the economy became overly dependent on mining. Domestic industry was secondary. Such domestic industry as developed, however, was based on the export earnings of oil which gave Venezuela the import capacity to buy machinery and raw materials needed for industrial growth. No middle-class group came to power before 1957 which used the tariffs, exchange controls, and the national budget to promote general industrialism as in Argentina, Brazil, Chile, Colombia, Mexico, and Uruguay. As a result, Venezuela now needs "crash programs" for economic diversification.

Notwithstanding the lack of conscious planning for industrial growth by the governments of Gomez and Jimenez, there was one compensating factor. These men were not anticapitalist, antiforeign, or anti-American. During the regime of Jimenez especially, the influx of foreign capital promoted a rapid rate of growth. One estimate of the average annual increase in the gross national product between 1950 and 1959 is 8.3 percent a year.[11] The percentage of increase in annual growth in the various sectors of the economy was estimated as follows:[11]

Oil	7.6
Agriculture	5.5
Mining	40.0
Manufactures	11.4
Power and water	19.2
Construction	8.4
Transportation	5.1
Commerce	9.8
Services	6.1
Housing	9.7

But these growth rate estimates are undoubtedly too high. The International Monetary Fund has estimated the total growth rate at 6.8 percent between 1948 and 1959. The mission to Venezuela which supplied the higher rate of 8.3 percent warns of the inadequacy of the Venezuelan statistical data on which their report was based. However, if Venezuela actually grew at 6 to 8 percent a year after World War II, the growth was not due to public planning and investment, but to the great influx of foreign capital, coming largely from the United States.

Perhaps Venezuela provides an important object lesson for Latin America. Without government planning and control, it grew faster than many of the other countries *because it permitted and encouraged a great inflow of foreign capital.* It may have refuted the belief that nations which are underdeveloped can rise more rapidly through the "bootstrap" method. But one is inclined to conclude that without great mining resources, Venezuela would not have attracted a great amount of American investment. Also, had the government pursued policies in which the great wealth from oil earnings was channeled into new domestic industrial investments, and had not allowed it to enrich Gomez and other politicians and be invested abroad, the results for Venezuela's economic growth would have been phenomenal. The growth would have been better balanced and the fruits of progress would have by now greatly increased the income of the average Venezuelan.

Thus the economic growth of Venezuela has been more affected by foreign investment than that of any other Latin American nation. Brazil, Chile, Colombia, and Peru have also received large amounts of foreign funds, but other factors such as inflation and exchange control played a large part in their growth. There has been virtually no inflation in Venezuela. Consumer prices rose only 8 percent between 1953 and 1959.

But the fact that foreign investment in Venezuela was largely in petroleum explains the difficulties that Venezuela began to experience after 1957. Petroleum investments declined in 1953, but they revived again in 1955 and were stimulated by the Suez crisis. However, as we have pointed out, the crisis ended in the middle of 1957 and petroleum investments slumped badly. Investors were dubious about the long-run prospects of Venezuelan oil. The supply of oil in the world now exceeded demand and the costs of oil production in Venezuela were almost double those in the Middle East. The decline in petroleum investments might have been offset by new direct investments in manufacturing. But Brazil, Mexico, Peru, and Chile attracted more American investment for this purpose than Venezuela, although some of the American manufacturing capital went there. Lack of mass purchasing power was one reason why Venezuela was by-passed.

At the same time that Americans were less attracted by investment in Venezuelan petroleum, the climate for investment in Venezuela deteriorated. American business interests, especially oil men, have been suspicious of Accion Democratica. They are afraid that it will turn to the left and engage in widespread expropriation of American capital. In addition, the threat of communism in Venezuela has become serious. As a result of these various factors deterring foreign investment and also causing a serious flight of domestic capital, Betancourt had either to restore the confidence of investors, both foreign and domestic, or resort to forced domestic saving and public investment.

It would seem that Venezuela must take a number of positive steps if it is to sustain and promote its industrial growth: (1) Reduction of its dependence on oil earnings for social overhead and domestic investment. (2) Encouragement of foreign investment by disavowing expropriation. (The establishment of a national petroleum corporation did not promote confidence.) (3) Equalization of income to some extent through more progressive taxation and higher wages so as to create a basis for greater purchasing power. (4) Discouragement of the foreign flight of domestic capital by restoring confidence, and, if necessary, by the continuation of the embargo imposed on the export of capital. (5) Development of public investment. (Venezuela has already made some progress in the fields of hydroelectric power and irrigation.) (6) Formulation of a sound national economic plan and the adoption of controls through credit and business regulations to carry it out. (7) Assistance for its programs of social investment and agricultural reform from the Alliance for Progress. (8) A rapid increase in education, both general and technical. (No advanced industrialism can be created with great illiteracy and the lack of technicians and efficient managers.)

Conclusions

In conclusion, Venezuela's future and the future of the moderate democratic regime of Accion Democratica depend on successful and rapid agricultural reform and the growth of balanced industrialism. The latter must be far less dependent on capital derived from petroleum earnings and much more dependent on domestic and foreign capital devoted to manufacturing and the development of hydroelectric power. Venezuela's prime needs are *capital* and *education*. It already has the land and the resources needed for a great economic future.

It may be added that Venezuela has consistently violated many of the precepts of economic development theory. It has attempted to industrialize without the growth of agricultural productivity. Industrialism requires a strong agricultural base. It has allowed unbalanced industrial development to occur. It has failed to provide for a rising level of income and purchasing power as a basis for the expansion of domestic industry. It has allowed domestic capital to go abroad, and it has failed to advance its social overhead investment rapidly enough to adapt the people to industrialism. It has also failed to cope with its great cultural dualism, and even today land reform is seriously retarded by the attitudes not only of large landowners but of the poor farm workers as well. Venezuela needs an ideological revolution. It needs also to accept some of the features of the economic policy revolution.

By 1963, however, the Betancourt government had begun to move in the direction of greater economic planning. A national planning office was established, and it drew up a four-year development plan with the assistance of a mission from the International Bank for Reconstruction and Development. The Venezuelan government seemed fully aware of the need for balanced industrial growth. The Venezuelans also were trying to establish a basic core of iron and steel production to aid the growth of their manufacturing industries. A new steel plant was built for the government on the Orinoco River at Matanzas by an Italian firm. The whole Guayana area near the juncture of the Orinoco and Caroni Rivers is being developed to produce steel, iron ore, and electric power. Industrial and power projects were coordinated by a government corporation, the *Corporacion Venezulana de Guayana*. If Venezuela can continue this form of economic planning, and simultaneously make progress in domestic capital accumulation, social development, and agricultural reform, it will have a bright future.

References

1. International Bank for Reconstruction and Development, *The Economic Development of Venezuela*, Johns Hopkins Press, Baltimore, 1961, p. 3. The Chase-Manhattan Bank figure for 1960 was $1,120.

2. Angel Falls, discovered in 1937 by Jimmy Angel, an American aviator. They are 3,212 feet high.

3. The United States had 34 billion barrels, and the Middle East, 181.4 billion.

4. He never married and had numerous illegitimate children, some of whom he richly endowed at public expense.

5. Cf. Herring, *op. cit.*, p. 468.

6. Herring, *op. cit.*, p. 470.

7. In all these countries, however, except Mexico, the triumph of the middle class meant mainly urban industrialization rather than land reform and the political power of the landlords remained great.

8. Lorenz Stucki, "Venezuela's Alternative to Castro," *Die Weltwoche*, April 7, 1961.

9. *Encuesta Agropecuaria Nacional*, 1956.

10. International Bank for Reconstruction and Development, *op. cit.*, p. 145.

11. International Bank for Reconstruction and Development, *op. cit.*, p. 28.

EIGHTEEN

CENTRAL AMERICA AND THE CARIBBEAN ISLANDS

MIDDLE LATIN AMERICA CONSISTS OF TWO GROUPS OF COUNTRIES, the Central American nations below Mexico and the larger islands of the Caribbean Sea. Most of these nations are oriented toward the United States, and are dependent on us for trade to a considerable degree. In the first group we have six nations, extending south from Mexico, Guatemala, El Salvador, Honduras, Nicaragua, Costa Rica, and Panama. Island Latin America consists of four countries, if Puerto Rico is included. But the latter is a part of the United States, and, strictly speaking, cannot be classified as a part of Latin America. The three independent nations are Cuba, Haiti, and the Dominican Republic. In terms of population Cuba, Guatemala, and Haiti are the largest, and Costa Rica and Panama the smallest of these Central American and Caribbean countries.

Most of the middle American nations have little in the way of resources. In Guatemala there is some iron ore and an intensive search is being made to discover oil. In El Salvador there is virtually nothing except good forests rich in mahogany. The Dominican Republic has some iron and bauxite. Puerto Rico and Nicaragua, apart from land, also lack resources. But Honduras, Costa Rica, Cuba, and Haiti have considerable reserves of minerals which have not yet been developed. In Honduras there is copper, lead, zinc, iron, and coal. Costa Rica has quartz, granite, oil, mercury, sulphur, and copper. In Cuba there are large deposits of iron ore, and in Haiti, copper, antimony, tin, and sulphur.

There are great differences among the central American and Caribbean countries as to population density and the rate of population growth. Cuba, the Dominican Republic, El Salvador, and Haiti are overpopulated, and in some of the countries—notably Costa Rica, the Dominican Republic, and El Salvador

Country	Population per Square Mile	Annual Rate of Growth
Costa Rica	57.2	4.0
Cuba	152.5	1.9
Dominican Republic	217.6	3.5
El Salvador	316.3	3.5
Guatemala	89.4	3.0
Haiti	327.1	1.2
Honduras	45.1	3.3
Nicaragua	25.4	3.4
Panama	36.6	2.9
Puerto Rico	68.5	— *

* The rate of growth of population in Puerto Rico cannot be fully estimated without taking account of those who have migrated to the continental United States. This is too difficult statistically to arrive at a good estimate of growth.

—the rate of population growth is very great. The table gives population densities and annual rates of growth in 1960.[1]

Industrialism has not progressed very far in most of these countries. Puerto Rico, Costa Rica, Panama, and Cuba have made the most progress. The rest of the countries have hardly advanced beyond a few small factories supplying a limited number of products used domestically. Per capita incomes are so low in most of the countries that there is little demand for manufactured goods. The incomes of these countries according to Professor Kindleberger ranged in 1953 from $296 per capita in Cuba to Haiti with $70 per capita. In the years from 1948 to 1959, some of the middle Latin American countries went ahead rapidly. In 1959 the per capita income of Costa Rica was the fourth highest in Latin America ($410). Per capita income in Cuba was either above that of Costa Rica or not far behind. The following are

Costa Rica	$ 425 *
Cuba	250
Dominican Republic	230
El Salvador	225
Guatemala	200
Haiti	110
Honduras	200
Nicaragua	170
Panama	400
Puerto Rico	622

* Excessive growth of population in Costa Rica is choking off the growth of per capita income. The Chase-Manhattan Bank even estimates that per capita income was only $333 in 1962.

estimated per capita incomes for 1962 based on production growth and population rates and on the economic consequences of the revolution in Cuba.[2]

Forms of government in middle Latin America reveal a great range also. At one extreme we have Cuba with a Marxist-Leninist dictatorship linked to the Soviet bloc. At the other extreme, we have Puerto Rico, a part of the United States with a semi-independent democratic commonwealth government, and Costa Rica which has had genuine democratic government for many years. In El Salvador a progressive military dictatorship controlled for several years until a free election was held in 1962. In Honduras there was until 1963 a democratic government with welfare-state characteristics, and in Nicaragua a government which is democratic in form but is actually controlled by the Somoza family.

A wide variation exists also in regard to literacy, schooling, and public health. Illiteracy of the population over ten years of age in 1959 was over 80 percent in Haiti, 61 to 75 percent in Guatemala, El Salvador, Honduras, Nicaragua, and the Dominican Republic, and 14 to 30 percent in Costa Rica, Panama, and Cuba. In Puerto Rico, illiteracy had fallen to 13 percent. In Costa Rica, Panama, Cuba, and Puerto Rico there are good public school systems, but in most of the other countries public education is limited and very poor.

The Economic Problems of Central America

The Central American states have many critical economic problems. There are the evils of monoculture, and the need for land reform; the lack of resources, industrialism, and capital; the needs for a common market and better roads and transportation facilities; the great need for social investment in education, health, and welfare; the problem of cultural dualism; the tendency of population to grow more rapidly than production; and the need for new energy sources such as hydroelectric power.

The middle Latin American countries are largely agricultural. Farming consists of two kinds—commercial farming of export crops, mostly, except in Costa Rica and Haiti, on large plantations, and subsistence farming on small plots of land. In some countries such as Honduras the majority of the population is engaged in subsistence agriculture. Export crops, however, vitally affect the general prosperity and development of these economies because they determine their import capacity. In central Latin America the most important export crops are coffee, bananas, and cotton. Of some importance also are cacao and sisal. Guatemala, Panama, and Honduras are banana countries and El Salvador and Nicaragua are coffee countries. Costa Rica and Guatemala have large exports of both commodities.

In 1960 the price of bananas fell to the lowest point in 18 years, 3.8 cents a pound. In 1961, however, the price had recovered to 6 cents due to the effects of bad weather and a disease which has spread from Panama. Thus, one of the problems of specializing in banana production is wide fluctuations in prices. But in addition there is long-run decline in the demand for bananas in the United States. Although demand has risen in Europe, the countries which depend so heavily on bananas for export earnings, such as Honduras and Panama, cannot hope to grow very much more on the basis of this new market.

A similar point may be made in regard to coffee. The world production of coffee has been increasing much more rapidly than the demand. Heavy dependence on coffee for export earnings not only subjects the countries involved to great fluctuations of income due to price changes but limits their rate of growth. The demand for coffee has been increasing by only 3 percent a year.

One solution for the problems of monoculture is agricultural diversification. Some of the Central American countries have turned to cotton, sisal, cacao, and other products. But demand in these fields is also limited. The best way out is to gradually reduce the reliance on export crops and turn to industrialism and domestic food production. But this requires capital and a growing domestic market. These countries need development programs and American capital.

Honduras and Nicaragua

Various problems of Central America are illustrated by the situations in Honduras and Nicaragua. In Honduras there is so little industrialism and urbanism that 83 percent of the people are farmers. In 1962 only 4 percent of the land was cultivated, however. Most of the agriculture was on a primitive subsistence level. Three quarters of the farms did not even have ploughs. Most of the houses were floorless mud huts. The roads were inadequate and half the children were receiving no education at all. About 65 percent of the population was illiterate. In Honduras there is only one important enterprise—the growing of bananas on plantations working for the American United and Standard Fruit Companies. This is declining because of the poor demand for bananas, and the insistence of the unions of banana workers on unproductively high wages and fringe benefits. The unions have made repeated demands which the companies cannot afford to meet, and they may soon be compelled to leave Honduras.[3] But there is no other way to earn money for commodity and capital imports.

Industrialism is almost nonexistent. There is a little light industry. In 1951 there were only 20,000 people employed in industrial establishments. These were mostly small-scale, employing on the average only five workers per establishment. This pathetic underdevelopment exists in spite of the fact that Honduras has a considerable amount of mineral wealth, including iron ore.

Beginning in 1950, the governments of Honduras have begun to give serious attention to the economic and social problems of the country. A central bank and a national development bank have been established. A new constitution was adopted in 1957 which provides for greater governmental centralization, extensive government regulation of the economy and new welfare measures. There was no need to provide land reform in the sense of land redistribution, however. Honduras, unlike El Salvador or Nicaragua, has never had much concentration of land tenure. Most of the people own land as a result of progressive agrarian laws enacted as early as 1835. Land has been given away or sold to the people at very low prices with the result that many Hondurans own land.

The government of the Liberal Party under President José Ramón Villeda Morales attempted to encourage development through planning and heavy deficit spending. A new labor and social security law was introduced in 1959. It provides even more comprehensive welfare benefits than exist in the United States. An example is the provision of full pay during illness for a period up to eight months.[5] But, as in the case of other Latin American countries such as Argentina and Chile, Honduras could not afford extensive social security. As a result, there has been a considerable amount of inflation with no great increase in production or income. Economic difficulties played a large part in the overthrow of Morales by the military in 1963.

The future of Honduras lies in economic planning and American aid. A national economic council has prepared a four-year development plan. On the basis of this plan, Honduras will obtain aid under the Alliance for Progress. With loans from the Inter-American Development Bank, Honduras had already begun her industrial program in 1962 by starting a hydroelectric project on the Rio Lindo.

The problems of Nicaragua are similar to those of Honduras except that in Nicaragua there is a problem of land concentration. In 1962 Nicaragua was considering an agrarian reform law which would authorize the expropriation of idle land and its distribution among the landless peasants. The owners were to be compensated by the *Instituto Nacional Agrario*. Nicaragua was planning reform along the lines of Venezuela, Colombia, and Peru. Nicaragua differs from Honduras also in that it has virtually no resources except land and forests. Nicaragua, however, is one of the few countries which has made progress in agricultural diversification. Cotton instead of coffee is now the leading export, and lumber exports are increasing. Both Nicaragua and Honduras have been severely criticized by Americans for lagging behind in economic planning.

Costa Rica

In the middle of Central America, Costa Rica stands out as the one country which has made considerable economic progress. The question is often asked: why has this one country in Central America gone ahead?

The reasons for Costa Rica's advancement are to be found in the early history of this small nation. In the beginning of the sixteenth century, fifty-five Spanish families moved into the Meseta Central, or central highlands. This region has an altitude of 3,000–4,000 feet, and a temperate to semitropical climate. By 1572, however, the Spaniards were faced with a difficult decision. They had to leave the country or give up the hacienda system. The small Indian population on which they relied for serf labor was dying out from the white man's diseases. The final decision to stay and farm the land themselves was unusual for Spaniards. As a result of the decision, Costa Rica became a country of small farms worked by their owners who were almost entirely white in racial origin. The small farms eventually proved more efficient than the haciendas.

In 1796 another important decision was made. The country needed exports to pay for imports of raw materials and manufactured goods. As an export product, the Costa Ricans decided to grow coffee, and they became the first coffee producers in Central America. The sale of coffee proved profitable, and incomes rose. The government, then located in Cartago, encouraged the growing population to move north, and take up new land for coffee planting. San José, which eventually became the capital, was founded. The pioneer movement of prospective coffee planters continued for some years. The excess population around Cartago was drained off, going first to the north, and then to the south also. Before Costa Rica turned to coffee it had been even poorer than Nicaragua.

It is apparent that a number of factors explain Costa Rica's advancement and higher income. First of all, small independent farming was more efficient than the system of large estates using Indian labor. Independent farming promoted democracy, and democracy led to the stress on education which is still great in Costa Rica. The early production of coffee also gave Costa Rica a head start. In addition, stable government, a by-product of democracy, encouraged the investment of foreign capital. The promoter Minor C. Kieth built a railroad from Limon on the Caribbean to San José. The government assisted transportation to San José by building many roads for coffee carts. Kieth added to his railroad traffic by establishing banana plantations in the Caribbean lowlands. These were worked by Negro labor brought from Jamaica. Further diversification occurred when cattle raising was started in the western lowlands near the Pacific. Labor in this area consists largely of *mestizos*. Costa Rica today has considerable agricultural diversity. In addition to coffee, bananas, and cattle, Costa Ricans raise much corn, sugar, rice, potatoes, beans, cotton, and cacao.

The history of Costa Rica seems to prove that any country in Central America could, by education and by habits of hard work and thrift, greatly raise its living standard even without large mineral resources or a goodly amount of foreign capital. Costa Rica has not followed the usual pattern of Latin America, and yet has advanced. There has been no inflation, no semi-fascist government, no deficit spending through erroneous use of Keynesian principles, and no great amount of economic planning. Apparently, Costa Rica has not needed these methods for its advancement.

Costa Rica, moreover, has been fortunate in not having two types of retarding factors which have plagued other Latin American countries. There is no large landowning class which can thwart agricultural progress and restrict education and welfare measures. There is also no elite of army officers to create dictatorships, support large landowners in their social backwardness, and live in corruption on the growing wealth of the nation. In fact, there is no army at all. Instead of the stultifying influence of landowners and generals, Costa Rica has had liberal democratic civilian leaders like José Figueres and Otilio Ulate. The former is one of the greatest democratic leaders in all Latin America. The great problem of Costa Rica today is the excessive growth of population.

Caribbean America: Haiti and the Dominican Republic

Haiti, one of the four Caribbean countries, is unique in Latin America. It has an almost completely Negro and mulatto population of French and African origins. It is Latin America's second poorest nation. Only Bolivia is poorer. It has the greatest population density in Latin America, but the slowest rate of population growth due to very poor health facilities. There is more illiteracy in Haiti than in any other part of Latin America. Although Haiti has enjoyed a considerable amount of tourism and has mineral resources, it has failed to develop economically. Coffee, sisal, cotton, and sugar are its chief exports. It has every problem mentioned in our list of middle American problems except excessive concentration of land holdings and monoculture.[5] Preston James has characterized the Haitians as follows: "The average rural Haitian is not a person of great ambition, nor one who takes naturally to the complexities of commercial life. . . . Only those things necessary to satisfy the fewest wants are produced. . . . The attitude toward the land and the use of the land is essentially African. Land ownership does not give prestige to the owner, and there is no urge to sell a surplus of things for profit."[6]

An enlightened government might conceivably give Haiti the "big push" it needs, but it would be working against the tremendous obstacle of a culture and cultural attitudes which are contrary to those needed for economic progress. Among these attitudes is a kind of antiforeignism and isolationism. In the past, foreign capital has not been encouraged and foreigners could not own land.

In recent years, Haiti has suffered from continuous trade deficits. Coffee earnings have declined. The tourist trade has been disappointing and little has been done to encourage it. The government, however, has undertaken to balance the economy through an austerity program, and has established a development body, the *Institut de Development Agricole et Industriel.* Loans have been made for development by the Inter-American Development Bank. Haiti has planned a TVA project in the Artibonite valley. It has also begun to accept Canadian capital on a concession basis to develop its copper resources. By 1963, under President François Duvalier, Haiti had become a backward, stagnant, and very repressive dictatorship.

The Dominican Republic which shares the other half of the island originally known as Hispaniola is now in a period of transition following the assassination of the dictator, Rafael Trujillo. Under Trujillo, who came to power in 1930, the Dominican Republic made considerable progress. For over twenty years the budget was balanced and the earnings from the exports of sugar, cacao, and coffee increased to over $100 million. Impressive public buildings and public works were erected. Santa Domingo was modernized and renamed Cuidad Trujillo in honor of the "Benefactor of the Fatherland." New, safe water supplies were developed, and good roads were built throughout the island. Public education and public health facilities increased. Considerable progress in industrialization occurred with the growth of food processing plants, distilleries, cement works and sugar mills. But the progress was made at the cost of freedom and at the cost of greatly enriching the Trujillo family. The growth in the national income did not find its way into the pockets of the masses. The future of the Dominican Republic depends on the ability of the nation to maintain progress without restrictions on freedom, and to establish democracy in a country which has not been educated for it. Failure of the government under its democratically elected president, Juan Bosch, to achieve these objectives nearly resulted in a Castro-like revolution. Before the fall of Bosch, the Dominican Republic had the full cooperation of the United States, a great asset. The trade embargo had been removed, and both governmental and private capital was flowing in.

Cuba

The sensational danger point in middle Latin America is, of course, Cuba. In this volume we do not have space to do justice to the economic and political influence of the Castro Revolution. In 1963, however, the influence of the revolution had declined to some extent. This resulted from the sordid revelations of refugees, the overtheatricalism of Castro, the visits of President Kennedy to Venezuela, Colombia, and Mexico, the improvement of economic conditions in other countries and the Alliance for Progress. Cuba had failed, at least for the time being, to serve as the focal point for similar revolutions in Venezuela, the Dominican Republic, Chile, Brazil, and Ecuador. Some believed that the Soviet Union had begun to regret its heavy investment in the Cuban revolution.

Castro had taken over the Cuban government on January 1, 1959 with the flight of Batista. Dr. Manuel Urrutia, an anti-communist liberal, had become president. But by July 1959 the communists had virtually gained control. Urrutia resigned, and Dr. Osvaldo Dorticos Torrado became president. Before this change, the revolution had concentrated on land reform and non-Marxist leftists were in control. The basic agrarian reform law was promulgated in May, 1959, and a National Institute of Agrarian Reform established. The large estates were expropriated without compensation. The sugar mills, of which American interests had owned about 40 percent, also were confiscated.

On October 13, 1960 the next stage of the revolution began. The government nationalized 383 large businesses and some banks.[7] Cuba openly proclaimed itself Marxist. The crowds began to shout Marxist slogans, and death was threatened for non-Marxists. Blas Roca, the Secretary General of the Communist Party in Cuba (P.S.P.), declared that the leadership of the workers (and of the country) rested with the Communist Party. Fidel Castro was now not the only leader, but merely the "maximum leader." The communist-controlled bureaucracy was taking over the actual functioning of the government. The public was increasingly controlled by Committees of Revolutionary Defense. The communist-controlled militia assumed the functions of the army, and the army was given the safer function of construction work. The sizable Cuban middle class fled in thousands, and Cuba was left short of technicians, managers, and professional men.

During the regime of Batista, Cuba had the fourth largest per capita income in Latin America. Considerable progress had been made, although the annual rate of growth was slow. A large and efficient middle class had developed. But incomes were very unequally distributed, land ownership was highly concentrated, and very little was being done to enhance the welfare of the landless sugar farmers. These conditions were the seeds of the revolution. Unlike Trujillo, Batista and his followers made little effort to aid the masses. Trujillo did a great deal more for both the economy and the common people of his country than Batista. The upper classes in Cuba were indifferent to the great danger of revolution, and the United States also shared in this indifference. Even after Castro assumed power, we seemed naively unaware of the political vacuum in Cuba, and the inevitable result—government by the Communist Party.

Many people wonder whether the Cuban socialist economy can survive. Before the revolution, Cuba was largely dependent on the United States. We bought most of its sugar and tobacco, and supplied it with large earnings from the tourist trade. We also supplied much business and industrial capital. The revolution caused Cuba to change from economic dependence on the United States to dependence on the Soviet Union. But the transition is difficult. The Soviet Union, which is now one of the largest beet sugar producers in the world, cannot be expected to continue to buy great quantities of Cuban cane sugar. However, out of the anticipated production of 6.5 million tons of sugar in 1961, the Soviet Union agreed to take 4.86 million tons. To finance the new four-year economic plan, Cuba needs to sell 6.5 million tons of sugar a year to Russia and other countries.

There are other difficulties besides the loss of the American sugar market. The embargo on American exports has created shortages. We were exporting rice, a staple of the Cuban diet, and machinery and machine parts. In 1961, machinery was breaking down badly without the American replacement parts needed for repairs.

Production in general began to decline. Cuba had lost many of its technicians and skilled workers. Sugar output collapsed and Cuba was unable even to supply the Soviet Union with the 4.8 million tons it had promised. Although there was much publicity as to the supply of machinery and technical aid gained from the Soviet Union, the amount is uncertain, and a good deal of it was military. By 1961, failures of production were openly admitted by government officials, and the workers and the new untrained managers were exhorted to work harder for the sake of the revolution.

Guevara announced in 1961 that 207 factories from the Soviet bloc would be put into operation by 1965. But in 1962 only three of these factories were operating.[8] Cuba continued to suffer from sabotage and absenteeism. The guerilla warfare against the regime could not be stopped. In the summer of 1961 Castro attempted to win over the remaining merchants and small industrialists. Limited property rights were restored, and an effort was made to remove some of the inequities caused by confiscations of property.

As in other communist countries, planning is of prime importance. A Cuban central planning committee was set up (Juceiplan). The committee consisted of Dr. Castro and three leading communists. Under the committee were six provincial planning committees and many local committees. The four-year economic plan has stressed diversification of agriculture, development of consumer-goods industries, elimination of the fat shortage, increase of electric power, and production of steel. The economic ministries were to administer the plan. The most important of these was the Ministry of Industries headed by Ernesto ("Che") Guevara. Together with Raúl Castro and Blas Roca, Guevara has exercised great influence on Cuban policies.

Whether the socialist economy will succeed in removing shortages, raising production, and improving the standard of living remains to be seen. It is also uncertain as to how much austerity the Cuban people can stand. In real terms, income has been at least halved. The regime is largely supported by the farm workers and the poorer elements in the population who believe Castro's extravagant promises of a bright future and who have relished the expropriation of the propertied classes. In 1964 Russia gave Cuba a new trade agreement designed to assist its long-run development and to prevent Cuba from becoming a satellite of Communist China.

Puerto Rico

In striking contrast to Cuba is the semi-Latin American country, Puerto Rico. Only a brief survey of the remarkable growth of this island can be given. Puerto Rico and its people are a part of the United States largely by choice. They have a degree of Latin American nationalism, but it is not sufficiently strong to offset the obvious advantages they enjoy from remaining a part of the United States. Consequently, the independence movement in Puerto Rico is weak.

In 1950 the per capita income of Puerto Rico was a little over $300. In 1963 it exceeded $900. From 1950 to 1963 gross national product grew more rapidly in Puerto Rico than in the continental United States. A growth for the period of 7.5 percent a year was sustained despite the depressions of 1953 and 1957–59. Puerto Rico advanced until it had the highest per capita income in Latin America except for Venezuela.[9] Although trade with the United States, which accounts for one third of the economic life of Puerto Rico, has increased only 2 percent, internal production has increased 9 percent. The economy is developing rapidly internally, and may become much less dependent on outside trade.

Economic growth in Puerto Rico can be attributed almost entirely to industrialism and tourism. Industrial growth is largely due to a heavy influx of capital investment from the United States. The inflow of capital, in its turn, is due to a number of factors: (1) liberal tax exemptions to attract business investment, (2) low wages, (3) the expanding internal market demand, and (4) the safety of investment since Puerto Rico is a part of the United States. The Chase-Manhattan Bank sums it up by saying that "new plants with modern techniques adapted to Puerto Rican conditions, plus modernization of older plants, and the growing number of skilled workers and technicians, has enabled most companies to maintain a strong competitive edge relative to their counterparts on the mainland."[10]

Investment has amounted to as much as 21 percent of the total income of Puerto Rico. By 1963 there were over 900 new industrial plants. Forty percent of these plants, moreover, were of local origin. Although investment from the continent has been great, local investment is now great also. Puerto Rico has passed the "take-off" point, and is growing indigenously at a rapid rate. Puerto Ricans, unlike other Latin Americans, have no inducement to invest abroad. Also, when money is made in Puerto Rico it is not wasted on lavish conspicuous consumption. The island is infected with an optimistic, aggressive business psychology. Although a certain amount of indolence and lack of ambition based on the old feudalistic land system still exists, modern attitudes are rapidly taking hold.

Between 1951 and 1961 Puerto Rico passed over the line between an agrarian and an industrial economy. In 1951 the net income of Puerto Rico derived from agriculture and manufacturing amounted to $310 million. Of this, $102 million came from sugar cultivation, $93 million from other forms of agriculture, and $115 million from manufacturing. In 1961, the net income from these three sources had grown to $519 million. But of this amount, only $71 million came from sugar cultivation, $128 million from other agriculture, and $320 million from manufacturing. Income from manufacturing had expanded 260 percent. Only 14 percent of *total* net income came from agriculture while 22 percent came from manufacturing. Thus Puerto Rico is becoming primarily a manufacturing and commercial economy. It no longer depends so heavily on agriculture, and agriculture itself has become more diversified. There is less emphasis on sugar cultivation, and much more emphasis on the production of food for domestic consumption.

Considering the size and character of Puerto Rico, these changes are decidedly in the right direction. As we have said, the country lacks resources. It is also too small to support a large population from agriculture. The obvious need is industrialization with a large capital investment devoted to light industry. Other needs are better education, housing, and sanitation, and a level of wages low enough to attract investment. As a result of following policies along these lines, capital investment in Puerto Rico reached $323 million in 1960, and the gross national product was $1,573 million.

The achievement of Puerto Rico is due in part to development planning under what has been called "Operation Bootstrap." Puerto Rico set up a development corporation which has the power to make loans for business enterprises and to undertake projects of its own. The development program was headed by Teodoro Moscoso who was later appointed chief of the Alliance for Progress division of AID by President Kennedy. The Puerto Rican development program has stressed industrial diversification. The government has assisted by providing a tenyear exemption from local taxation which was extended for three years. Some firms are now at the end of thirteen years of tax exemption. In spite of this, there seems to be no tendency to move out after local taxes are imposed. The Puerto Rican Chamber of Commerce has also played a part by providing much information as to business opportunities. The United States Government has assisted through financial and technical aid. It has also allowed Puerto Rico to import raw materials for industrial purposes free of customs duties.

Despite Puerto Rico's advance, it has a number of serious problems. One of these is the concentration of land tenure. This is especially the case in the sugar plantations. At one time, half of the sugar in Puerto Rico came from the plantations of four large companies. Another problem is unemployment. The population has grown at a faster rate than the economy could cope with in either agricultural or industrial employment. A great amount of unemployment has resulted. Between 1950 and 1960 it averaged 13 to 15 percent a year. In 1961, however, it fell to 11 percent. Some of the unskilled migrate seasonally or permanently to the United States, and there also has been migration of trained workers seeking higher paid jobs. In recent years, however, the trained workers have found better employment at home, and the migration consists largely of the unskilled. In 1960 there were 750,000 Puerto Ricans in New York City alone.

Puerto Rico provides valuable lessons for Latin American development. The progress of this island proves the great value of six factors: (1) better education, (2) foreign capital, (3) domestic saving and capital accumulation, (4) diversification of both industry and agriculture, (5) stable government which guarantees property rights, and (6) a progressive business-minded attitude on the part of the people. Puerto Ricans today insist that they are Americans with the ambitions and attitudes that prevail in the rest of the United States. This is largely true. It explains the use of the above six factors to bring progress to the island of Borinquen.

References

1. William Benton, *Voice of Latin America*, Harper and Brothers, New York, 1961, p. 23.

2. These are the author's estimates based on an independent income analysis.

3. William S. Stokes, "Honduras: Dilemma of Development," *Current History*, February 1962, pp. 83–84.

4. Stokes, *op. cit.*, p. 87.

5. Most of the land in Haiti is held in small plots which grow even smaller with division at the death of the owners. The Haitian elite, along with the original French, lost the great estates.

6. Preston James, *Latin America*, Odyssey Press, New York, 1942, p. 771.

7. Altogether, the Cuban government has confiscated over $1 billion of American property including sugar land, sugar mills, and other business property.

8. David D. Burks, "Economic Prospects for Cuba," *Current History*, February 1962, p. 81.

9. "Puerto Rico Moves Ahead," *Latin American Business Highlights*, Chase-Manhattan Bank, 4th quarter 1961, p. 7.

10. *Ibid.*, p. 8.

V

The Future of
Latin America

NINETEEN

THE FUTURE NEEDS OF
LATIN AMERICA

WE HAVE NOW SURVEYED THE ECONOMIC PROBLEMS OF LATIN America—as they affect all or most of the nations, and in their specific applications to each nation. The past and the present have been discussed, but what of the future? Will it be bright or dark, capitalist or communist, democratic or fascist? Latin America is in transition from conditions and policies which have prevailed for a century or more. The outcome is not clear. It is especially difficult to predict how Latin Americans will solve their problems in the long run.

There are however, a number of certainties in the Latin American scene. There is no doubt that a social revolution is taking place in which the lower classes, having become aware of their lowly state, are now convinced that it can be greatly improved. Through liberal, radical, fascist, and communist leadership, they are becoming politically active in their own behalf. It is certain also that nationalism is growing stronger, and with it, a great urge for economic and political independence. Both anti-Yankeeism and pro-communism are by-products of this new nationalism. Finally, it is evident that the social revolution has reached a critical stage in half of the countries, notably Argentina, Bolivia, Brazil, Chile, Colombia, Cuba, the Dominican Republic, Guatemala, Ecuador, Honduras, Peru, and Venezuela.

The crisis in the social revolution arises from the failure to solve long-standing economic problems in a period in world history when social change has become imperative. Economic growth which was considerable between 1945 and 1957 has stagnated, and in some countries per capita income has actually declined. Instead of going forward, some of the nations have gone backward at a time when the need for progress was most

267

urgent. Economic independence, another prime objective, has not been achieved.

From the point of view we have expressed in these pages, there is an ideal way out for Latin America, consisting of the economic policy revolution and the acceptance of a sound theory of economic development as previously described in Chapter 6. Latin America would do well to follow this theory and a comprehensive plan based on it. But whether this point of view is right or wrong for Latin America, the willingness of the nations to accept it is by no means certain. Their acceptance of the economic policy revolution in the years 1930–57 was fragmentary and intermittent.

Political and Social Needs

By 1960 most of the governments of Latin America had become democratic or semidemocratic and a new and optimistic leadership had appeared which represented the political middle. It was not fascist or communist, nor did it represent the old conservative forces, the *hacendados,* and the military. The new leaders believed in democracy and the promotion of the general welfare, and they represented liberal business, the middle classes, and the poor farmers and workers. They were the so-called "new men" who had risen from the ranks in government, business, and the unions, and were anxious for both economic and social progress. They did not want undue interference from either the United States or the Soviet Union. But their nationalism was not of the anti-Yankee variety and they wanted loans and technical aid from the United States and other countries. Although believing basically in capitalism, they favored a large measure of government economic control, planning, and government enterprise. In other words, they advocated a mixed private and public economy following much of the economic policy revolution program.

It is our contention that if these men are allowed to lead, Latin America will have a great future. But the optimism which prevailed in 1960 and 1961 had rude shocks in 1962. In Argentina there was the victory of Perónism at the polls, the removal of Frondizi and the return of military dictatorship. In Brazil there was the resignation of Quadros, the split of power between the nationalist-communist Goulart and the Congress, and the triumph of Goulart in the selection of Brochada da Rocha as premier. In Peru the army, in typical Latin American fashion, prevented the election of either de la Torre or Odria to the presidency and assumed dictatorial power under a junta originally headed by General Ricardo Perez Godoy.[1] In Venezuela a series of disturbances and uprisings by communists threatened the regime of President Betancourt. In the Dominican Republic the people, after the overthrow of the Trujillo regime, were unable to establish immediately a truly democratic government. Finally, in the first free election in over thirty years, a liberal, Juan Bosch, became president. But his regime failed despite the vigorous support of the United States. Although Castro's influence declined, it continued to be an active force for communism in Mexico and in other parts of Latin America such as Brazil, Chile, Ecuador, and Venezuela. Communists continued to exert great influence over the Latin American labor movement and to propagandize the Andean Indians.

In 1963 some improvements occurred. Semidemocratic elections were held in Argentina and Peru, resulting in the selection of reasonably moderate presidents, Arturo Illia and Balaunde Terry. But military coups occurred in the Dominican Republic, Ecuador, Guatemala, and Honduras. If these changes, however, do not destroy middle-class leadership, progress may yet occur. Whether under democracy or dictatorship, it is essential that the "new men" lead.

It is essential also that the "new men" accept sound economic theory. The continuation of excessive inflation and adherence to Keynesian theory will only lead to disaster for the new middle-class control and the ultimate triumph of communism or fascism. Latin America sorely needs to accept the type of economics of the periphery developed by Prebisch, which stresses the promotion of industrialization both of manufacturing and agriculture through government economic planning. The middle-class leadership will not offset communism nor speed economic and social progress without a "big push," and this in turn cannot be achieved without bold planning and a great deal of domestic saving as well as foreign capital and aid.

The new middle-class leaders must also be realistic. They were not entirely so at Punta del Este. For example, the annual rate of growth proposed was too low to take sufficiently into account the serious population problem of Latin America. Because of rapid population growth, the annual rate of production increase needed is 5 to 10 percent. Moreover, realism consists also in accepting the fact that to grow at 5 to 10 percent, investment must amount annually to 10 to 20 percent of the gross national product. This rate of investment cannot be maintained through excessive inflation since it requires a large amount of *real* domestic saving. The Latin American nations must obtain a large amount of capital the hard way through taxation, consumer saving, and low wages because inflation, when it becomes excessive, destroys *real* saving. Wages rise too high, capital flees or goes into speculation, savings institutions collapse, taxes are evaded, and even the ploughing back of profit in business declines.

The Middle-class Dilemma

The salvation of Latin America rests with the middle classes. They are not only the chief defense against communism, but the source of the education, economic incentive, and economic management that Latin America needs. Except in some countries, however, the middle classes are still small and to obtain and hold power they must gain the support of workers and small farmers. At times this has happened, as in the election of Frondizi in Argentina, Quadros, Dutro, and Vargas in Brazil, Betancourt in Venezuela—and in fact, in the case of most of the men occupying the presidencies of Latin American nations in 1960.

But the necessity of increasing saving through taxation and low wages to promote industrial growth ultimately tends to alienate the working class and the poor farmers. In the great period of growth in the United States after 1865, the middle classes could count on a large part of agriculture and labor to keep them in power. The middle classes in Latin America are not in this fortunate position. They face a dilemma. Unless they stay in power, they can accomplish nothing, but they cannot control on the basis of middle-class votes alone. A number of choices are open to them. On the one hand, they can turn to the left, expropriate land and foreign capital, provide more expensive social security, raise wages and become neutralist or anti-American. In these ways, they may be able to hold farm tenant and labor support. In part, these were the tactics of Quadros. But Frondizi, in the beginning of his presidency, was unwilling to turn to the left, and when he finally did by supporting the election of Perónists, he fell victim to the military forces.

Another choice that the middle classes have is to turn to the armed forces. With their aid, they could rule as the *hacendados* did before them. But this means dictatorship. It not only goes against the principles of the liberal elements in the middle classes which favor democracy, but it is of dubious long-run value. Ultimately, the armies may be infiltrated by leftist influences. Army dictatorships are not as secure as they once were. Another danger is that the leading generals may decide to run the country in their own narrow interests.

Yet another alternative is the acceptance of a limited form of democracy and the subordination of the army. This solution is fascism or near-fascism. Near-fascism of this sort originated with men like Obregon and Calles in Mexico, Vargas in Brazil, and Trujillo in the Dominican Republic. An emotional paternalistic leadership is established by which the leader obtains the support of the lower classes, but follows policies dictated by the middle classes. Under this near-fascism in Mexico and Brazil, there was a degree of civil liberty, but there was also a good deal of suppression, some of it brutal. The modern middle-class liberal does not find this solution to his taste.

The Interim Stage

It is possible that democracy, as we know it in the United States, is premature in Latin America except for countries like Uruguay, Chile, and Costa Rica, where it has been firmly established for many years. Democracy is not based on democratic principles, ideals, and traditions alone. All Latin America has democratic traditions. But democracy requires long-standing democratic practice, widespread education, the subordination of the military forces to civilian government, strong middle classes, and a noncommunist, or nonsyndicalist labor movement. Most of Latin America lacks these requirements. Another requirement is belief in capitalism as the basic means of material progress. If there is socialism or statism, there must be a reasonable coexistence established between them and capitalism. Capitalism, which provides the individualism in economic life fundamental to democracy, must not be unimportant or exist merely by sufferance. But here again there is a dubious situation in Latin America, since the masses are not sure whether they want capitalism. They come from a feudalistic land system, and many of their experiences with a money economy have been unfortunate.

It is not unlikely, therefore, that in these current years false starts will be made. The austerity and development programs may prove too unpopular with the workers and the poor farmers. Without education, they are an easy prey for demagoguery of the left. There is also a ready-made scapegoat in the United States, and the communists and nationalists can take full propaganda advantage of bad economic conditions to attack both us and the capitalism we represent. Latin America, moreover, is appealed to by dramatic personalities such as Castro, Perón, Toledano, Haya de la Torre, and Prestes. Liberal middle-class leaders like Frondizi do not have a strong personal attraction. As a result, their austere efforts to control for the general welfare may not be accepted by labor and poor farmers who are accustomed to uneconomic wage increases and public handouts. The poor will agree to economic sacrifices only when led by personally attractive and dramatic revolutionaries like Fidel Castro. But when socially dangerous men like Castro or Haya de la Torre win at the polls, conservatives, including the landowners and the upper middle class, turn to the army to void the elections. Middle-class rule, unless it gets the political support of the masses, may thus result in military dictatorship.

Economic Needs

Although the situation in Latin America is a composite of political, social, and economic factors, we believe that the major difficulties are economic. To deal with these difficulties more statistical knowledge is needed, and the policies adopted by the various governments must be based on a sound general economic theory. Gradual economic change can usually be left to the direction of businessmen. But rapid change is now sought in Latin America, making government control and planning necessary. Governments must step in and determine economic policies, and these, in their turn, can be successful only if they have a solid theoretical foundation. We have examined the economic problems of Latin America in relation to a fundamental economic theory outlined in Chapter 6. It is now possible to summarize the conclusions which were derived from this theory as we surveyed the problems in the various countries.

1. The tendency at times for export prices and the terms of trade to decline makes it impossible for Latin American nations to grow rapidly by importing capital paid for by export earnings.
2. Neither agriculture nor industry can grow and raise the standard of living rapidly without capital. Capital accumulation is essential.
3. An increase in production and productivity in agriculture, if devoted to export production, would not appreciably raise the standard of living in Latin America. Much more coffee, sugar, bananas, cacao, and cotton would so depress the prices of these commodities as largely to offset the advantages gained from increased output.
4. The way to a higher standard of living in Latin America lies through (a) the growth of industrialism, (b) the development of home markets and Latin American common markets, and (c) a great increase of domestic food production.
5. To achieve a rapid rate of growth in these three respects, there must be (a) economic *balance,* (b) a *big push,* and (c) a final *take-off.*
6. The achievement of balance requires *economic planning, government enterprise,* and *economic nationalism* through tariffs, exchange control, and the prevention of flights of capital.
7. The big push can come about only through a combination of foreign loans and aid, and forced saving through low wages and *moderate* inflation. It cannot be derived entirely from the available loan capital in Latin America or from export earnings. They are both too small.
8. No Latin American nation can progress steadily or rapidly until it has "taken off." In other words, domestic saving, both voluntary and involuntary, must become large and continuous. Two things are necessary for this result: (a) a large and enterprising class of businessmen willing to invest the savings and (b) a government

which is favorable to business and maintains political and economic
stability. Both for domestic capital accumulation and the attraction
of foreign capital, the investment climate must be favorable.

9. Social progress must accompany economic progress. Neither can
proceed without the other. But neither should be emphasized at
the expense of the other. In Latin America, economic progress
through the growth of business enterprise has often been sacrificed
to superficial measures for social progress. Even the way the
Alliance for Progress was implemented in 1962 and 1963 promoted
social progress at the expense of economic progress.

10. There are no less than seven different kinds of balance required
in Latin America. An examination of the countries reveals imbalance in all seven. There is imbalance between (a) social investment and economic investment, (b) agriculture and industry, (c)
export and domestic trade, (d) mining and manufacturing, (e)
heavy and light industry, (f) public and private enterprise, and
(g) wages and profits. Balance must be maintained in these seven
areas. But the free-price system, even if it functioned universally
and effectively in Latin America, could hardly be expected to
accomplish this result in view of the underdeveloped character of
the countries. Thus a large measure of central planning and direction is needed.

The conclusions we have listed reveal some of the basic economic needs of Latin America. But there are also other needs.
Resources must be developed, new land opened up for cultivation, and vast increases made in transportation and communication. New power resources are urgently needed, and the rate of
population growth must be kept below the rate of production
growth. Vast improvements are required in health, housing, and
general and technical education. One almost universal need is
the removal of illiteracy. But economic policies designed to promote general economic growth will do more to meet these needs
than *specific* efforts to meet them. In our opinion, it is essential
to focus attention on general coordinated economic growth
rather than on separate problems, largely social in character,
such as housing, health, and education. Underdeveloped countries which become too specific and "social" in their objectives
are in danger of making social advances without adequate clothing, food and electric power. Social development requires economic development. If a choice must be made, the latter should
be emphasized.

The Ideal Country

With the economic needs we have outlined in mind, we can conceive of an ideal country which follows sound political and economic precepts. Let us call our ideal nation *Ventura*. First of all, Ventura is controlled politically by a large middle class consisting of both old and new middle-class elements.[2] The older elements are the small independent farmers, professional men, and business enterprisers. The leading force consists of these enterprisers, the so-called "entrepreneurial class" referred to earlier. The new middle-class elements are composed of white-collar employees, managers and corporate executives. In Ventura, both elements in the middle class are strong, but the entrepreneurial group leads, and the emphasis is on business enterprise rather than white-collar bureaucracy.

In Ventura, the government is stable and honest. It maintains order, encourages business, and avoids expropriation. But its main goal is rapid simultaneous economic and social development, with emphasis on the former. It stresses economic planning and capital accumulation. It is not nationalistic to the point of rejecting foreign capital or technicians. Through its economic plans, it encourages the balanced growth of industry and agriculture. Wages are not so high that growth is discouraged by low profits, or so low that there is a lack of domestic buying power. Capital accumulation proceeds at the rate of 10 to 20 percent of the gross national product a year. This high rate is reached by the encouragement of direct foreign investment and domestic saving. When domestic saving on a voluntary basis is not high enough, involuntary saving is induced through regressive taxes and a moderate degree of inflation.

Nationalistic economic planning by the Ventura government projects ahead the growth of roads, telephones, schools, public housing, technical education, and public health in one planning budget. In another, it projects the growth of a home market in food, and provides new land, machinery, and education for farmers. In yet another Ventura budget, there is a plan for the growth of mining and both heavy and light industries. A fourth budget provides for the development of natural resources. To achieve the budgets, both public and private projects have been begun. Capital is obtained from government development banks, the ploughing back of profits, tax funds loaned to business, and foreign direct investments, loans and aid. The economy in Ventura is a mixed economy, and more socialist and planned than that of the United States. Support of the program is aroused by nationalistic propaganda. The tariff system and foreign exchange are designed to promote domestic industry, and yet Ventura belongs to a Latin American common market.

No nation in Latin America entirely resembles Ventura. Mexico falls short of the ideal, since its dictatorial government is almost fascistic and its socialism frightens foreign capital. The oil expropriations have never been forgotten, and Mexico is too eager to insure domestic control of businesses started by foreigners to allay their fears. Unfortunately, however, most other Latin American nations are even farther from Ventura. Costa Rica and Puerto Rico are notable exceptions. In recent years, Venezuela under Betancourt has come closer to the desired pattern and great hope has been aroused by economic progress in Peru.

The Basic Problem of Capital

In our opinion, insufficient capital is the most important problem in Latin America. How can more capital be obtained and directed into diversified investments that will lead to rapid and balanced economic growth? No other question deserves greater attention by Latin Americans. Concern over housing, poor health, illiteracy, economic inequality, and landlessness should not distract the leaders of these countries from their paramount need. Above all, *they must obtain more capital.* Although social progress should go hand in hand with economic progress, the latter is the foundation of the former. If economic progress cannot be made rapidly without sacrifices in social progress, *social progress should be sacrificed. But economic progress must not be sacrificed for social progress because this will mean the retardation of both.*

Thus the main issue in Latin America is not whether social progress is more important than economic progress, or even whether it is equally important. The main issue concerns the accumulation of capital. Should capital be obtained through (*a*) domestic saving, (*b*) reinvestment of earnings, (*c*) direct foreign investment, (d) foreign private loans, (e) foreign government loans, (g) foreign aid, or (h) export earnings? An examination of the economic history of Latin America since World War I reveals that direct foreign investment and export earnings caused a great economic boom in the fifties, but were unable to sustain rapid economic growth. Since 1960, foreign government loans and foreign aid have been too small to substitute for the decline in private direct foreign investment and in export earnings. They have barely offset the flight of capital.

For rapid economic growth, Latin America needs $12 to $16 billions of capital a year. In recent years, new direct foreign investment has fallen to half a billion dollars a year. Much of this new capital has been offset by the flight of capital both foreign and domestic. It has been hard for Latin American nations even to prevent balance-of-payment deficits. Moreover, the Alliance for Progress funds in 1962 and 1963 were going too much into social rather than economic projects. As a result of the changes in the last five years, three conclusions seem obvious: (1) Latin America must greatly speed up domestic capital accumulation; (2) direct private foreign investment must be revived on a scale larger than ever before; and (3) Alliance for Progress funds must be directed to a much greater extent into industry.

The first of these conclusions is of paramount importance. The ultimate salvation of Latin America surely lies in greatly expanded domestic saving and investment. Foreign capital and aid can hardly be expected to supply more than $5 billion a year, and, as we have pointed out, a real take-off in Latin America requires at least $12 billions of investment a year. Thus, out of a gross national product of $80 to $100 a year, Latin America must save at least 10 percent.

Two methods thus far have proved effective as means of domestic capital accumulation in most of the countries, the re-investment by domestic business of large earnings made possible by low wages and inflation, and government loans of capital to private business or to public enterprises also made possible by low wages, deficits, and inflation. The austerity counterpart is high taxes. Through high taxes, a government could force saving and invest the capital by loans to private businesses and public enterprises.

In either austerity or inflation, wages have to be kept low. Thus in Brazil, Chile, Colombia, Mexico, and Peru, inflation speeded capital accumulation before inflation became excessive *because wages were kept low.* But in Argentina, higher wages negated capital accumulation despite inflation. Excessive inflation finally retarded progress in Brazil, Chile, Colombia, Mexico, and Peru also. In Puerto Rico and Costa Rica, however, advancement has occurred through domestic capital accumulation without inflation, and the good results have been due partly to low wages and partly to the development of individual saving and vigorous domestic business enterprise. Puerto Rico also has had the great advantage of American capital from the continent.

If Latin America will not take the austerity road to capital accumulation, it must accomplish its objectives through inflation, or be content with slow progress slightly accelerated by foreign aid and foreign direct investments. Since most of the Latin American nations that have shown the greatest domestic economic growth have not been able to apply austerity successfully, inflation is the policy they are more likely to follow. But what is the role of inflation in capital accumulation? Can it be used continuously, or is it only capable of serving as a temporary short-run device? Also, can it be kept moderate and under control?

The Role of Inflation in Capital Formation

It is clear that inflation becomes the leading device for domestic capital accumulation when an economy is very poor. In rich countries, saving on a large scale is much easier. Incomes are not only large enough to provide comfort, but a surplus that can be laid aside for contingencies and future needs and money pours into banks, savings institutions, new issues of securities and insurance. The problem often is not insufficient saving, but greater saving than the economy is willing to invest at levels of full employment. Thus the primary cause of inflation in Latin America is low real income, and the consequent inability to obtain enough capital to meet the needs of both social and economic progress from voluntary saving by individuals. Consequently, forced saving must be resorted to, and inflation is the obvious means of inducing it.

But inflation has two basic weaknesses as a forced-saving and investment device: (1) it can go too far and destroy both saving and investment, and (2) it can result, even when moderate, in profits which are sent abroad, or used for land speculation rather than for business capital. Thus the first requisite in using inflation for capital formation is moderation. But what is moderation?

In attempting to answer this question it is first necessary to point out that inflation is a disguised form of income redistribution. It shifts income from those with fixed incomes, and wage earners and salaried people generally, to the holders of physical assets and those whose income is in the form of profits. When this occurs in a relatively slow or moderate fashion, the higher profits caused by the inflation will encourage *productive* use of property and lead to further investment in business. However, if the rise in prices becomes too great, it is more profitable to *hold property than to use it productively*, and it pays to give up business for speculation. Also, real incomes of workers decline to the point where productivity is impaired because of bad physical conditions or a decline in incentive. Changes in prices and costs become unpredictable, and business is further impaired by risk. In general, inflation becomes excessive when production begins to be replaced by property holding and speculation.

Historically, the years 1955 to 1958 are significant as illustrative of the shift from moderate to excessive inflation. In these years, Colombia, Mexico, and Peru crossed the line and inflation became too great. All three countries were growing rapidly and inflation each year had been 10 percent or less. Between 1955 and 1958, however, the rate of inflation rose above 10 percent. In Peru and Colombia it increased to 20 percent. It is our belief that inflation becomes excessive once it rises above 10 percent a year. A country using inflation as a means of capital formation, therefore, should hold the annual rise in prices down to 10 percent.

The degree of inflation is harmful only insofar as it shifts capital away from production or reduces productivity. However, an inflation rate much greater than 10 percent a year in Brazil and Chile did not curb production because conditions peculiar to these countries continued to make business, in contrast to speculation, profitable. Not the least of these was the great lag in wages. But other factors were involved. Even a rise of prices above 10 percent a year may not hamper production if these factors operate. They consist of a rapid rise in domestic food and raw-material production, prohibitions on the export of capital and taxes that discourage speculation.

In unadvanced countries, labor costs are vitally affected by food costs. If food production increases rapidly as industrial production and prices increase, wages need not be increased very rapidly and labor costs will remain low. Business, in this case, may be more attractive than mere speculation. A business not only earns high profits from operations but has speculative profit from the rising money value of the business properties. In Argentina and Chile, however, food production did not rise rapidly. In Chile, food costs became 60 percent of wages for the lowest income groups. In Argentina, agriculture was disrupted in an effort to promote industrialism and food prices rose. When food production grows rapidly, a much higher level of inflation can be supported without causing a decline in business activity.[3]

Conclusions

In conclusion, Latin America must rapidly industrialize through self-induced domestic capital formation. A combination of economic nationalism, socialism, planning and moderate inflation are needed for this purpose. But the emphasis must remain capitalistic. Capitalism is the most efficient means of raising the standard of living of the average man in a hurry, no matter how underdeveloped a nation is. Thus the economic regimes of the new Latin America should be basically capitalist.

As has been said earlier, Latin America will have to do most of the job of economic development on its own. There is no easy road to economic success. No amount of foreign aid or direct investment can enable Latin Americans to avoid the necessity for domestic saving. Also, both the austerity and inflationary methods of promoting saving are virtually the same. There is merely a choice between open taxation or disguised taxation through inflation. But the austerity must not be confined to the poor. The rich must be curbed in their extravagance, their penchant for investment in real estate, and their desire to "play it safe" by taking large parts of their wealth abroad. They must be imbued with the capitalistic spirit of business enterprise and slough off the decadent vestiges of the old feudal land system.

Latin America needs a Peter the Great to cut off the beards and strip off the long coats of the Latin American "economic boyars."

But whatever Americans may think, Latin Americans can and will solve their problems in their own way. Even though we believe that they should follow capitalist principles, we cannot expect them to adopt laissez-faire and complete free enterprise. They will choose to progress through a nationalist-socialist-capitalist complex which will arouse the fear of some Americans. Since there is a social revolution in progress in Latin America which has reached the crisis stage, even capitalism must be promoted in a revolutionary context. It must be "planned" and for "the good of the masses." It must be supported for social rather than individualistic reasons. It cannot be advocated merely on a logical basis, and it must become a faith, intimately connected with the desire of the masses for self-betterment.

In the last analysis, the needs of Latin America are psychological. In this respect, the history of Mexico since 1917 is most significant. The Mexican revolution created a democratic faith. Although Mexico has not become politically democratic in the American sense, it has accepted democratic goals, and has gradually fused capitalism with the democratic and socialistic concepts of the revolution. This Mexican socialistic revolutionary capitalism had, until 1959, caused a phenomenal rise in production and the standard of living. If Mexico can be taken as a guide, progress in Latin America would seem to require some such fusion of capitalism and socialism in the other nations. As in Mexico, businessmen should support democratic and revolutionary goals. American businessmen in Latin America especially need to support these goals since they, more than any other businessmen, symbolize capitalism. If the propaganda of the communists is substantiated because capitalism turns out to benefit only the wealthy few, Latin America will be ripe for communism.

Finally, Latin America needs the capitalistic leadership of the "new men" of the middle class. But under a mixed capitalist-socialist system, these men must plan. To plan intelligently for economic development they must follow a sound theory of development. We must plan with them following the same theory. Specifically, this means that the Alliance for Progress should work through a joint planning committee consisting of our economists and Latin American economists, both from the vari-

ous governments and from the two common-market organizations. A comprehensive joint plan must be developed and based
on sound theory. It should not be done (1) by us alone, (2) on
a piecemeal basis, or (3) be dependent upon specific unilateral
agreements between the United States and various Latin American nations concerning their willingness to make specific tax,
land, and monetary reforms. The whole philosophy of our Alliance for Progress planning is inappropriate when analyzed in
terms of the need for over-all economic planning in Latin
America.

References

1. President Perez Godoy was removed by the army on March 2, 1963.
Lindley Lopez who was less of a dictator and better disposed toward the
United States became president.

2. For an analysis of the old and new middle class, see C. Wright Mills,
White Collar, Oxford University Press, *New York, 1951*.

3. Cf. R. J. Alexander, *Labor Relations in Argentina, Brazil, and Chile*,
McGraw-Hill, New York, 1962, p. 372.

TWENTY

WHICH ROAD WILL
LATIN AMERICA TAKE?

IT IS OBVIOUSLY DANGEROUS TO ATTEMPT TO PREDICT POLITICAL and economic changes. Even when marked trends are discernible, as was the case in Latin America in the late 1950s, they may suddenly be reversed, because of the appearance of new and unforeseen circumstances. In 1957 Latin America seemed well on the road toward rapid industrial progress. The old agrarian feudalism was being replaced by the growth of cities and business enterprise. But by 1960 the revolution in Cuba and the collapse of the great economic boom created uncertainty.

Between 1961 and 1963 the uncertainty increased. The people's revolution in Cuba turned communist. Democratic regimes in Argentina and Peru were replaced by military dictatorships and a military coup removed the president of Ecuador. Quadros resigned suddenly as president of Brazil, and was succeeded by Goulart. A fierce struggle for power followed between conservatives, neutralists, and communists. Although undemocratic governments were overthrown in the Dominican Republic and El Salvador, free elections were delayed for a long time. In 1963 Guatemala, the only country in the world ever to overthrow a communist regime, returned to military rule. In that year also, military coups overturned the democratic regimes in the Dominican Republic and Honduras under Bosch and Morales and the government of Haiti under Duvalier became a repressive dictatorship.

In predicting change, one is tempted to indulge in wishful thinking. Liberals, especially, are prone to this weakness. But what one thinks *should* happen will not *necessarily* happen unless the wishful thinking is based on sound social theory. For example, one might conclude from these pages that the economic policy revolution reveals a valid social theory for Latin America, and that, for this reason, Latin Americans will eventually adopt the policy revolution in its entirety. Conceivably this might happen merely because no other program has a sound theoretical foundation. The combination of capitalism, economic national- ism, and socialism it represents offers the best solution for Latin America's basic problem of accelerating economic growth.

But the adoption of sound policies may require too much education, and take too long. In the meantime, the pressures of the social revolution are strong, and the more dramatic national- istic measures may win popular support. There is also the danger of revolutions spearheaded by *penetracionistas* from Cuba and supported by communist rank-and-file elements in the military forces. Once in power, it will be virtually impossible to dislodge these Castro-like governments. Their removal would require military intervention by the United States, and we are not yet prepared to intervene. Yet apart from military invasion, communist regimes do not collapse. Their economic policies may be unsound as long-run means of benefiting the common people, but they can remain indefinitely in power through totalitarian methods of control.

Notwithstanding the possibility of communist revolutions, however, the future of Latin America undoubtedly depends on the adoption of sound economic theory, and the theory behind the economic policy revolution is valid for Latin America. But wise policies and planning for development do not come about automatically. They must be implemented by economic classes, in this case the middle classes. No other social groups in Latin America are likely to favor the economic policy revolution in the broad context required for its success. One must conclude, therefore, that the future of Latin America depends not only on the prevention of communist revolutions but on the fortunes of the middle elements in Latin American society. The para- mount question about Latin America concerns these elements. Will they be able to obtain and retain power?

This question resolves itself into a number of subordinate questions which are partly political and partly economic. For example, we are concerned politically with the alternative to middle-class rule. If these classes fail, is the alternative rule by communists, fascists, cliques of conservative wealthy business- men, or the old reactionary combination of the landlords and the army generals? Also at bottom, the success or failure of middle-class government will be determined by economics. Can the middle class solve the basic economic problems of Latin America?

Their ability to succeed economically is closely related to other questions. Can they not only preserve capitalism, but make it work to the advantage of the common people? To do this, they must cause a rapid growth in domestic capital investment. Can they bring about a "take-off" through domestic capital accumulation? To what extent can or will foreign direct investment revive to assist the "take-off"? To what extent also will the "take-off" be promoted by the programs of the Alliance for Progress? Will these programs succeed or fail in promoting a much-needed increase in the rate of economic growth?

The Political Questions

Thus the future of Latin America has political and economic aspects centering around the future and effectiveness of the middle classes. Their political success depends largely on their economic success. Can they retain power by solving the critical economic problems of Latin America?

It is essentially these classes which assumed power in Latin America after the fall of the dictators from 1954 to 1960. The problems they faced were extremely difficult—the failures of the partially adopted economic policy revolution, the decline in export prices, the decline in foreign direct investments, the collapse of the economic boom, severe inflation, deficits in trade balances, growing unemployment, and the threat of communism. As a result, they sought heavy financial aid from the United States to meet the depression and inflation crises, to revive the economic boom and the high rate of growth, and to stay in power by meeting these problems with our aid.

But the basic way out of all these difficulties, as we have emphasized repeatedly in previous chapters, is rapid domestic capital accumulation. Foreign aid and foreign direct investment can only serve to supplement and accelerate domestic investment which is the real solution for the economic problems of Latin America. Before 1960 Mexico, Brazil, Chile, Colombia, and Peru had made considerable progress in domestic capital accumulation. But this was achieved through a policy of low real wages induced by inflation. The wage demands of organized labor were met by higher *money* wages which were offset by inflation. The "fiction" of higher wages was maintained through inflating the currency.

Capital accumulation through inflation, however, has had serious drawbacks. Inflation must be held down to 10 percent a year or it stifles saving and economic growth, and this has proved difficult in Argentina, Chile, and Uruguay and virtually impossible in Brazil. In the end, also, inflation which is more rapid than 10 percent a year antagonizes labor. In addition, it is opposed by foreign businessmen, by international loan agencies, and by the United States Government.

But if, as in Argentina, an austerity program is adopted and money wages are held down, the middle classes lose the support of labor and the poor farmers. Their chance of holding power becomes dim, and they are likely to turn to dictatorship. This alternative may be opposed by the middle classes themselves, and in the confusion, the military forces sometimes take over for purposes all their own. Inflation control, wage control, higher taxes, and other aspects of austerity are unpopular, and if they are pursued by any government in Latin America the chances of its survival are poor. Middle-class governments may lose power if they follow too closely the footsteps of Frondizi and Quadros in countries that are already accustomed to inflation.

In some countries, however, which are still relatively unindustrialized or have not had much inflation, such as Colombia, Ecuador, Peru, and Venezuela, it may be possible for the middle classes to retain power by concentrating on the land problem. Betancourt, for example, counted heavily on the poor farmers for support. But to obtain this type of agrarian backing, a government must proceed rapidly with land reform and tighten its control over the army. Failure to provide land reform, after making promises to carry it out, can easily play into the hands of the communists. Failure to hold onto the army may also prove fatal to middle-class government because landlords are bound to be alienated by extensive land reform. There is a long history in Latin America of dictatorships brought about by a political alliance between the landowners and the military. In Colombia, Peru, and Venezuela, however, the liberals have been wise in adopting land-reform policies that call for expropriation only of unused land. These countries are also fortunate in having a great deal of unused or reclaimable land which can be turned over to the landless. Thus it may be possible to satisfy the poor farmers without unduly alienating the landlords.

The middle classes may also be able to hold power in countries where they constitute a considerable part of the population such as Argentina, Mexico, Chile, Costa Rica, and Uruguay. In these countries also, there is considerable democratic tradition and middle-class ideology. Moreover, in countries like Honduras where there is no great concentration of land ownership, the poor farmers may accept the leadership of the middle classes merely because of their education and status. In Mexico, a combination of factors is involved. The middle classes are large and the farm population continues to accept the present essentially middle-class government because of its revolutionary traditions and its success in promoting economic development as well as because of its intellectual prestige.

In summary, the middle classes could hold power in Latin America if they follow a policy of moderate inflation, retain the support of the army, avoid alienating the large landowners, and gain the support of the poor farmers through land reform. They can also hold power where they are large proportionately to the total population and are supported by the masses because of their education, revolutionary traditions, and success in promoting economic growth. Specifically, their chances of political power are greatest in Mexico, Costa Rica, Chile, Colombia, and Uruguay. They are dubious in Argentina, Brazil, Guatemala, Nicaragua, Venezuela, Ecuador, the Dominican Republic, Bolivia, and Peru. They are nonexistent in Cuba, Haiti, and Paraguay.

If the middle classes fail in all but the first five countries mentioned, what are the alternatives? In the long run, the most probable alternative is communism. There is no other way out for backward countries when the middle classes fail, or when capitalism is in reality rejected. In the short run, however, there are a number of alternatives. The short run could be a period of "borrowed time," which, if wisely used, could still stave off communism. Some of the characteristics of this period of "borrowed time" are already apparent.

The first step taken after middle-class, liberal, capitalist government fails is military dictatorship. This step has already been taken in Argentina, the Dominican Republic, Ecuador, Honduras, Salvador, Guatemala, and Peru. Through military regimes, the policies of the middle classes could be continued, and to a large extent this has been true in these countries since their military coups. Argentina, Peru, and Salvador have returned to semi-democratically elected presidencies. Fortunately, the Kennedy Administration realized that insistence on immediate return to democratic government in these countries would lead to chaos, and work against the very policies that we favor in Latin America. It was not so wise in its attitude toward the military coups in Guatemala, the Dominican Republic, and Honduras. Despite our understandable preference for democratic government, it may be naive to support free elections at times when the only result will be communism or fascism.

But military regimes have many dangers. In both Argentina and Peru there was evidence that the balance of power could be upset, and the rival military cliques threatened to become more interested in their respective ambitions than in promoting the general interests of the nation along middle-class lines. Top military men, moreover, are likely to be conservative. Once in power, they may come under the influence of the very wealthy and the landlords. If military regimes are captured by these groups, the old Latin American pattern will be restored. Not only will progress be retarded, but the stage set for communist people's revolutions. The reactionary character of the Batista regime and our blind indifference to the consequences of it go far toward explaining the Castro revolution. We in the United States may have played a decisive role in causing Cuban communism. American business and sugar interests collaborated with Batista. They were singularly unaware of the dire consequences of this collaboration, not only for the Cuban people but even for themselves. More recently, our insistence on supporting the government of Dr. Bosch which was backed by American businessmen almost resulted in communism. Only the military coup—not our policies—prevented communism and removed the corrupt and inefficient regime of Dr. Bosch.

Another danger of military rule is communist infiltration of the lower officers and the army rank and file. A "people's" revolution can occur in the army itself. The result of such a revolution can be communism or fascism. In Argentina under Perón, it led to fascism; in Cuba under Castro, to communism. Abortive attempts have been made by army groups to establish communism in Venezuela and a return to Perónism in Argentina. In Brazil, a conservative military dictatorship proved difficult because of leftist army infiltration which may grow strong enough in the future to establish Castroism. In 1963 there were already three communists in the Brazilian cabinet.

In conclusion, the only desirable alternative to the failure of middle-class democracy in Latin America is military dictatorship in behalf of the middle classes. But for the reasons outlined, military dictatorships of this character are unstable and unlikely to follow the interests of the middle classes in the long run. They are devices to borrow time, time which is precious indeed because of the social revolution in Latin America. The masses will not wait for social and economic betterment. Any government must provide improvements rapidly or succumb to some form of totalitarianism which can force the people to accept a low standard of living in return for promises of better things to come, and the satisfactions of "sending people to the wall," expropriating the wealthy, the orgies of revolutionary harangue and anti-Americanism, and the building of a few more schools and hospitals.

The Economic Questions

In the end, as we have said, the political future of Latin American depends on the economic effectiveness of the middle classes. Can they bring about quickly a real economic "take-off"?

In 1963 the prospects of a rapid "take-off" in Latin America were not great. Most of the countries were inching their way out of the depression which had hit them in 1960 and 1961. Loans were sought to balance payment deficits and to prevent default on short-term debts. Argentina, Brazil, Chile, and Uruguay continued to struggle unsuccessfully to arrest inflation spirals that had already gone too far. The Alliance for Progress had not met with enthusiasm, and it failed even to offset the economic decline and flight of capital. It was too slow in getting started and suffered from lack of good leadership and planning. Many of the Latin American nations rejected the Alliance and turned again to exports as their main hope for further economic development. In general, President Kennedy had failed to provide effective leadership in Latin America. His personality was against him and his choice of advisors on Latin America unfortunate. It remains to be seen whether President Johnson will do better.

But the depression in Latin America is bound to give way to recovery and advancement, especially in Mexico, Colombia, Venezuela, Chile, and Peru. In Brazil also, the basis for rapid economic advancement exists. The real cause for optimism, however, is the rise of the "new men," especially the new businessmen. If, wages can be held down, and if businessmen aggressively invest their profits in new business enterprises, the "take-off" may occur in most of the larger Latin American nations. But this will require a period of political stability of at least five years, under political regimes, either democratic or dictatorial, which are favorable to business enterprise. The Latin American situation is circular. Economic progress depends on stable government, but stable government depends on economic progress. However, the situation is also cumulative. As progress is made, it will become increasingly easier to maintain stable government and make further progress.

American Business and Latin America

Of considerable seriousness for Latin America is the ambivalent attitude of American business toward it. American capital has been greatly discouraged by the Cuban revolution, the danger of communism in Brazil and Venezuela, the expropriations and uncontrolled inflation in Brazil, the cancellation of oil concessions in Argentina, the Panamanian crisis, the lack of tax incentives and the widespread anti-Yankeeism. Millions of dollars of American capital have been withdrawn. But business was somewhat heartened by the Alliance for Progress. At the outset of this program American business supported President Kennedy's leadership. They saw in the program a means of maintaining in power pro-American middle-class governments and the defeat of communism. They also believed that the Alliance for Progress could be used as an inducement for tax and fiscal reforms and as a stimulus to capital investment and more exports to Latin America.

In 1962, after the establishment of the Alliance for Progress, a business committee of 25 members was chosen to advise the Administration. A meeting was held with the President at the White House, and it was assumed that the committee, known at COMAP[1], would organize the business community in support of the Alliance and restrain the flight of American capital from the Latin American nations.

During 1962, however, the flight of capital was resumed, and a rift developed between the President and businessmen over Latin American policy. They had been sceptical of the Alliance for Progress from the beginning. Little effort had been made under the Alliance to encourage the expansion of private investment, either local or foreign. The collapse of the boom in Latin America which placed the liberal governments in jeopardy and encouraged communism had been due in no small measure to the decline of investment. Despite the fact that the Alliance program assumes an annual net private direct investment from the United States of only $300 million, nothing was done to restore even this small amount of net capital inflow. During the first year and a half of the Alliance for Progress, more American capital was taken out of Latin America than went into it. About a billion dollars fled from Argentina alone. President Kennedy's first reaction to the outflow consisted merely of lecturing businessmen on the need to supply capital to Latin America in order to forestall communism.

In the early days of COMAP, a number of subcommittees were formed to investigate new investment possibilities in various parts of Latin America. Very little resulted from these efforts. When Peter Grace later assumed the chairmanship, the committee turned its attention to the risks of investment resulting from currency depreciation, various trade restrictions and outright expropriation.[2] Not only were American businessmen facing these dangers, but the rate of return on capital had fallen considerably below earnings in Western Europe and other parts of the world.

Added to the rift between the President and business was a growing difference of opinion about policy among the businessmen themselves. Peter Grace urged greater emphasis on business investment in the Alliance for Progress stimulated (1) by United States tax deductions for earnings in Latin America, and (2) by granting $2.5 billion of Alliance aid a year to Latin America for imports of raw materials and equipment *in connection with industrial development alone.* This heavy emphasis on business investment finally resulted in a report of the committee written almost exclusively by Grace and to which prominent conservative committee members strongly objected.[3]

The dissenting view had been circulated by three members of the committee—David Rockefeller, Walter B. Wriston, and Emilio G. Collado—before the report appeared. They believed that aid should be provided only to countries which earnestly endeavored to create a favorable climate for American private investment. The late President was urged to state publicly that the primary purpose of the Alliance for Progress was the promotion of private business investment. But Grace and his followers in the committee were unwilling to confine the Alliance for Progress to a program promoting private investment, although they differed strongly with the Kennedy Administration because of its virtual neglect of government-supported business investment, its granting of aid solely on a government-to-government basis, its lack of general over-all economic planning, and its overemphasis on social development.

Failure of our own government to enlist the support of business for the Alliance for Progress was serious indeed, especially when it was accompanied by failure to get support from the larger Latin American countries where the greatest opportunities for business investment exist. It constituted an additional cause of the decline in direct investments and the flight of capital. In 1963 it was hard to find any reason for optimism concerning the revival of direct investment. But American business had invested heavily in Latin America in the 1950s. If in the next few years middle-class government prevails in most of the countries, excessive inflation is ended, reasonable government stability is achieved, expropriation of American business property is stopped, and communism fails to get a strong foothold, business investment may revive. The Latin American governments can do much in creating a favorable climate for investment, both through the protection of foreign property and through tax reductions. Unless there is a revival of foreign investment, however, the chances of an economic "take-off" are negligible. We state this opinion despite optimistic predictions at the end of 1963 that a great boom would start in 1964 due to Alliance for Progress spending and the greater political stability of Latin America.

The Shortcomings of the Alliance for Progress

By 1963 the Alliance for Progress itself was proving a disappointment. It had not kindled the imagination or aroused the enthusiasm of the people of either North or South America. It was bitterly attacked in Argentina and Brazil and aroused only mild enthusiasm in countries such as Colombia and Venezuela which are closely attached to the United States. The Alliance also suffered from waning enthusiasm in the United States.

But the major difficulty arose in Washington from poor leadership. The true significance of the Alliance as a balanced program seeking to promote both economic and social development was not understood. As a balanced program, it requires much intelligent economic planning in cooperation with Latin Americans and with major emphasis on regional economic development. Our government has attempted to implement the program without adequate planning either national or regional, and with the major emphasis on social development. To be sure, social projects are much easier to plan, obtain support more readily in the United States and Latin America, and have an immediate political value as concrete evidence of social betterment through the aid of the United States. But the long-run consequences of a program which improves housing, sanitation, and education without causing rapid general economic growth may be disastrous. We are in the odd position of trying to prove to the people of Latin America that capitalism is a better system than communism while failing to stimulate economic growth *through capitalism*. One begins to wonder whether the provision of the means for social developmentthrough American aid is different in any fundamental respect from the provision of such aid by Soviet Russia in Cuba, except that the money comes from two different countries.

Unless the Alliance for Progress program shifts more strongly to the support of economic development and private investment, it may have political significance but will fail as the fulfillment of the economic policy revolution. The policy revolution was fully embodied in the Charter of Punta del Este. It is basically a program of accelerated economic growth through controlled and planned capitalism, and involves an increase in saving and investment. It is essentially a great, broad program designed to increase the rate of economic growth. In the first twenty months of the administration of the program, however, this essential point seems to have been missed. There was little indication in 1963 that the Kennedy Administration would emphasize economic development or cooperate with those American businessmen who are most experienced in Latin American affairs and could supply leadership in promoting economic development.

But the situation is a highly complicated one, and it is easy for those not in the midst of it to find points to criticize. Also, the government is not alone at fault. The business community has many shortcomings in its approach to Latin American problems. The worst of these are (1) a cynical hopelessness about progress in Latin America and the assumption that it is going communist anyway, (2) the quid-pro-quo attitude that regards aid as a payment for allegiance to free enterprise, and (3) the assumption that Latin America must clean house through budgetary, tax, and land reforms before it will be decent enough for us to do business with through grants-in-aid, a form of inter-American puritanism.

These three attitudes, which are common among American businessmen, greatly weaken our chances of effective economic and political leadership in Latin America, and, for that matter, in other parts of the world. The first of these, hopelessness, has made us run out of Latin America before too many communist shots have been fired. Although the danger of communism is great, it is not great enough to justify a great flight of American capital. The flight itself makes the danger greater. The second, the quid-pro-quo attitude, has made us lose friends and not influence people throughout the world. Basically, it is a form of provincialism. We cannot accept deviations from our principles in other countries, and vainly hope that the rest of the world can be saved through our missionary zeal and accept our way of life. In short, if we are to promote capitalism in the world, we must be content to promote a different form of capitalism than our own—a controlled capitalism. But how many businessmen are content with this compromise? Moreover, much as we might like to do it, we cannot buy allegiance to our economic system nor can we buy alliance and friendship.

The Problem of Compliance

The third, or clean-house attitude, is related to the second, or insistence on the acceptance of free enterprise. Prevention of inflation, the balanced budget, tax reform, and individualistic small farming through land reform are all related to the free-enterprise philosophy. Business has insisted on acceptance of these principles as a condition of both private foreign investment and Alliance for Progress aid. This business viewpoint triumphed at Punta del Este. It is partly an insistence on a quid-pro-quo for aid, but it also involves the belief that we should assist only those nations which introduce reforms consistent with the free-enterprise philosophy. There is, of course, a liberal aspect to this type of reasoning. Tax reform may result in a fairer allocation of tax burdens, and greater income for the poorer parts of the population. Inflation control and land reform will also aid those with middle and lower incomes.

But how much reform can business and our government reasonably expect? The reform record of all of the countries since 1961 is poor. Shall we withhold aid until it is much better? If so, we will have to withhold aid for a long time, and this is an invitation to communism. Let us examine the record in some of the countries.

Argentina went into a severe economic crisis in 1962 after the removal of Frondizi. The continuation of austerity was possible only under military dictatorship. Unemployment and bankruptcies reached record levels, and labor unrest became acute. The foreign debt proved a severe burden, and the national treasury was virtually empty. Both the government and private industry defaulted on loans. The cost of living rose 32 percent and industrial production dropped 20 percent.[3] Production continued to fall and prices rose 20 percent in 1963. Unemployment was 8 percent. Under these very adverse circumstances, with both political and economic instability, Argentina was hardly in a position to balance its budget, introduce elaborate tax reforms, and reform the land system. Argentina, as a consequence, has received virtually no new private investment and little Alliance aid.

The situation in Brazil was no better except that production neither rose nor declined. But, as Juan de Onis has pointed out, all of the four most advanced countries in South America, Argentina, Brazil, Chile, and Colombia were in serious difficulties in 1962, and this was still the case for the first three in 1963. They could not get started again on the road to rapid growth. They could barely keep their heads above water. Brazil in 1962 came to the end of the road for extreme inflation. Both the leftist government of Goulart and the businessmen were painfully forced to realize that they could not make further economic progress until inflation was brought under control. A financial breakdown was imminent with disastrous revolutionary consequences. At this juncture, Goulart's finance minister, Dr. Francisco Santiago Dantas, developed a conservative stabilization and development program. As a result, the United States loaned Brazil $84 million of emergency funds. But despite this slight attempt to control inflation, it continued at a serious rate. Prices rose 62 percent in 1963.

A similar chain of events prevented much reform in Chile. The government of President Alessandri unpegged the exchange rates and introduced austerity measures. An exchange crisis developed with an acute shortage of dollars, and despite attempts to balance the budget, the cost of living rose 27.7 percent in 1962, giving rise to strikes and union pressure to raise wages.[4] Alessandri tried to resist these wage demands, but a 15 percent general wage increase had to be granted to appease the unions. The American-owned copper companies had to allow an even greater increase of 42 percent. In the meantime, Chile attempted to obtain $200 million of United States aid so that her new ten-year industrial development program could be started. Although the Chilean program was approved by the United States, no funds were received in 1962. In an effort to indicate good faith in carrying out the pledges of the Charter of Punta del Este, Chile increased her property-tax assessments, and began in a minor way to introduce land reforms. But the over-all picture was not bright for either tax and land reform, or even inflation control, due to the political pressure of landowners on the one hand and organized labor on the other. In 1963 things went from bad to worse in Chile. Prices rose 50 percent and exports declined. However, production grew by 6 percent.

These compliance problems have their counterpart in still other countries. Bolivia, for example, went to work immediately to prepare a ten-year development plan for aid under the Alliance for Progress, but a very ambitious and unrealistic plan was finally presented. As a result, no substantial aid was granted in 1962. Not only was the plan ill-conceived, but Bolivia had made no headway in introducing reforms in public administration and taxation. Production in the nationalized tin mines lagged seriously and powerful union leaders continued to insist on unrealistic wages policies. But despite many difficulties, the Bolivian trade balance was maintained, and the government deficit reduced. By 1963, however, Bolivia had achieved currency stability, a great accomplishment for a country that had had such a notorious inflation.[5]

In Uruguay also, little had been done by 1963 beyond raising a few taxes and prohibiting luxury imports. Inflation was still rampant and the building boom had collapsed. A host of economic problems beset the nation. In Mexico, no serious effort was made to introduce much needed reforms in tax collection, but Mexican production grew and inflation was moderate. Before the fall of Ydigoras in Guatemala, financial irresponsibility here also was extreme. But the new military government of Colonel Peralta Azurdia aroused great hope among the businessmen for administrative reforms.

In Colombia, progress in reform has hardly been any greater than in the other countries, although the large and energetic business class of this nation continues to inspire confidence in the United States. Another reason for confidence in Colombia is its relative political stability. But the nation suffered serious unbalance in 1962 because of the drop in the value of its coffee exports, which are the chief basis of imports of industrial equipment and raw materials. Some progress was made in meeting the trade deficit through foreign credits and through a 27 percent devaluation of the peso. But national spending continued to outrun income by over $100 million a year, and as Kathleen McLaughlin points out, "while the belt was being tightened in the front, it was being loosened in the back."[6] It was the old story all over again of labor-union pressure for wage increases. President Valencia could not resist the pressure, and the cost of living rose 18 percent in the first three months of 1963.

The situation in Peru under the military dictatorship was much better. Land reforms were introduced. All uncultivated land was taken over by government decree. A National Planning Institute was created to stimulate industrial growth, and considerable progress was made in tax reform. The economy continued to grow at a rapid although somewhat slower rate.[7] Both private capital and Alliance for Progress Aid poured into Peru. Businessmen, both foreign and domestic, had confidence in the military junta.

In Venezuela in 1962 and 1963 the situation was also hopeful in that Betancourt rapidly introduced land and tax reforms. But communist-inspired violence frightened both American and Venezuelan businessmen. The flight of capital was a serious problem and the rate of growth slowed down. The party of Betancourt triumphed in the 1963 elections and the situation may be greatly improved due to more political stability. Production grew 4 percent in 1963 and there was virtually no inflation.

In this brief survey of the compliance problem, several conclusions are evident. Very little can be expected soon in Latin America in the nature of tax and land reform and even in inflation control. Certainly, Alliance for Progress aid should not be made dependent upon marked advances in these fields. Perhaps the token achievements of passing new tax laws, improving collections somewhat through expert aid supplied by our Internal Revenue Service, and the beginnings of wise land reforms should be enough to qualify for aid. The problem is a delicate one because Latin American governments are confronted with the need to win elections with the support of wealthy businessmen and landowners. They need also to attract the capital of these people into domestic investment. Under the circumstances, we cannot press too hard for reform lest we promote the overturn of the very middle-class governments we wish to support.

General Conclusions

As we have said at the outset, the future of Latin America is difficult to predict, but we hold certain strong convictions about it. We believe that Latin America is sufficiently imbued with democratic ideology and nationalism to resist communism, at least of the Russian and Chinese varieties, if capitalism and the middle classes are given a reasonable chance to prove their ability to better the lot of the masses. This means that the hope of Latin America depends on the middle classes and their retention of political power. This, in turn, depends upon (1) the prevention of communist minorities from seizing power through unfair tactics, and (2) upon the effectiveness of the middle classes in solving the economic and social problems of Latin America.

The problems of social development are now in grave danger of being considered as superior to and apart from the problems of economic development. Without adequate attention to economic development, Latin America will be lost to communism or fascism. The Alliance for Progress must shift its emphasis to economic development, and there must be effective cooperation between the American businessmen interested in Latin America and the Federal government. Coordination between business and government on this matter has failed, and the implications of this failure are serious indeed. If we do not promote a form of socialized capitalism in Latin America, it will accomplish little to provide temporary short-run aid. Even the Alliance for Progress, if it continues for ten years, becomes in effect a short-run program if it does no more than meet crises in the balance of payments and promote social development. The short run is obscuring the importance of the long run, and superficial aspects of aid the importance of those that are fundamental.

We return at this point to our original theme. The economic policy revolution worked out by Mexico and Uruguay was fundamental as a solution for both the economic and social problems of Latin America. It was based on valid development theory, and was a natural result of the cultural and economic history of Latin America. This approach to Latin America's problems was embodied in the Act of Bogota, and the Charter of Punta del Este and represents the best thinking of the "new men" in Latin America. It is the contribution of the real but unavowed leadership of Mexico and represents the social outlook of the new elements in the middle classes throughout Latin America. We should understand it for what it is, and assist realistically in carrying out its basic policies. However, in 1963 we in the United States, although playing a crucial role in creating and implementing the Alliance for Progress, failed to understand it and to support its basic economics.

The future of the Latin American world depends, therefore, on two things: (1) the ability of the United States to provide a leadership based on economic as well as political understanding, and (2) on the ability of the Latin American middle classes to carry out the implications of the economic policy revolution. *Above all, we should realize our debt to Mexico. Its creative act of combining Latin American nationalism with capitalism and socialism in a workable combination emphasizing capitalism not only deserves our respect but should be promoted by us as the primary means of advancing the future economic and political welfare of Latin America.* Enlarged by the economic theory outlined earlier in this book and implemented by a comprehensive economic plan, it is the way out for Latin America. It is the way to defeat communism and promote rapid economic progress. Will it be taken? Not unless our people understand it and approve it and our government in cooperation with the planning groups of the Latin American common markets provides the necessary leadership.

Thus far our leadership has failed. Latin Americans in Panama, Guatemala, Honduras, Haiti, Cuba, the Dominican Republic, Argentina, and Brazil have rejected our leadership. They have turned from the Alliance for Progress to internal programs, to their own planning in the common markets, and to reliance again on export earnings as a source of capital. But the administration of President Johnson at its beginning revealed signs of providing the leadership his predecessor could not provide. The appointment of Thomas Mann as Johnson's chief assistant in Latin American policy was especially significant.

There are several reasons why the appointment of Mann was a hopeful sign. The new administrator wanted American business to play a larger role in policy determination, and he placed great emphasis on economic development and the growth of capitalism in Latin America. Also, his extensive experience with Mexico suggested that he might favor some aspects of the economic policy revolution. Soon after Mann assumed his new duties, Presidents Johnson and Mateos met, presumably to discuss broader matters than the few minor problems that exist between the two nations. In addition, Mann supported the new planning steering committee established after the conference in Sao Paulo in November, 1963, which brings the Latin

American nations into joint policy determination with the United States in the Alliance for Progress program. Perhaps under President Johnson our leadership, through greater realism, will at last become effective, although there will be less idealism and drama than under the late President Kennedy. But to quote the revered Bard, "this is a consummation devoutly to be wished," in fact, most devoutly.

References

1. Commerce Committee for the Alliance for Progress.
2. Cf. *Business Week,* Feb. 23, 1963, p. 27.
3. Cf. *New York Times,* Apr. 8, 1963, p. 1.
3. Cf. Edward C. Burks, *New York Times,* Apr. 8, 1963, p. 49.
4. Charles Griffin, *New York Times,* Apr. 8, 1963.
5. Cf. Alberto K. Bailey, *New York Times,* Apr. 8, 1963.
6. Cf. *New York Times,* Apr. 8, 1963, p. 72.
7. The Peruvian growth rate of the gross national product had reached 8 percent in 1960. It was probably still 5 percent in 1962 and 1963.

INDEX